A Place
for
Noah

JOSH GREENFELD

A Place for Noah

HOLT, RINEHART and WINSTON

New York

Copyright © 1978 by Josh Greenfeld

Published simultaneously in Canada by Holt, Rinehart and Winston of Canada, Limited.

Library of Congress Cataloging in Publication Data
Greenfeld, Josh.
    A place for Noah.
    Continues the author's A child called Noah.
    1. Brain-damaged children—Biography. 2. Greenfeld, Noah Jiro, 1966–   I. Title.
RJ496.B7G73   362.7'8'2   77–13354
ISBN 0–03–089896-x

Designer: Kathy Peck
Printed in the United States of America

A slightly different version of the Introduction appeared in *The New York Times* on June 29, 1977.

10 9 8 7 6 5 4 3

For my sons:
Noah,
who is not a metaphor.
And Karl,
who knows that.

Noah Noah everywhere
he goes around just like air.
And when you hear his sacred tune
you know he'll come around the room.
And when he comes to stay
he will stay his way.

—KARL GREENFELD, AGE NINE, 1974

*A Place
for
Noah*

INTRODUCTION

Many people wonder what to name their baby. I still don't know what to call my eleven-year-old son. It is six years since I wrote *A Child Called Noah*. My son was then five years old and had finally seemed to achieve that great pinnacle, toilet training. He was capable of a few words of reward-induced imitative speech, but generally behaved pretty much like a one-year-old with poor sleeping habits and bizarre wakeful activities. His idea of play was flexing and unflexing his hands before his eyes, picking at infinitesimal shreds of lint on the floor, and bouncing up and down on sofas and couches and beds—or endlessly rocking. He seldom interacted with anybody or anything.

We wondered about his hearing and his sight—whether he was actually suffering any perceptional losses—but these faculties seemed untestable. We did notice that though at times he could not seem to hear a loud sound right next to him, he could at other times respond to a quiet whisper from across a room. In the same way he often did not see what lay immediately below his eyes, but seemed to know what lay around a corner.

His intelligence, far below par, was both uneven and untestable. Perhaps the most definite thing we could say about his condition was the label most frequently assigned to it: *autistic*. I no longer consider—or call—my son Noah autistic. This does not mean his condition has improved markedly. It does mean, however, that my perception of his condition has clarified immeasurably. And I no longer distract myself with the use of a term that implies meaning but defies definition. The word *autism* means self-involved—and who isn't?

But it neither specifies a cause nor locates a source, even though its Greek root oozes with scientific promise.

My son Noah was—and is—brain-damaged. He suffers from severe developmental disabilities and acute deprivation in his fine motor processes; he is definitely mentally retarded and naturally has a behavior problem. We have yet to discover the exact reasons—which area of the brain and what perceptional faculties are not functioning properly.

But encircling him with an Orwellian word such as *autism*—one that cosmeticizes rather than communicates—is no help. As a writer I should have known to be wary of so murky a word, of any attempt to conquer with language an uncharted province of science.

Yet, ironically, just as autism does not really exist as a unique and disparate form of brain damage, the games some people play with the term are only too real, and the effects of its use are all too damaging. Thus, many psychogenic-oriented professionals have managed to keep an organic malady within their own alleged esoteric expertise. Thus, certain parents of brain-damaged and retarded children—unable to face the realities and stigmas of the old words—have found an elitist designation, or diagnosis, for their children, requiring more funding, more staffing, more attention.

But, to me, by far the cruelest effect of the glamorous term *autism* is the specious hope it promises for a miraculous cure.

Books and articles keep crossing my desk, rhapsodizing over various cures encountered or uncovered. In recent years I have witnessed some changes for the better—and some changes for the worse—in many brain-damaged children, but I have yet to see

2

the evidence of any single dramatic cure with my own eyes. Oh that there were one! Meanwhile, this proliferating genre of literature, though perhaps designed with the best of intentions, actually too often inflicts only guilt upon those closest to these children—their parents and their teachers.

How is my own son Noah now? He is doing better than he has done, but not as well as I would have hoped. If I had once seen his malady as transient, I now know it to be permanent. But I still must deal with it on a transient—or existential—basis. I still both enjoy Noah and endure him. Which is, after all, the way most of us fundamentally treat one another.

I am sometimes asked if Noah's presence has changed the nature of our family life. Obviously, it has. But since I cannot imagine the way our life might have been without him, I don't know in what way. I know it might have been easier, and I have to think it might have been better—otherwise all my other values fly out the window.

I have become completely disappointed—or disenchanted—with both orthodox medicine and public education. I have discovered that those areas which are of life and death concern to me are too often treated by their practitioners as merely self-promoting hypes and hustles. I suppose I have had to learn the hard way that most of the people whom our society delegates to know and care about children like my son Noah neither really know nor genuinely begin to care.

I have looked into joining some of the national organizations of concerned parents, but usually I found these groups too involved with the politics or ego trips of their leaders and not concerned enough with the children themselves. Anyway, I have never been much of a joiner and to have a "loner" child make me become an organization man would have been a final irony.

And as for Noah's future—I prefer not to think about it. Which puts me very much in step with the rest of society. For anyone with stomach enough to visit the kind of state hospital to which Noah will eventually be consigned—call him brain-damaged or autistic—knows he has no future at all.

When I last wrote about Noah in June of 1971 his brother,

3

Karl, was six and a half and had just completed the first grade; I was a working writer and my wife, Foumi, who had been a painter when we married, was just beginning to write herself and had sold a few articles to some of Japan's leading magazines. After spending a winter in California, where Dr. Ivar Lovaas, a psychologist at UCLA—and his students—had worked with Noah and instructed us in behavior modification, we had come home to Croton-on-Hudson, New York, a village thirty miles north of Manhattan, where we lived in a house overlooking the Hudson River.

The behavior modification tasks were divided between Foumi and myself. Since I am the native-born American I would work on speech, trying to get Noah to imitate sounds. Foumi would concentrate on the nonverbal areas, those areas calling for visual or physical cues. We also had just initiated Noah to a regime of megavitamins—heavy dosages of certain vitamins daily.

This book, then, begins where *A Child Called Noah* ends. Again, I have gone back and thumbed through the pages of my journal. Again, I have transcribed my day-to-day hopes and fears and confusions. Again, I think these entries, though often muddled and uninformed, can best indicate who we are as individuals and the nature and quality of the experience we as a family have been through.

And if I seem angrier on these pages than I once was—so be it. I am angrier. But some days, it seems, my rage is all that I have left.

PACIFIC PALISADES, CALIFORNIA
JULY 1977

4

1

July 4, 1971

Independence Day. Independence for whom? Not for us. Just as we begin to get self-congratulatory, to mark our small but epic milestones, Noah reminds us that we all still have a long way to go. We thought we were, for the most part, through with the toilet cleanup details that no matter how much we rationalize and intellectualize are utterly demoralizing. But last night Noah let loose again in his training pants—his second accident of the day.

July 5, 1971

We celebrated the Fourth of July with a teriyaki barbecue picnic at the Hiraokas. Karl played with Takeshi, their six-year-old son, and their two-and-a-half-year-old son, Toshi, joined in. Noah remained the odd child out, plucking away at the grass, pressing his head ostrichlike into the rolling lawn.

I did some good work with Noah this evening. I closeted myself in my study with him and a bowl of potato chips. And when he said what I wanted him to say I rewarded him with a sliver. He did say "Daddy" a few times and I got an occasional "I want" out of him. But what I'll do now, I've decided, is concentrate on verbal signals for the toilet functions, "pee-pee" and "uh-uh." If he learns nothing else that's what I want him to know.

A friend has been staying with us for the past few days. Whenever we have a guest Noah passes into the background and Karl surges to the forefront. He talks incessantly, wants to hear—or overhear—every particle of "adult conversation" and partake in all adult activities.

We've been giving Noah vitamins, a try at orthomolecular therapy, and we're coming to a Catch-22 position. As he becomes generally more aware, perhaps because of the vitamins, he is less apt to drink the beverages that we've spiked with them. I don't care that much if he doesn't take the vitamins—I don't think they've been that effective—but it does bother Foumi. Which, in turn, has to bother me.

I took Karl, Noah, and Mark, a neighbor's four-year-old, to the lake yesterday. Noah never joined in their activities, swimming and dam building and tunnel making on the beach. I wondered whether I should try to force Noah to join in. Instead, I decided to leave him alone, to let him do whatever he wanted to do. He just wandered farther and farther away from me, sand fingering and glee prancing, and never making social contact of any kind, until finally I had to run after him and bring him back.

Karl played "camping" with Mark, and it was painful for me to watch them. Because, as they were stacking blankets and pillows on our playroom floor, Noah was bouncing on the couch nearby, "camping" in his own world.

But then Karl did make me laugh. He put his baseball cap on Noah and handed him a bat, and said: "I'm in the Little League, but you're in the autistic league."

July 21, 1971
A sad, cyclic thought: We're not doing enough for Noah in the way of education, but education cannot do enough for Noah either.

July 24, 1971
Foumi and I were talking about the future. There will be a school operating on behavior modification principles opening in Santa Barbara. There is the lure of the sun, of a fresh, new geographical experience. Yes, I feel the call of the Coast. And all the mediocrity in me yearns to answer it.

July 25, 1971
At the lake yesterday Noah tugged at his penis and pulled at his pants so I was able to catch him before a urination and a defecation. Small victories. But it is trying to be with him. I could not go into the water and play with Karl. When I was in the water with Noah he was all cute and cuddly. But on the beach he was less active and less inquisitive than a one-year-old baby. Noah just sat there running sand through his fingers and turning his head from side to side. And, as always, whenever I spend

7

more than two hours with him, I begin to feel trapped, as if I were caught in a never ending journey with only the vaguest of destinations.

July 28, 1971

Noah had no vitamins at all yesterday and he had no crying jags either. He even seemed much better off.

July 30, 1971

A typical summer day: We get up at 8:15 and push-prod Karl into dressing and eating his breakfast as we prepare his sandwich lunch. At 9:00 I drive him off to his summer camp. I return home about 9:20 and help Foumi with Noah. At 10:00 I drive him to his summer school. By 10:30 I'm at my desk in the office I rent in downtown Croton looking at *The New York Times*, enjoying a second cup of coffee, and finally getting my own short workday started.

At 3:20 I pick up Karl and drive him home—Noah is home already, having been taxied back from school. And then I work with Noah, help Foumi in the garden, or take the boys swimming. We have dinner between 6:00 and 7:00 and the next two and a half hours are spent urging Karl to look at a book, urging Noah to look at anything; bathing them, playing with them, until it is their bedtime. It is a very boring day—until I consider the alternatives.

July 31, 1971

Noah did a marvelous thing. He took off his pants, went upstairs, and sat on the toilet bowl, where he delivered a movement. Learning for him is still such a painfully slow and uneven process. But he *is* learning.

Meanwhile, Foumi and I have decided, on this muggy, hot, humid, impossible day, to go to Los Angeles again for the winter. And in the spring, when we return to New York, we'll decide on our next move.

August 3, 1971

The rainy season—my brain is sloggily, sloshily inundated—and we're all under the weather. Noah is a daily chore, Foumi and I are at each other constantly, and Karl is a pain. This morning Karl didn't even go to camp. He had awakened before us and treated himself to a Big Wheels cupcake before breakfast so I said that he could not have another one in his lunch sack for dessert. He then tearfully decided he wouldn't go to camp. "Fine," I said. "You can use some study time to freshen up your math." The result: It took him five hours to do two pages of simple math.

Neither guilt nor compulsion, I know, are spurs enough to get a child to work. But I'm not sure of any other way, either. Upon the recommendation of his teacher, Karl is supposed to go into an open-school classroom this September. But Foumi is beginning to have second thoughts about it; the lack of a clear description of the exact program disconcerts her. And she is right. My training as a writer tells me that if something has no discernible center, no recognizable core, and defies concrete description, one must be wary: there may be nothing there at all.

August 9, 1971

Our Japanese friends, the Hiraokas, were over for a last supper. Today they are off to California and a new job assignment. As always, Karl enjoyed playing with their boys, and I enjoyed watching Toshi, their youngest, demonstrating that marvelous transformation from baby to boy, a phenomenon that continues to elude Noah.

August 12, 1971

Foumi's had another article published in the *Shukan Asahi*, Japan's leading weekly, and already she's complaining like an old pro about how mercilessly it was cut.

Karl meanwhile upholds the artistic end of the family, drawing nightly in his room. But he too has a tough attitude. I remember before Grandma went back to Japan last winter she asked him for some of his drawings. "Do your own drawings," he replied.

August 14, 1971

I think of a vacation, of a new car, of a future in which I can be purely creative. What an indulgent fantasy! I feel young and fearful, ready to begin the pursuit of a conscious definition of self again. And ready, too, to fail again.

August 15, 1971

Yesterday morning I awoke to Noah's "I want Daddy." I would have swum the Atlantic to answer that call.

August 18, 1971

A friend came over, tears in her eyes. She had discovered that her teenage daughter was on drugs. We had a talk and told her to "cool it" for a while with her daughter while gradually applying a stricter behavioral code. Our friend has been a very lenient, modern parent. And as we listened to her lament, it struck us again that the laissez-faire environment of an open school might not be the best thing for Karl.

August 22, 1971

The summer mugginess has returned and the kids are home all day, their summer programs over. Noah has backslid: he urinated on the living-room couch last night, the playroom sofa the night before. And to make me feel even worse, I had a call from the mother of a fifteen-year-old boy who has begun to have seizures after a life in autism. "Make arrangements for your kid before he reaches adolescence," she warned, "because after that nobody wants him. All the miracle workers give up." Since Noah is five now that means we should figure on having him for another five or six years at best. Or worst.

Having him: He sits in the sandbox out back and lets the sand run through his fingers and then he wanders down the patio-terrace steps to the lawn that leads to the front of our house, picking at the grass. Beneath the deck he squats and examines the gravel and then retraces his route back to the sandbox. No constructive play on his own. But he can pile blocks on top of each other under Foumi's supervision.

Karl, meanwhile, can play checkers, break his watch by overwinding it, and get a bloody nose fighting. And just now, in the after-dinner twilight, he's calling to show me how high he can pump in the swing I've hung from the bottom of the deck.

August 24, 1971

The family Greenfeld went shopping for back-to-school clothing and Noah behaved very well. Indeed, for all his afflictions, we treated him like the normal kid brother. We bought most of the new stuff for Karl; Noah will get his brother's hand-me-downs.

August 25, 1971

Autumn is in the air. Chilly mornings, cold toes, great sleeping and eating weather. Another season. But the same Noah. One therapy or another, it does not matter. He cannot quite communicate, his brain just can't cut it. I must accept it—there is really no hope.

August 28, 1971

In the storm last night one of our locust trees split and fell, sliding down, tearing the gutters off the roof of a neighbor's house, rippling his brand-new aluminum siding. The insurance will take care of the damage, but it's still a pain. I have other locusts standing there, every bit as big, every bit as vulnerable. I will have to have them cut down soon.

But now I'm seriously thinking of moving. Not for just the winter. But really uprooting ourselves. Perhaps my trees are telling me something.

August 29, 1971

I'll never understand how Noah's bladder works. Two nights ago he drank nothing at dinner, urinated a great deal before sleep, woke up once during the night and was taken to the toilet, and then wet himself before morning. Last night he drank prodigiously during and after dinner, urinated but a drop before bedtime, then slept through the night and woke up dry.

August 31, 1971

Roberta, a local Foumi-trained therapist, has had Noah doing some great stuff with blocks, piling them into impressive edifices upon her cues. But he still won't initiate an action, he has to be prodded every step of the way.

September 2, 1971

This morning when Noah saw Foumi coming down the stairs he went to her and hugged her. I would have to call that initiating an action.

September 3, 1971

The suburban bubble has burst. I'll be glad to get out of here. Because we're living with the worst kind of bigots: those who are unable to acknowledge their prejudices—or to imagine that such prejudices reside in their children.

Karl has been having a bad time lately, the kids on the block are ostracizing him. Foumi, who can sense her invisibility in the eyes of others, could also sense the root of Karl's bad times —his Japanese face, his autistic kid brother. He is the different one on the block.

I mentioned this to one of the parents. He said we were reading into a situation. Perhaps we are. But it's something we just can't close the book on.

I don't like the idea that because of Noah whatever we say is treated as something derived from some extreme and bizarre

12

point of view. Not to be believed. Not to be taken seriously. Most people do not realize that vivid extremes are the only things that can give definition to all those blurry gray areas that are still not in focus.

September 6, 1971

We went to an annual Labor Day picnic. And Karl loved it, popping girls' balloons as he roamed the grounds. And Noah behaved marvelously compared to last year and two years ago when he was a bother to behold. This year he discovered the sandbox by himself and went and played there.

I ran into a psychiatrist whom I had gone to high school with. He said that he was not a Freudian; that he had heard of children who, having stopped talking, had learned how to talk again; that he even knew of children like Noah who had gone on to college.

I doubt it. I don't believe it. But it is still something to dream.

September 7, 1971

Roberta had Noah playing patty-cake and filling his pail in the sandpile.

September 8, 1971

Noah urinated three times in his training pants before falling asleep. The third time I yelled at him. "You keep this up," I said, "you're going straight to an institution."

Immediately I heard Karl crying in his room. "What's the matter with you?" I called out.

Karl came to the bathroom door where I was changing Noah. "Don't send Noah to an institution," he sniffled. "I love Noah."

When I told Foumi about the incident, she sniffled even more than Karl. "If we didn't have Karl," she cried, "we would send Noah away and forget about him."

True, I thought. And almost cried myself.

13

September 9, 1971
Karl came home from school complaining again about the open school, the integrated classroom combining kindergarten, first-grade, and second-grade students. He said it was boring, that he didn't learn anything, that all he did was play. What did he play with, I asked. "Blocks," he said. "By the time I get to high school I'll be very good with blocks."

I thought the line was funny and repeated it to his teacher. "Even at high school age," she said with a straight face, "there are still insights to be derived out of blocks."

September 10, 1971
Last evening I decided to call Ivar Lovaas, the behaviorist psychology professor at UCLA who had worked with Noah last winter. I told him about Noah and what he was doing, and Ivar was pleased with how far Noah seems to have come. He said there probably wasn't much more they could do for Noah at UCLA than what we're doing, but that if we came out to Los Angeles for a day or two he could better judge. I was most concerned that since Noah's behavior was inconsistent we sometimes treated him inconsistently. Ivar said not to worry.

So, in a sense reinforced, I relaxed with Noah and he responded. I was able to get some awfully good "Daddies" out of him.

September 11, 1971
There is no logical reason why we shouldn't eventually move to California. The weather here is absurd—today it's suddenly hot and muggy again. And I'm not happy with the school situation here for either child. Today Noah's school sent home some of *his* artwork. Ridiculous stuff. I know he didn't do it.

September 12, 1971
Everyone seems to make the same mistake about President Nixon that I used to make as a draftee about my career army sergeants.

14

We assume there must be a cleverness behind a deviousness that is so obvious. And there never is.

Karl forgot his lunch so I ran it over to school. It was 9:30 and the teacher was asking him, "What do you want to do today?" He shrugged. I watched him finally go over to the "weighing table." "Yesterday," the teacher told me proudly, "we measured the room."

"What are you going to do today?" I asked. "Weigh it?"

But what am I complaining about? Karl amazes me with his vocabulary—how he uses certain words—and with his craftiness —how he gets me to pay for things despite his allowance.

Noah, on the other hand, is static. "Love is feedback," as Skinner says. And we don't get any from Noah. In fact, sometimes his singsong vacuousness gets on my nerves, the what-to-do-with-Noah problem overwhelms me, and suddenly I just want to strike out at him. Can I help it if I don't always love him as much as I want to?

Foumi speaks of her pleasure in the changes in Noah. I see no changes. I despair when I am with him. I want to get away from him, to get him out of my life.

I took Noah to the barber so we could get samples of his hair for some sort of mineral-tracer test the vitamin doctor wants to run on him. After the haircut he doesn't even look cute to me. I want to put him away in some residence. It may not be the best thing for him, but it will be the best thing for me.

Each afternoon Roberta works with Noah, mostly with blocks. Both of my kids building with blocks. When Karl does it I'm discouraged; when Noah does it I'm supposed to be hopeful. Hopeful of what? The older he gets, the more pessimistic—or realistic—I become. Even though he's improving I've reached a leveling off in my feelings about him.

September 22, 1971

I went to a meeting at Noah's school last night. Again more talk of money raising than of treatments and cures, educational techniques, and the securing of good teachers.

I'm not at all satisfied with Noah's teacher this year. I observed her the other day. She's young, intense, humorless, and goes too fast, expecting everything and nothing from the kids at the same time. She whizzes them from one activity to the next. If I know anything at all about these kids it's that you have to teach them very slowly.

September 23, 1971

Yesterday Noah. Today Karl. There was a meeting of the parents of Karl's open-school class. Coffee and cake were served, but I'm not sure we were. The director of the program seemed nicer than I recalled, the parents more intelligent, but the program even more unintelligible. Obviously Karl isn't learning very much. Just as obviously he is having a good time. So we're confused, still don't know what to do about the situation.

I mentioned this confusion to my literary agent. She laughed and told me how her stepson had once returned from the progressive Greenwich Village school he attended, complaining, "I wish I could stop working with clay and start reading."

Special—or normal—I'm afraid education is always a problem.

September 24, 1971

Noah's new teacher sent home a note saying his luncheon peanut butter sandwich was good—since he enjoyed it—but that his meat sandwich was "Unsatisfactory"—since he didn't eat it. I sent back a note explaining our nutritional policies, that the peanut butter sandwich was the reward for eating the meat sandwich.

Unsatisfactory might be more the term I would use to describe her teaching. I know she's young—just out of college—and goes on classroom theory rather than hard-wrought experience. But worse: she does not know she does not know.

Last night Noah awakened me at four. He was wet and I changed him. But he never went back to sleep. I realize now that I should not have changed him, but let him soak in his own urine until morning. Next time I'll do that.

Or was he just hungry? Is that what kept him awake? Poor kid. I tend to blame him for everything and he can't tell me anything. Not even when he's hungry.

September 25, 1971

I'm getting hometown sentimental about Croton. There is a lovely *Our Town* feeling about this place. I enjoy climbing the cemetery on the hill near the library, standing amid the pre–Revolutionary War gravestones, and looking down at a high school football practice, and out at the river in the distance.

But then I remind myself that most of the people here are phony liberals, more interested in voguish problems than real ones, in stylish attitudes than in deeply felt concerns. Otherwise, how could a kid like Karl become an anathema on our block?

September 28, 1971

I'm furious with Noah's teacher. I watched as she encouraged him to knock over his blocks so as to "express himself aggressively." What bullshit! And after all the hard work Foumi and Roberta put in getting Noah to build with blocks. And Noah has had three toilet lapses in the three weeks of school. That's more than he had at school all last winter in California.

I spoke to the director, seeking to unburden myself. He told me I did not understand the problems of running a school, that the teacher was the best he could get. "Sure," he told me, "an

17

experienced teacher would be better. But we can't get one at our salary levels."

I understand the problems of education. I remember a choreographer once telling me that if you understood theater, you understood ballet. In the same way I think if you understand your own learning experiences, you can understand any educational experience—even the most special one.

And I can't get out of my mind's eye the look of Noah in school today. He seemed constantly confused and out of place —not alert at all.

September 29, 1971

Karl was funny about Yom Kippur: "If I'm half-American and half-Japanese, half-Asian and half–North American; half-Mongolian and half-Caucasian, half-Buddhist and half-Jewish, then can the Jewish half of me stay home from school today?"

Holiday or not, I tried to teach Noah. But I got too riled, too angry, and finally I slapped him. My sin.

So it really was a Yom Kippur day. Agnostic that I am, I almost yearned to take my aching ass—and heart—to a synagogue in Brooklyn and commune with my father's spirit.

September 30, 1971

We visited a special school in Connecticut, quartered in a large, ramshackle house, and there were chickens and rabbits in a truck garden. Each room in the house was full of toys and musical instruments and painting materials and the children were lavished with attention on a one-to-one basis.

The director was a sturdy Yankee woman who obviously loved the children. She could not accept the notion of punishment in any form and spoke in Freudian terms of their delicate, bruisable egos. I watched a child pushing a teacher roughly out of a room. I was appalled. But the teacher was delighted. "What progress," she said, clapping her hands. "Notice how well he's communicating."

Her school, the director told us, was a last resort for the children. The next stop was a state institution where nothing would be done.

The local district picks up a tab of up to $7,000 per year for each kid, and provides transportation. If we have to send Noah to a psychogenic—or Freudian-oriented—place it's a lot better than the one he's at. It would mean having to move to Connecticut, though.

October 1, 1971

Noah has been sleeping better and Foumi thinks it's because of an increased dosage of pantothenic acid—or calcium pantothenate. She also has decided, after reading a book by Glenn Doman, that we should talk very clearly to Noah, loudly and slowly, as if he were a two-year-old.

October 4, 1971

We visited the Van Cortlandt Manor, a nearby colonial restoration. Noah liked the garden, Karl liked the history, and they both seemed to like the idea of the family doing something together. And so did I. We just don't get out as a group enough.

October 5, 1971

Noah bangs occasionally on his toy piano. So I took him to my office where there is an upright in the reception room, and he proceeded to bang upon it. Perhaps we should get him a piano—and a music teacher.

Meanwhile, Foumi has also begun the Doman-Delacato way of teaching reading to babies. She's posted a large printed MOMMY on the wall of Noah's room. And she'll ask him to touch it when he says it.

October 8, 1971

Noah was wet this morning when he awoke. He'd had entirely too many toilet accidents lately—both at home and at school.

October 10, 1971

We went to Phillipsburg Manor, continuing our get-away visits to the local colonial restorations. Karl enjoyed himself, taking pictures of the geese and the swan. But Noah was quite impatient and mainly kept dragging ass. He did sit still for a twenty-minute movie, which surprised us.

October 11, 1971

Noah was playing with the knob control on the fan. He pulled it off and dropped it on the floor. Foumi told him to pick it up. He did and tried to put it back in place. A step forward.

But later he repeatedly took his pants off. A step backward. And his speech has all but stopped. I had to point out to Roberta, our Foumi-trained therapist, who is getting a bit frustrated, that for every step forward Noah takes, there is another one backward—and two to the side.

October 12, 1971

A lovely autumn day, a piny scent of winter in the air. We completed our grand tour of the Hudson River Valley colonial restorations with a trip to Sunnyside, Washington Irving's domicile. We enjoyed walking along the grounds, the leaves crisp beneath our feet, the swans swimming about us. And afterward we stopped off to visit friends who live nearby. Noah seemed very aware of his surroundings and was particularly respectful of their Siamese cat. In fact, when I asked Noah to say "I do" if he wanted to go home, he quickly said it twice.

October 13, 1971

This afternoon there was an indoctrination program at Noah's school to meet the teacher we had already met. Foumi didn't have the heart to go but I felt one of us should, otherwise something might be held against poor Noah.

I listened to the teacher limn the routine, which included a

20

lot of free play. I asked her if she believed in behavior modification—the molding of behavior through rewards and punishments. "Definitely not," she said. When I came home I
immediately called Alys Harris, the director of the school Noah
had attended in Los Angeles last winter. She assured me they
would have a place for Noah when we return to California in
December.

October 17, 1971

The leaves have turned on the streets nearby and I walk each day
under an umbrella of brown-flecked yellow. I've acquired a
new rocking chair for my office. The more I think of leaving
here, the more comfortable I become.

October 18, 1971

I was in Manhattan all day and when I came home I found Noah
busy emptying a tissue box and Karl complaining that the TV
set wasn't working right. Still, whenever I go into the city I
come home looking forward to seeing the children. While I am
in the city, however, I often wish that I were still young and
alone, living in a cold-water Greenwich Village apartment,
dreaming of becoming a playwright.

October 19, 1971

A ray of California hope rises here in the East. We went to see
another school in Connecticut. The site belonged to a college
for nuns, and the teacher, a sister, had six aides to help work
with nine children. The director is a local state university psychology professor who believes in operant conditioning, though
not quite as much as we do. But there seemed to be living
examples of results all about. One kid could read even better
than Karl; other kids were echolaliac—automatically repeating
whatever they heard; and some were as bad off as Noah—but
they were all being worked with and they were all alert. In

21

particular, I noticed a black boy who moved and gurgled and smiled just like Noah. It would be a good idea to return in six months and look at him again, to observe what progress, if any, he has made.

This morning I looked at some Connecticut real estate ads, though Foumi wasn't as taken with the Connecticut school as I was. She didn't like the way the teachers shied away from punishment and adverse stimuli and the fact that they didn't stress the importance of establishing eye contact. Yet neither did they seem to cheer and reinforce positive accomplishments enough. And the teachers on the whole, Foumi felt, lacked the self-confidence of an Alys Harris.

October 20, 1971

The old are the best therapists. They really know how to reward and flatter a child. When Mr. Rose, our septuagenarian cab driver, picked up Noah this morning, I told Noah to say "Good morning." But Noah said nothing. Mr. Rose smiled down at Noah and said: "He likes to say 'Hi,' not 'Good morning.'" And sure enough, Noah said "Hi."

October 23, 1971

Noah can now easily pull apart and push together the plastic beads they tried so hard to get him to do at UCLA. And if he knocks over a trash basket, we can get him to right it again. And he can build with blocks, which builds our hopes.

October 24, 1971

Family mishaps: (1) Karl had left a black crayon in his pants so we spent half the night trying to get the dryer clean; (2) Foumi's lately taken to drinking a white wine and cider mixture. Noah happened by, sampled the drink, and downed it all. For the rest of the evening he was thoroughly irascible, crying wildly, never quite knowing where he was at.

October 25, 1971

The Monday morning blahs: I feel alienated from my own youth but not yet caught up with the truth of my middle age. My elbow aches constantly and I think I have arthritis there just like a fellow left-hander from Brooklyn—Sandy Koufax.

Meanwhile, I did work with Noah over the weekend. Though the speech went badly, as usual—I barely could get him to repeat an "uh"—he did build well with his blocks and he was generally more interested in his toys, especially his little piano. Perhaps he is finally developing a sense of his own things.

October 26, 1971

Karl was talking about his classmates and his friends. I asked him who his best friend was. "Noah," he said.

But then Foumi tells me she saw Karl play-wrestling with Noah on the floor the other day and cautioned him about smothering Noah. "If a policeman saw you doing that," she warned, "he'd think you were killing him." "Wouldn't you be glad if I killed him?" said Karl. "Then you wouldn't have to worry about taking care of him."

October 27, 1971

Drove out to Connecticut to visit a prominent playwright I know. But as we sat and talked in his studio he told me one thing I did not know. He has a son with mongolism—Down's syndrome. "I took one look at the baby, at the palm of his hand, and I knew. This was three years ago. The doctor said wait and see. I said, 'No way.' I knew once the child was in my house I was done for. So I put him in a nursing home straight from the hospital. You see, I had a Down's syndrome cousin. Ruined the family. Brought the family down trying to care for him. Where is my son now? In the state institution not far from here. He's a healthy kid and we visit him, but it's different—it's not as if we became attached to him from day one."

23

October 28, 1971

Noah gave Roberta a tough time during speech therapy, refusing to open his mouth at all. But then last night he came sauntering into the bathroom and said "Hi, Daddy." And before he went to bed he issued forth a "Good night."

I'm convinced that Noah someday will come to speech on his own. There is something about him, in spite of all his dumbness that seizes the shortcut position and won't abandon it. Thus, once he says something, he sees no need to ever say it again. Perhaps not only is he more educable than we thought, but, ultimately, much smarter than we think.

October 29, 1971

Karl was a pain, trying on costumes for Halloween, never being satisfied with any of them. Then he woke me in the middle of the night complaining tearfully that he could not sleep, he was having a nightmare about the Headless Horseman. I mumbled something to Foumi about how he was doing all these numbers just to get attention. She told me not to be so Freudian, and reminded me that we had just visited Washington Irving's home.

Noah had to bring a costume to his school too. And we had thought it would be just a waste. But he was amused as he watched Karl put on his mask. And Foumi thinks she can see the outlines of a sense of humor forming. He certainly knows how to keep us guessing.

November 1, 1971

Last night I took an unmasked Noah—along with his masked brother—trick-or-treating. At first Noah resisted, preferring to ride in the car rather than walk down the block. But as he got farther and farther away from the house his protests waned. And he seemed to enjoy the idea of knocking on doors, ringing doorbells, visiting houses, and finding people glad to see him. But most of all, I think, he liked the idea of doing something with Karl. By the end of the evening I even had him toting his own trick-or-treat bag.

This afternoon was another story. I came home to find a path of feces and urine from Noah's room to the john. And Foumi told me she had urged Noah to go to the bathroom just ten minutes before.

November 6, 1971

Noah can learn quickly. Show him how to push the light switch twice and he'll do it himself. Perhaps he just does not like the testing process, which is often confused with the learning process. Most children don't like to be tested.

November 7, 1971

I never thought I would get so involved in education. But I realize that those in charge of the systems know so little—and really care even less. And worst of all, they're all suckers for the hypes I've learned the hard way to ignore.

November 8, 1971

He has to be pushed and prodded every step of the way. To get dressed. To come downstairs. To eat breakfast. To take his vitamins. To put on his coat. To get him off to school each morning exhausts us. Noah? No, Karl.

Noah, who can do puzzles in his absent way, is just like any other inattentive, uncurious, intensely lovable two-year-old—who happens to be five and a half. But he tries, God love him, he tries. He just can't always seem to connect. The other day I taught him how to put the light on and off. I next asked him to jump. Immediately he ritualized the whole thing—he would jump and then play with the light switch.

November 11, 1971

Let me record my encounters with education during the past few days. A week ago we went to see Karl's class. It was open school week—"open" in the old sense, to visitors. And we were dismayed at what we saw—confusion without creativity, entertainment more than education. So we walked about the school looking for second-grade alternatives for Karl. We saw a class for those with learning disabilities that seemed too clinical. We saw two traditional, one-teacher–one-classroom situations. One was dull; the other was duller. Finally, we found a structured class taught by a young, warm, vibrant teacher.

So the next day when I dropped Karl off at school, I asked his open-school teacher, who was idly picking out chords on her guitar, what his reading level was. "I'm not interested in reading levels"—she looked up—"I'm interested in where his head is at." Among other things, I told her that meant we had different and incompatible philosophies. "In that case," she said, "you better take Karl out of our class."

I took her at her word. I went to see the assistant principal. I told him I would like to have Karl transferred. He told me it would be no problem and I came home relieved, and self-congratulatory.

But the next day Karl's teacher was on the phone: we should have a meeting, an in-depth conference. We should consider the whole child, Karl was developing wonderfully. In short, we should give open school another chance. "No way," I said. My mind was made up. I was determined to transfer Karl out of her room and the assistant principal had given his permission. She said the assistant principal did not have the power to give such permission, only the principal could, and she doubted if he would.

Which turned out to be so. The principal proceeded to give us a hard time. At first he said he could not transfer Karl at all. Finally he said he would transfer Karl only to the class we had found the dullest—for no reason. He was just being ornery.

I became angry. I called the district principal. He didn't return my calls. I tracked him down at a meeting. He wiggled out a back door when he saw me. I left word at his office that I was keeping Karl out of school until I heard from him.

Last night I did reach him at his home. I complained about the pettiness and vindictiveness of his staff and of the principal. He said he could not allow parents to dictate educational policy and he would back his principal every step of the way.

"Okay," I said. "I'm going to hold you personally responsible for Karl's education this year if it doesn't work out."

"What does that mean?" he asked.

"Whatever you think it means," I said.

"Are you threatening me?"

"You're damned right."

"I'm going to write a memorandum about this conversation," he said.

"Include in it," I said, "how you kept avoiding me when I tried to see you."

And on and on it went, until he did say he would talk the matter over with the principal and get back to me.

This morning he did not call me. I called him. He was away from his desk.

But then the principal called. He'd take Karl out of the open school and put him in the class we wanted on the condition that I would sign a letter stating the move was against all their professional recommendations.

"Certainly," I said.

This incident has taught me much. I thought we had trouble with education for Noah because of his special problems. I've now learned that even normal education is a hassle. The open school was a closed society. The administration, the principal, the teacher did not care about the individual child. They were all too busy scoring points for each other. Any bureaucracy is frightening; the educational bureaucracy doubly so—kids are at stake.

Karl appreciates our concern, understands that we are as worried about his potential development as we are about Noah's. Yesterday he said to Foumi: "Why don't you get Noah's class changed too? You don't think his teacher is good for him."

Tilting with bureaucracy is enervating. Raising children, normal or abnormal, is agonizing. I can't stand governmental functionaries. I've always hated capitalism because I know it's just forty master thieves. But socialism, I'm afraid, would be just forty petty clerks. What is my political dream now?

27

November 12, 1971

A new friend of Karl's was over while Roberta was working with Noah. The friend observed for a while curiously. Karl explained that Noah was autistic, that he had a bad brain. "We're lucky," he told his new friend, "we have good brains."

November 13, 1971

Noah is making sounds again! Various starts at words, shards, of echolalia. He knows—or tries: "Rice," "Come on," "Daddy," "I want," "I do," "Hi," "Mommy."

And in my study he'll touch the word DADDY I have pasted on the wall when I say "Touch Daddy." And in his room he'll touch the word MOMMY pasted there when I say "Touch Mommy."

November 14, 1971

Cool breeze, autumn leaves, it's a lovely, glorious, never-want-to-leave-Croton day. Yesterday we drove out to Long Island to visit some friends and Noah did not have a good time. He's reached a period where he doesn't like to leave home. Perhaps that means he is more aware of his environment. I still can't tell whether a troublesome incident or interlude is a good sign or a bad one.

November 15, 1971

Karl's new teacher has wisely placed him in a cluster among old friends. And I like the look of the work Karl has begun to bring home. It *is* "work" and has teacher comments written on it.

November 16, 1971

Karl continues to like his new class. The teacher doesn't seem to be a great brain but she does spark vitality. And yesterday

for the first time in eons Karl was drawing nonobjectively—
and beautifully.

I watch Noah guardedly. It is only a question of time before
we will have to put him away. He is simply too retarded, too
unable to take care of himself on an elementary level. The decision will somehow make itself. As Karl gets older it will just be
easier for him to accept Noah's departure from the family picture. And as Noah gets older he will leave the cute stage, as
surely as the kitten becomes the cat. And it will be easier
for us too.

November 17, 1971
Today we saw the future, Noah's future. We went to Letchworth Village, a fifty-year-old New York State institution in
Rockland County. The masonry is fantastic, the rolling hills
impressive, but the facilities were overcrowded—with four
thousand patients—and understaffed, there seemed scarcely
enough help about. And the place reeked institution—the smell
of urine and lye; the harsh green painted walls; the dirty windows; the begrudging attitude and incompetence of unin-
spired civil service.

First the social worker took us to one of their custodial
wards: sixty old women in odd clothes sitting in a day room,
all manner of freaks calling for a Hogarth, a Daumier, to sketch
them. It was bath day but the place still stank. Half of the
"children," as they were called, even though some were into
their sixties and seventies, had to be fed; others weren't even
toilet trained. And there were just seven people to take care
of them.

After that things seemed to get better. But that's the way,
I'd been warned, institutional tours are orchestrated. Immediately they show you the worst—something dramatically bad—
so you think they are honest. And then the scenes improve as the
tour unfolds. Until gradually you feel as if there is hope; indeed, as if some sort of progress had been achieved right
before your very eyes.

29

We visited several classrooms and "rec" rooms; an occupational therapy room; and finally a "cottage" where some fifty children slept in a crowded dormitory. It seemed impossible for any individual, even a normal one, to take roots there.

When I came home I looked at Noah. I had seen his fate—sooner or later he will have to go to one of these places. I thought about it and shuddered. My impression of Letchworth was worse than my memory of a visit to Dachau. I vowed I would have to send Noah to a better place, one where he would not be so irrevocably and irretrievably lost.

November 18, 1971

Foumi calls the scene at Letchworth—the old women, disfigured, with bulging stomachs, double malnutrition chins, and skinny beanpole arms—a "surreal heaven": "They were all so gentle and had nothing to do."

November 19, 1971

I've been working extra hard with Noah. He drifts back quickly without backup, without brushups. It is difficult for him to distinguish exact instructions. Once I begin asking him to give me something, he will give me the same object over and over again, no matter what I ask for. He is like a computer offering the same printout no matter how the program is altered.

Karl has been doing such creative artwork since coming out of the open school. He has an eye for color, a feel for design. He is his mother's son.

And Noah, I'm afraid, is mine.

November 20, 1971

Children are so literal. Foumi decided to go into the city to see an exhibition of American Indian art. We were surprised when Karl insisted on going with her. When they came home she told me how utterly disappointed he was. He had expected to see exact likenesses of American Indians—so many cigar-store Indians lined up in neat rows.

November 26, 1971

We had a half-dozen kids in for Karl's seventh birthday party. Noah spent the afternoon with Roberta, out of sight, so Karl could have his day.

November 27, 1971

I came home to find Foumi in tears, overburdened suddenly by Noah. And I fell into despair too. His speech remains minimal, his self-care haphazard, and the problem increases as winter approaches. This afternoon he was urinating all over the place.

Last night we tried to explain our dark mood to Karl and he was boyishly baffled. He could not understand that we were different from other families. He cried when we told him that Noah would never be better.

November 28, 1971

If Foumi is near the breaking point so am I. This afternoon I was pushing Noah on the swing and now it was slowing down. I thought I would surprise him with another push. And I did. Hard. He wasn't holding on tightly to the swing ropes and he slammed to the ground, his head snapping back as he did so. I expected to hear him crying. But there was no sound. And I thought: What if he's dead? What an ideal solution!

It was all in a split second. By the time I reached him Noah was crying loudly.

November 29, 1971

Ever since we've been to Letchworth Village I move in the same cloud of uric-acid–lye stench that permeated the wards there. And I see no way out. I'm boxed into an untenable situation. We must keep Noah at home as long as we can, otherwise we destroy his life. But we cannot keep him at home too long, otherwise we destroy our lives. Poor kid! It's him against us.

December 4, 1971

Foumi had a good day with Noah, teaching him to put out his tongue. And touch his nose. The only problem is that as he learns a new thing he proceeds to forget the last thing he learned. Leaky, freaky kid, head moving from side to side as he continually sings the gibberish song of himself.

December 5, 1971

Our meal routines have changed. We now allow Noah to eat with us. Because if he first eats by himself he'll sit down with us anyway and have a second meal. And we worry about his getting too fat, especially the way he wolfs down anything he likes.

December 6, 1971

We're leaving in ten days. Going to California again. So many arrangements to make, so much packing to do. I don't see how we'll manage to get it all done.

December 7, 1971

Noah talks less. I just haven't been keeping up with his speech; instead I've been trying operant conditioning only in terms of visual imitations. If the other things come first, perhaps speech will follow.

A note from Lovaas at UCLA. He says they're looking forward to seeing Noah again.

December 10, 1971

Karl is sick, a heavy cold, and it brings out the essential child in him—an endearing helplessness, a fetching dependency. I always thought the beauty of childhood was its transiency. But everything about Noah spiritually has no transiency, may be forever fixed, no matter how tall he grows, how hardened his skin becomes. And yet there will always be something beautiful about him to me. Could the grotesque then be but the lasting presence of beauty?

December 14, 1971

I'm reminded again of the unreality of it all. I flew with a presidential aspirant to Canton, Ohio, yesterday for a *Life* magazine article I'm writing, and returned today. And it is as if I've been away a light-year. When I walked in the door this evening I was delighted to see Karl. But dismayed to see Noah. He just stared at me a little quizzically but without any great interest, and the delight of return was soon gone.

December 15, 1971

Kids are real. Kids are hard. Before going to sleep last night Karl said, " I don't mind if you put Noah in an institution, as long as you adopt a new brother for me."

December 16, 1971

A gift-from-the-gods day: suddenly blue skies. Sunny, warm, un-Decemberish. As if the weather were trying to bribe us to stay here. But we're all packed, ready to go. Last night we had the neighbors in for a good-bye-and-please-watch-the-house-while-we're-gone evening. And this morning I feel the excitement of imminent travel, the anticipation of adventure.

I look forward to California. And not for Noah's sake alone.

$$\bigodot 2$$

December 29, 1971

We've spent a week on the run, leaving New York, flying out here to L.A., hoteling it. Noah has been a tremendous problem, watering down the transient floors, adjusting—or rather not adjusting—to the new situation. And Foumi swears she'll never make the relocation trip again. But I have found us a house to rent, a block from the school Karl went to last year. And once the holidays are over and school starts, perhaps the kids will stop running us ragged.

December 31, 1971

We've rented furniture, moved into our rented house, and I'm driving about in a rented car. The only thing I don't seem to have rented is kids. Oh that I could exchange them, send them back—especially the defective one. And so the year ends with me whimpering, the typewriter keys pathetically banging, and only the bell at the end of the line appropriately ringing.

January 3, 1972

The kids are squared away. I took Noah to his old school this morning, Alys Harris greeted him warmly, and he seemed at home immediately. And then I took Karl to his school. The principal remembered him and placed him in a class with many kids he knew from last year.

January 4, 1972

Karl is delighted with his school, his class, his teacher. His only complaint: He has to sit at his desk all day. And Noah had a good first day of school. He went to the bathroom and performed on cue, but Alys reports that she did have to chastise him for crumpling up his work paper. Alys is the indomitable New England schoolmarm, insisting that her children be students. Which is the only way to be, I guess.

January 5, 1972

We took Noah to UCLA. Lovaas and his students looked him over and were quite impressed with his puzzle-solving abilities —Foumi's turf. In fact, when I told one of the students that Foumi had done well but that I had failed in my speech assignments, she succinctly observed: "Yeah, you blew it."

But we weren't as impressed—Foumi and I—with Lovaas and his students as we had been last year. We almost feel that there is little they can teach us now, that they have more to learn from us.

January 6, 1972

Noah had his first working session at UCLA since our return. And we were quite pleased, watching Meredith, who had worked with him last year, work with him again. She proceeded more slowly than we had remembered, more patiently, and seemed to get more out of him as she rewarded him with a sliver of potato chip for the tight-lipped *mmm* sounds and the open-mouthed *ahs* she coaxed out of him. I left feeling good.

35

And Alys Harris told me she thought she heard Noah say "Mrs. Harris" this afternoon at school. He also hugged her for the first time since he's been back in her class.

January 8, 1972
As I was driving Noah home from school, I saw Karl walking down the street with a new friend. I stopped and picked them up. Karl pointed to Noah, bouncing beside me. "That's my brother," he explained. "He's autistic." And then he and his friend resumed their trade talks about bubble-gum baseball cards.

January 10, 1972
The boys are tumbling in the next room but Noah seems to have begun to resent Karl's roughhousing with him. A good sign. He also seems to have enjoyed going shopping with the family yesterday at the Century City Shopping Mall. Another good sign. But two good signs do not the great leap forward make.

January 12, 1972
Noah's therapists at UCLA are more patient with Noah than we are at home. But they cannot make any useful suggestions about how to improve his eating patterns, how to get him to eat a little of everything on his plate, not just the starchy foods.

January 13, 1972
When I arrive at Noah's school or UCLA these days to pick him up, he often greets me with a gleeful shriek of "Daddy."

January 17, 1972
Children do imitate. Foumi seems to have come down with the flu so last night I slept on one of the couches in the living room.

36

This morning I found Karl fast asleep on the other couch. Evidently, he had awakened during the night, found me in the living room, taken his pillow and blanket, and joined me. I have to be careful. His mimicry assigns a greater responsibility to me than Noah's.

January 18, 1972

Foumi's flu is making me sick. As I take full care of the kids, we both realize how much she's been doing. Which leads to her making Women's Lib noises. I know her role is not an easy one. But neither is mine. In a way I would love to put on an apron, go into the kitchen, and not have to worry about making a living. I think money worries are even more deadening to the psyche than mundane chores.

January 19, 1972

A Lovaas student has been assigned to come to the house a few afternoons a week and work with Noah.

January 23, 1972

Karl and I went to see *The RA Expedition*, a documentary showing how, thousands of years ago, Africans could possibly have built rafts capable of sailing to America. And Karl pleased me with his sense of humor: *RA I* has failed to reach America. Next sails *RA II*. And the Norwegian narrator, artificially trying to build up suspense, warns ominously, "Now the raft is in the hurricane zone." Karl, deep in the seat next to me, laughed and said in a mock Norwegian accent, "Make way for RA Three."

January 31, 1972

We went to Santa Barbara. A prospective school for Noah there is still in the formative stages. We met the woman who will be

37

the teacher, and liked her. I would not mind settling there at all.

Noah's report card from school:

Noah showed no apprehension upon reentering school. He is much stronger physically and is active and varied in his outdoor play.

It appears that he may have been in a more permissive environment during the past year as he has had a few tantrums when not allowed to have his own way.

He is beginning to conform to our structure again, and is quite cooperative identifying and matching symbols and colors.

Noah enjoys the class and is beginning to interact more. We are happy to have him with us again.

February 2, 1972

I've always told Karl that one of the advantages of his binational position is a choice of citizenship when he grows up. He also knows that both Foumi and I view nationalism as a negative rather than a positive force in the world today. So I was not surprised when his teacher reported that he is refusing to make the pledge to the flag in school each day. But I was pleasantly surprised to hear her say that she is glad that Karl is so outspoken in his refusal, that she feels it is good for the other kids to know that not everybody pledges allegiance to the flag.

February 3, 1972

Noah is toughening up. He really unloaded a pretty good shot at Karl today when Karl tried roughhousing with him. Karl took it quite well too.

February 4, 1972

They've started an experiment with Noah at UCLA. There is a theory that an autistic child can use only one sense, or one perceptional faculty, at a time. He cannot look at you, for example, and listen to you simultaneously. It is as if his communications headquarters can handle only one set of input or sensory stimuli at a time. The theory also postulates, however, that he is more sensitive to that one set of stimuli. In other words, what he sees, he sees even more clearly than normal.

To test the theory, some of the doctoral candidates have set up an apparatus that looks like a pinball machine scoreboard. They have it wired to flash various squares of light. Each time a square of light is flashed Noah is being conditioned to touch it. Gradually, they plan to dim the light squares and hope even the dimmest of lights will be a sufficient cue for Noah to touch the appropriate square. So science marches on over a cluster of potato chips fed to a still-babbling baby of five and a half.

February 5, 1972

I don't mind the use of Noah for scientific purposes at UCLA —but not in my house. The Lovaas student who comes here isn't working out. He seems more interested in conducting experiments with Noah than in teaching him.

February 7, 1972

I hate the room I'm working in—the green swirling wallpaper, the rumpled unmade beds, the messy, cluttered rug. I'm not sure I want to live in California, the great American dreamland. The school in Santa Barbara seems as if it will be okay for Noah. He's becoming more and more difficult, tantrumming at odd hours, grabbing and pulling hair for no fathomable reason.

February 8, 1972

I had a long talk about Noah with Lovaas. He shrugged sympathetically and finally said, "Look, there are people willing to devote themselves to such children. You and Foumi ought to find such people and place Noah in their hands."

I don't need Noah as a raison d'être. But neither can I see a life without Noah—not just yet.

February 9, 1972

We went to see a psychiatrist at UCLA's Neuropsychiatric Institute. He's an alleged specialist in autism. He spoke softly of autism being an organic affliction, a biochemical condition rather than a psychogenic one (a malady stemming from mental conflict or emotional unrest). But the analyst's couch in his office told us which corner he was in, that he was viewing autism as a brain disease in order to hold down the psychogenic fort.

It's all a grim joke! Organized medicine tosses the problem of autism into the hands of the psychiatrists in order to preserve its healing monopoly. And then the psychiatrists toss it right back in order to preserve their particular franchise.

February 10, 1972

Noah is running a fever. Last night, while he was in the bathroom, I brought him two aspirins. But I dropped one. I picked it off the floor, threw it in the toilet and flushed it down. I handed him the other one. He promptly threw it in the toilet.

February 14, 1972

We visited the Neuropsychiatric Institute's school at UCLA. The teaching facilities are marvelous—shops, homerooms, a recreational deck, occupational therapy rooms, but all unreal, like exhibitions at a trade fair. It's all only for kids while they're being tested. The project grants that finance it all put the emphasis on a kind of publish-or-perish research rather than on doing something for the children themselves. I just hope that someday parents will be given a voice in the governmental dispensations of scientific largesses. The hell with new-model promises. We're the consumers in dire need of services for the old defective models.

February 15, 1972

At Lovaas's training grounds speech is still an agonizingly slow process for Noah. He can say "Mmmm." He can say "Ah." But he can't put them together into "Ma." What he can do, though, is "object discrimination"—drop pennies into one container, marbles into another. Literally, small change.

February 16, 1972

In the mornings at his school I delight in watching Noah soar on the swings. He has learned to pump with his feet. He doesn't jump well, though. And he still can't throw a ball with much energy or direction. But then his old man wasn't a great athlete either.

I also get great joy each morning watching from our diningroom window as Karl runs up the hill toward school one block away. That's the ideal distance, I've decided, for every family to live, because a kid is so territorial, so much more secure being close to his school. For that reason alone I could be against busing—if I weren't so against those who are against busing.

February 17, 1972

We observed Alys Harris at Noah's school and as usual were impressed. She has control over the class, even when her back is turned. While she works with one child, the others patiently wait. Any command she issues, such as "Sit down," is obeyed immediately. And without the help of any aides, she even had the kids doing various physical activities: Carrying a die on a spoon. Walking around a rope. Jumping over two-by-fours laid out on the ground like a stepladder.

Noah couldn't do them very well. But then I think he was distracted, observing us as we observed him.

February 23, 1972

A trip up to the San Francisco Bay area, visiting old friends. We had warned them about Noah, but they were game. I doubt if they'll be that game again. Noah had an accident one afternoon on their teenage daughter's bed and was up screeching most of another night.

February 28, 1972

Yesterday was my forty-fourth birthday. I received no formal gift from Noah, but some great informal ones. At one point during the morning he suddenly disappeared. I looked about the house—his room, Karl's room, our room. Couldn't find him. Then I slowly opened his bathroom door. And there he was, sitting proudly, his pants pulled down, on the toilet.

He also spoke. In the afternoon we went shopping at the May Company. I was temporarily separated from him as I began to browse on my own. Immediately Noah cried out: "Daddy!"

And he was very funny too. When I took him into a fitting-room booth with me he started to pull down his pants. The booth does look like a bathroom of sorts, I guess.

February 29, 1972

For over two years we've been trying to eliminate Noah's "self-stimming"—or self-stimulation—his jumping, his bouncing, his finger flexing, his bizarre, repetitive movements. For an organism to stay alive, the behaviorists had told us, it must be stimulated. And if it doesn't receive stimulation from the outside world, it stimulates itself. At the same time, the behaviorists theorized, while the organism is stimulating itself it cannot receive stimulation from the outside world. So Noah's self-stimulation was an obstacle to his learning speech—or anything else.

But today I learned something discouraging from a Lovaas student at UCLA. She's doing a study which reveals that the stopping of self-stimulation does not necessarily result in improved speech. It seems that every time the behaviorists try to find a principle other than a pragmatic one, they're in trouble.

March 2, 1972

We now have two high school students who come to help us. They're much more useful than any of Lovaas's UCLA students.

March 6, 1972

Sunday, shitty Sunday. Even though Noah seemed to have a slight intestinal flu yesterday morning we tried to overlook it. The hyperactivist parents of a four-year-old autistic boy in the San Fernando Valley had been beseeching us to visit them for weeks. We went. A mistake. On the drive out, Noah went in his pants. At their house he went twice more, once wiping himself with their bedspread. And then their boy began to go with a loose stomach of his own. It reached the point of being almost funny.

During the hectic interludes we tried to speak of the need for humane residences for these kids. A word I hate, *institution*, kept popping up. But I know the establishment of another institution is no solution. Bricks replacing bricks is not necessarily progress. These parents, I'm afraid, have energy but lack education, imagination, and original direction. On the practical level, I still wonder what I want most for Noah. I know working for the establishment of another day school doesn't make sense to me. I know a residential school can too easily become an institution, providing more custodial shelter than educational nurture. I guess ideally the best solution for us is a live-in Anne Sullivan who discovers—or uncovers—in Noah another Helen Keller.

Right now while Noah is little I can still hope and dream for a lot. Yet I also have a recurring image of Noah, no longer a kitten, prowling through a life of endless hospital corridors.

March 8, 1972

Alys Harris, Noah's teacher, remains the perennial optimist. This morning she told me that Noah is trying very hard to talk.

43

But for a year and a half he's been like that. And while we once thought that large doses of vitamins such as niacinamide and drugs such as Deaner might help bring Noah to speech, we're gradually giving up on that approach. Which leaves us on a kind of Sisyphean treadmill. If Noah isn't constantly tutored, he loses what he has. But any emphasis placed on learning a new skill reduces the review time necessary to retain an old one.

March 10, 1972

Last week, after Karl's teacher reported he was misbehaving, we decided to give Karl a behavior modification scorecard on which each day the teacher would check his behavior as being GOOD or BAD. Karl understood that when it was checked BAD he would be punished by being deprived of playtime.

For three days it worked. The first two days he came home with a check on the GOOD. On the third day he came home with a check between the GOOD and the BAD. And yesterday he didn't bring the card home at all, saying, "The teacher lost it." I called the school and spoke with her. He was right. Now I have to figure out a system of rewards and punishments for her.

March 11, 1972

Ivar Lovaas and I were sitting in a booth yesterday watching one of his behavior modification student therapists work with Noah. "Money," announced Ivar, "is going out of style as a reinforcer."

"What's coming in?" I asked.

"Love," he said. "Love is again the key contingency."

"Who's the therapist offering love as a contingency?" I asked.

"God," said Ivar.

March 12, 1972

I detect a slight drift toward California values in me and I have to be wary of it. It is a belief in the primacy that the movie medium has over the literary medium, an almost climatic sense that entertainment is somehow more important than truth.

March 13, 1972

Karl told me that a new school friend had told him that his father was a screenwriter. "And what did you say your father did?"

"I said," said Karl, "my father was a regular writer."

This regular writer went to a Hollywood reception at a studio executive's house on Saturday, a catered picnic luncheon in Bel-Air. There were umbrellaed tables set up all over the garden. The host must have thought Foumi was a maid, or a governess in charge of Karl; he ignored her so completely.

I told Karl to sit at a particular table while I picked up some food for him. It turned out to be the table of the "heavies," the successful producers and hot directors; everyone clustering about it while the other tables were empty. And so I returned with my plateful of hamburgers and burritos to find an unhappy Karl uncomfortably sandwiched between two fat asses.

March 14, 1972

We continued our education in special education by visiting the Special Education Program of the Santa Monica School System. And we were duly impressed by what they called the "engineered classroom": The setup was structured, but there were places for "exploration" such as in the open classroom. However, unlike the open classroom, it had a center, a core, with a constant learning activity. And the kids were quiet.

The program was much too advanced for Noah at present. But oh that one day Noah could belong in such a program!

March 16, 1972

It gives me such a charge to watch Karl from the window as he kick-walks down the street, does a one-hand twirl around a light pole, tiptoes along the curbstone, leaps up onto a garden embankment and then broad jumps off it as far as he can.

March 17, 1972

I don't know how much these UCLA student therapists know but they can't know very much if they can't tell when a kid has to go to the bathroom. Yesterday afternoon, at his session, Noah rose and went to the door. The student therapist told Noah to return to his seat. But he had that look on his face, that squirm in his ass. I got him to the john and—just as I got his pants down—he could no longer hold it in. So some of it got on his underwear.

Still, he did better than the student experts.

March 18, 1972

I've come to a small conclusion: This society is not geared for anyone who is in anything less than perfect health, all assertions that we are living in a welfare state to the contrary.

March 20, 1972

I had lunch with one of the kids from the block I grew up on in Brooklyn. He's a record-company salesman now, fat, loud, vulgar, aggressive—just as I remembered him. He told me that one of the kids, who had become a cop, had multiple sclerosis and was now confined to a wheelchair; that the girl down the block, the tomboy who could punch a ball as far as any other kid, became a gym teacher and then died of cancer; that another girl, the quiet sister of a friend, had died of a mysterious and rare blood ailment.

I always thought of death as far removed from my own childhood, from my old block. But if it has caught up with some of the other kids, it may be catching up with this kid too.

March 22, 1972

It must be even worse to have a child who comes part of the way, develops a small vocabulary and a few traces of normalcy, than it is to have one who makes no progress at all. In that case one really doesn't know what to do with the kid; he has so much more to lose by being institutionalized.

March 24, 1972

I've stopped working with Noah on speech. I stopped because I was ineffective. I'm no Anne Sullivan even though I tried using the same methods with Noah as she had used with Helen Keller: a structured system of immediate rewards and punishments to teach the child to monitor and control his own behavior. I still think the failure was in the therapist, not the therapy. Because if Anne Sullivan had merely hug-loved Helen Keller profusely in the laissez-faire psychogenic style, Helen Keller would have remained an anonymous, multihandicapped autistic child.

March 25, 1972

We had a visitor last night who had not seen Noah for over a year. She noted how much more alert he was, how increasingly aware of his environment he had become. It takes a visitor to note such phenomena, I guess. I have observed that in the experiments they're running on him at UCLA Noah has improved in touching the square with the light . . . though he still protests vigorously as he does so.

March 26, 1972

During meals whenever I try to use food as an operant conditioning reward, Noah resents it terribly. And I can't say I blame him.

March 27, 1972

Karl has formed an inseparable friendship with a little six-and-a-half-year-old towheaded kid who is already worldly smart. He is the youngest of three brothers and—unlike Karl—he can size up a situation immediately, realistically. To Karl, of course, he must be a substitute for the kid brother he does not really have.

March 28, 1972

We had a go, Foumi and I, because of Noah. Foumi was keeping him up, waiting for his bowel movement. I figured he might fall asleep in his clothes so I put him in his sleeper. But neglected to inform Foumi of that fact.

Soon I heard Noah jumping on his bed and when I went into his room to investigate I immediately smelled the cause: excrement in his pants, excrement on the bed, excrement smeared everywhere. And so, loading up the washing machine, washing Noah down, changing the sheets and blankets, wiping the crap off the walls and the rug and the chairs, and doing all the shit-cleaning work our tired flesh has become heir to, we began a series of mutual recriminations.

I blamed the incident on Foumi.

She said it was my fault, that I never tell people what I'm doing.

I said that I had been trying to be helpful.

Helpful to whom? she screamed. Noah was my responsibility as much as he was hers.

And on and on it went.

Until, as usual, I ended up thinking of putting Noah away. But where?

March 29, 1972

If Noah is not making significant, really significant, strides within two years, I've decided, we'll definitely institutionalize him.

We had twenty-four hours away from Noah, spending a day and night in Santa Barbara, while we left him in the charge of our two high school helpers. In our hotel room this morning, as we all lay in bed relishing our restful, uninterrupted sleep, I asked: "Who misses Noah?" Foumi and Karl and I all looked up at each other. But none of us gave an answer.

When we returned this afternoon we were greeted by a sulky Noah with a "screw you" expression on his face. But this evening he has been affectionate, sidling up to us and then leaning up against us like a cat. And just a moment ago he distinctly said the word *strawberry*.

April 3, 1972

Bodil, a Norwegian grad student studying with Lovaas, has begun to work with Noah. She teaches him in steps, breaking down the simplest acts because Noah is unable to make the usual connections. For example, if you want him to place a coin on the table and then turn it over, you have to teach him two distinct movements.

In speech she's trying to get him to make "mmm" sounds against the flat of his hand and soft "p" sounds against a cupped hand. In this way, theoretically he can learn to monitor the sounds he makes by both the position of his hand and the breath expired against it.

April 5, 1972

The Norwegian girl has Noah making match-ups. He's doing well placing spoons with spoons and forks with forks. But no matter what she does he's not responding very well to her efforts to induce speech.

49

April 6, 1972

I learned of an autistic child who not only did not make progress on vitamins, but actually regressed—so a parent told me. That's all Noah has to do now—regress.

April 7, 1972

I tried to be tough with Noah. I decided I wouldn't give him his milk last night until he said "I want milk." But I settled for an "I."

April 11, 1972

As I walked into the house last night I heard Foumi screaming in the kitchen. There was Noah clawing at her while she was trying to sauté some meat for a spaghetti sauce. And Karl was crying at the back door, his clothes soaked and muddy. I felt like Superman to the rescue.

April 12, 1972

Noah can be cute. But Karl can be even cuter. He can use words, he can make jokes, and, most important, he constantly develops, unfolds. His teacher tells me he has improved tremendously and that she is very pleased "with the contributions he's making in class." Karl's on a presidential kick now, reading about their lives, fascinated with their history. I distressed him inordinately, though, when I informed him that George Washington had slaves. But he has to learn to live with the truth, wrinkles and all.

April 14, 1972

Tonight Karl is on his first sleep-over, staying with his tow-headed little friend. All evening I have been half awaiting an I-want-to-go-home call from him. But it has not come. So perhaps at last he's come of age. What age? I do not know.

April 15, 1972

I was in the park with Noah when he noticed a mother giving her child some juice. Noah then said "juice," and ran to grab the cup. He began to climb onto the mother as if she were a statue. I rescued both the beverage and the woman from my attacking son. But once more, even in the bright afternoon sunlight, the future of Noah looked dim to me.

April 16, 1972

We've been looking at houses lately. And the real estate salesman who took us around yesterday looked vaguely familiar to me. At the end of the day he gave me his card. I read, "Bruce Bennett."

The name rang a bell and I said, "Didn't you once play Tarzan?"

He nodded.

I turned to Karl and explained. "When I was a boy he was Tarzan."

Karl looked at me in utter disbelief: "When you were a boy Tarzan was a realtor?"

April 17, 1972

Karl's interest in presidential history has, if anything, increased. He rattles off lists of those born in Virginia, those who came from Ohio, those whose names are John. I wonder if he's compensating for the fact that because he wasn't born in this country he can never dream of becoming President himself.

April 18, 1972

When I gave Karl his bath tonight I realized with a pang that one day he will be bigger and taller than me.

We've definitely decided to move here permanently even though living in Los Angeles presents problems—the air, the commercial climate, the anti-art ambience. But it also proposes some solutions: Noah's schooling, Foumi's unhappiness with a cold climate.

A blow from the East. I had written Noah's school telling them we would be back at the end of the month and hoped there would be a place for Noah there.

The reply from the director:

> Dear Mr. and Mrs. Greenfeld:
> I have received your letter requesting readmission for Noah. I regret to inform you that at this time the program is fully subscribed to.

Etc., etc.

Beautiful. What are we supposed to do now? Perhaps we should stay here and not even go back there anymore—except to move.

I feel awful. I feel my freedom has been impinged. Restricted. With a normal child one can come and go and always find a school. With a special child, one is literally always coming and going.

I called the American Civil Liberties Union in New York. I told them my child might very well be denied an education because he is autistic, that I wanted to go to court about it, and would the ACLU be interested in supporting me. No, I was told, they weren't interested in such a case.

I spoke to the director of Noah's school in New York again, after threatening legal action on my own. And somehow, suddenly, a place has opened up for Noah; I have been assured that they can take him back after all. But as I prepare to return home, I still feel put out, discriminated against, and begin to understand what members of a minority have to go through.

April 28, 1972

Our last day in L.A. We had a farewell conference with Lovaas, the key words unspoken but sensed. He feels he let us down this time, and we do feel a bit let down.

$$\widehat{3}$$

May 3, 1972

I was putting suitcases away in the basement when I came across some old letters from the time I was in the hospital with polio twenty-four years ago. In rereading them I saw how everyone thought I had suffered some great misfortune at the time. And I had. I could not walk.

But I soon knew that I was not so badly hit, that though I was afflicted with the dreaded disease of polio I would recover to a large degree. And I did.

And then I thought about Noah and how he would never recover and how we would never get over him. He's an affliction here to stay, one that continually unfolds.

May 4, 1972

After dinner last night I had severe chest pains. Worse than any I ever had before. Different, too. Tight across the top of my chest. For a half hour I endured them. Then I complained to

Foumi and she called our doctor. He told her there was nothing to worry about. After all I had no weight problems and I was still in my thirties. No, Foumi told him, I was forty-four.

He asked to talk to me.

I described the pain and he said he'd meet me at the hospital.

My neighbor Tom drove me there—and left me there at my insistence. In the emergency room a technician gave me a cardiogram, an intern took my blood pressure. Soon my doctor arrived.

He had stopped at his office to pick up my last cardiogram from the files. He read the new cardiogram and compared it to the old one. He took my blood pressure. And he told me my heart was all right, that I was probably suffering from a spasm in the esophagus.

When he drove me home I asked him why he had become so concerned when he found out my age. "At your age," he said, "you don't screw around. Any pain in the chest can be the big one."

Later Foumi and I talked it over: the strain of Noah could bring on a real heart attack.

May 7, 1972

Noah was up all night chirping and I was ready to kill him this morning. And Foumi and I, our nerves tired, insomniacal, have been on the combative verge all day long.

May 8, 1972

Hooray for Crest. At the dentist's today, Karl had two cavities. But Noah none. Which is a great relief. Because if he had any there was no way he would keep his mouth open so that the dentist could work on him—even with a local anesthesia. He would have to be put out completely.

55

May 9, 1972

Foumi thinks that somehow, someday, Noah will get to meaningful speech. In general she has greater long-range hopes for him than I have.

May 10, 1972

Changing schools again may be bad for Karl academically, but being home is certainly great for his appetite. This afternoon when he came home from school he had three bags of Cheez Doodles; at dinner he ate a big bowl of spaghetti and a generous portion of salad. And then an hour later he wanted a grilled cheese sandwich.

May 11, 1972

Noah literally almost knocked me out this evening, butting his head against me. I had wanted him to stop playing with Foumi's purse. He refused. I took it away from him. He still wanted it and lashed out, scratching me. I held his hands. Then he drove his head with force up into my chin.

And I'm sure he knew what he was doing.

May 12, 1972

Roberta is excellent when it comes to working with Noah on visual imitations. But I get the feeling that she, too, has all but given up in speech.

May 13, 1972

Karl's teacher called yesterday. She had found him alone at lunchtime in the classroom, crying, slamming his school-cafeteria-lunch sandwich to the floor, exclaiming: "This is no good. They don't know how to make lunches here." And she thought it might be more than just a sandwich that was troubling him.

I talked to him after he came home. He said he didn't like

the kids, that they treated him mean; he wished he could go back to California; and that the lunch *was* rotten.

I feel sorry for the kid, uprooting him the way we do because of his brother. But I also have to be wary of letting him use Noah as an excuse of any sort. His teacher also had told me that Karl complained that Noah had been keeping him up at night. Noah has—but not that much.

May 16, 1972

As I rode the Central along the Hudson this morning I was amazed by the filth, the generally seedy quality of both the train and the view. It's really hard to adjust to the East after having lived in California. But it does feel good to be far removed from the lures of the movie business.

Now if I could only remove myself from the tugs of Noah. He is still a problem. He scratches, he pinches, he strikes out. But even worse, he still breaks my heart.

May 17, 1972

Foumi thinks that when Noah suddenly lashes out and clutches at someone he might be having incipient seizures. We should look into some of the drugs used on epileptics.

May 18, 1972

Our close friends are still having a problem with their teenage daughter. She's slipping off to Greenwich Village and slipping into trouble—the freaky hippie drug scene where she pops pills and sleeps with less-than-whole people.

My friends don't know what to do about it. My heart goes out to them. The ordinary development of kids isn't so ordinary either.

May 19, 1972

I've moved into my new office, atop a pharmacy cornering on the two cross streets that comprise downtown Croton. I

57

look out my window and see the high school kids, all a blurry blond to me, gathered before the delicatessen eating their sandwiches. I open the windows and hear them shouting to each other and wonder if they know, munching on their bologna, the roll bread squirting between their teeth, the bottles of soda in their hands, that these are the indelible years of their lives.

May 20, 1972

Another assassination attempt. I have the radio on, awaiting further news of George Wallace's condition. He was shot in a shopping center in Maryland. I never liked the man but I truly hope that he does not end up paralyzed. I know a little of the life of the handicapped and do not wish it on anyone.

May 21, 1972

Roberta had Noah jumping successfully. Something he had not done well before. She laid out three blocks on the floor and he jumped over them. And he was so delighted with his accomplishment that he smiled shyly. I then tried to get him to flash a peace sign—but his digital coordination is just too poor; all he could do was waggle his hand generally—not hold up the specific fingers.

May 23, 1972

Noah is ill; Karl is unhappy, rebelling against the idea that he has to learn multiplication tables; Foumi is complaining about the muggy weather. In returning East I've not exactly found Nirvana.

May 27, 1972

When I drove into Dom's gas station this morning, his brother Pete, cleaning my windshield, observed Noah sitting beside me.

"How's the little fellow?" Pete asked. "How's he coming along?"

"Slowly," I said.

"I can't stand it when kids are sick," Pete said. He went back to the pump, shaking his head, and then turned around and said to me from the depth of his Catholic being, "You better take care of this little fellow, Josh. He's a cute little fellow and you better take care of him."

May 28, 1972

Our neighbors have a new dog. They keep him out all night in their backyard just below us. This morning Noah awoke to the dog's barking, came downstairs, divested himself of his clothing, and urinated on the kitchen floor. But that is not the point.

That dog's barking has been disturbing all of us lately. And when I called the neighbor, with whom we'd always been on the best of terms, to suggest that keeping that dog in the backyard all night wasn't working out for us, she was less than gracious. "I hope you move soon," she said.

May 29, 1972

Noah continues to amaze me with his sibling jealousy: his eyes dart back and forth between his dessert plate and Karl's, comparing quantities. At such moments, you couldn't ask Noah to be more aware of his environment.

Karl, too, continues to amaze me. He can remember inconsequential facts in history such as George Washington's father's name or the fact that Alcock and Brown were the first to fly the Atlantic nonstop. But he can't remember how much four times nine is.

May 30, 1972

I tried talking to our neighbor again about their barking dog and she was completely intransigent.

May 31, 1972

Foumi has been working on a book in Japanese and yesterday she exploded at me. A friend had come over so that I could help him with his novel. And Foumi was jealous. "You spend time on your friend's book. But not mine." "His book," I explained, "is written in my language." But there was no stopping her. And soon she was off into a Women's Lib bit, complaining that she does not have enough time to finish her book.

I'm getting a little fed up with Women's Lib. I think it's an unrealistic view of society. Justly or unjustly one can only deal in society on situational terms, one has to live with the symptoms even as the root causes are being examined. It may not be fair but I can't help it if my time—at the moment—is worth far more than hers in the marketplace.

Foumi also complained about my creation taking precedence over hers. What creation? Two thin books, one mentally crippled kid, another skinny son—the sum total of my creation.

Hell, I want my liberation.

June 1, 1972

Presidential-year politics has caught up with the Greenfelds. We convened a family meeting this morning on our bed. Karl was elected president. Only he and Noah were eligible for that high office since they are the only ones born into the family. As the new president, Karl pledged to learn the multiplication tables—the platform he had run on. Noah, as vice-president, will continue to try to say "ah."

June 3, 1972

Karl suggested at breakfast that he didn't want me to go to his class picnic. But I put in an appearance anyway. And though he treated me most casually—just waved a weak hello to me—I could tell he was glad that I came.

June 4, 1972

Noah has not progressed dramatically this year. Next year, by this time, I will have placed him in an institution. He is a very severely retarded child. Forget the autism and the schizophrenia, he's a damned retard and I have to get rid of him.

June 5, 1972

When Karl and Noah and I take our evening constitutional, Noah constantly holds up, stopping and dawdling, talking to the trees and the grass, but then he always comes running after us.

June 6, 1972

I had a long talk with an editor I know who has a twenty-two-year-old retarded daughter. She also has epilepsy and has been taking medication that controls it. But now he's worried that she might have some sort of incipient paranoia. Lately, she cannot sleep at night, imagines people are constantly walking back and forth on the ledge outside her window.

We don't have the problem of imaginary people outside our window. We still have that real dog whose barking woke us all this morning. I'll go and complain to the neighbors again, putting it as nicely as I can.

June 7, 1972

I almost poked the social worker at Noah's school. Foumi and I went there for an obligatory meeting with him. When he began by asking if our attitude toward Noah was different from our attitude toward Karl, I turned to Foumi and said: "Let's get out of here." It was obvious to me that he didn't understand the first thing about the problem of a Noah and was reaching for some old Freudian tract-or-track.

Foumi told me to stop being my usual impatient self and actually tried to answer the man. But he kept on going down the psychogenic line. And when he got to "Why do you think a disturbance from Noah upsets you more than one from Karl?"

61

I was on my feet telling him to shut his mouth unless he wanted my fist to shut it for him.

He tried a new tack. "How can I possibly help you?"

"Instead of asking stupid questions," I said, "you could look for an institution that would commit itself to providing lifetime care for Noah."

"Do you mean to say you are prepared to give up your parenthood?" he asked.

This time Foumi was on her feet, pulling on my arm.

The man was an anachronism in our lives. And perhaps I let out all the hostility I had built up toward all the social workers we had dealt with in the past on the poor guy. But he also brought it on himself, so insecure and nervous that his own facial tic never stopped working as he subjected us to the ridiculous scene.

June 8, 1972

I enjoy overhearing the talks that Karl has with Roberta, Noah's tutor. Karl tells her he wants to be a historian, for example, but he isn't sure historians are well paid. (I think he thinks historians are people who stand around and list names of Presidents and give dates of battles.) He doesn't want to get married and have children because kids only bug their parents. He isn't even sure he wants to become an adult.

"There are advantages in being an adult," Roberta suggests.

"Like what?"

"You can eat whatever you like," she says. "What do you like?"

"Chocolate pudding. But I don't know how to make it."

"Well, you could find a wife who loves you and makes all the chocolate pudding you want."

"And spaghetti?"

"And spaghetti."

Suddenly, Karl changes the subject to prejudice. "Would you mind," he asks, "if somebody called you a Jap?"

"No," says Roberta.

"That's because you're not Japanese. But when people call

me Jap it's because they have prejudice. They don't like me because I'm Japanese, and they want to hurt my feelings. And I know I shouldn't let it bother me—but it does hurt my feelings. And when my feelings are hurt I cry. That's how I am."

June 9, 1972

Noah likes jumping over an extended rope. The only problem is Karl keeps inserting himself. But it's good in that way too. Because Noah learns to await his turn politely.

June 10, 1972

At breakfast Karl was complaining about his life, even talked about wishing he had a heart attack and died. I gave him hell for that kind of talk. Foumi told me afterward to calm down, not to worry, that she thinks he's just trying out tidbits of overheard adult conversation.

June 12, 1972

I ran into a friend I had not seen for almost a year. "How is Noah?" he asked. "How is he getting on compared to last year?" I had to think about my answer. Noah is better at dressing himself—or at least participating in the process; at toileting; has stronger wants; and seems more aware of things. He even has a favorite toy, the music-box radio. But still he always has to be watched—for toilet hints, for dirt eating, for sudden disrobing.

My friend told me of someone he knew who kept a special child in his home until the child was fifteen.

"And then what happened?"

"He put him in an institution."

I must have shuddered.

"Don't worry." My friend patted me on the shoulder. "As Noah gets older and less beautiful it will be easier to part with him."

I hope that is so. I hope a child's looks change before his

parents' eyes. Unlike the fact that a parent's looks never change to a child. I hope so. But I doubt it.

June 14, 1972

When I came home from the city Noah was sitting on the steps, waiting for me to take him for a car ride. He knew I knew that's what he wanted. But I had no desire to go for a ride. And so he was greatly annoyed. How important is cognitive communication anyway?

June 15, 1972

It's one of those warm June days on which I get that graduating-from-high-school feeling of luminous innocence—or is it imminence? I stand at the threshold of my own identity. And what a marvelous identity it will be.

June 17, 1972

A father-and-sons day. This afternoon Karl and I watched the Soap Box Derby eliminations in Ossining. Karl had a hot dog, a soda, an ice cream sandwich, and some candy. Then his tooth fell out.

When we came home, he and Noah and I took a walk together. "I like Noah," Karl decided.

June 18, 1972

Sleep is a major problem again. Noah continues to murder sleep. Up at five, jumping and whining and yelping, impossible to quiet. I go around in a stupor all day.

And it isn't easy writing in a stupor. Especially when I have to write for a living and dream of writing as an art. I know I will never get ahead financially because insecurity costs, and with Noah I can never be secure. Our last two winters in California have exhausted our savings. And I have no idea of the additional Noah expenses that lie ahead—except that they will be never ending. I also know that if the problems now posed by Noah often seem intolerable, without money they would be impossible.

And yet the dream of my youth lingers still: I will find the time, I will find the way, I will develop my craft, I will write something worthwhile.

But I can't do it in a stupor. Or is the dream only part of the stupor?

June 19, 1972

My friend's pill-popping teenage daughter ran away from home again. Yesterday he heard she was in Philadelphia, drove there to reclaim her, and then, helplessly, put her into the county mental institution. I don't think that's the place for her. And I hate seeing him so distraught.

June 21, 1972

The first day of summer: A rainy morning. A sense of continual desperation when it comes to Noah. A joyous promise of renewal in Karl. And a lingering malaise when it comes to my own writing. I look out my window at the high school kids and wonder when I will ever try out for the varsity.

June 23, 1972

Karl has the habit of resisting with speech rather than complying with deed. He immediately goes to his strength, his tendency to be glib. He's afraid to learn anything he doesn't have a grip on already—which precludes everything new. For example, he does not want to learn, he claims, how to swim or ride a bicycle, yet complains that he can do neither. When I try to teach him either, he says I'm a bad teacher. Which is true. I tease more naturally than I teach. So he's got me there, and not with his glibness.

We took a trip to Boston. I wanted Karl to see Boston before we move to California both because of American history and my own history. And Karl enjoyed visiting the frigate *Constitution* and walking along the Freedom Trail. More important, he enjoyed the swan boats in the Boston Public Gardens as much as I had as a child growing up in nearby Malden.

Noah was a good traveler but a bad sleeper. Over the three-day period he did a lot of nocturnal bouncing on our hotel beds. And we've returned as tired as if we had journeyed a thousand miles.

June 30, 1972
At our family meeting this morning on my bed I asked: "Who's president?"

"Noah," Karl said. "He was reelected."

"Again?" I asked.

"Yes," said Karl. "Noah's been president more than Franklin D. Roosevelt."

Such stuff Karl knows. But still not seven times seven.

July 1, 1972
We decided—Karl and I did—to have an all-boys birthday party for Noah at my office. We bought some cookies and milk and nuts and Karl sat at my desk reading a history book, while Noah bounced on my cot playing with what Karl described as "Noah's idea of paradise," a rubber band. We sang "Happy Birthday" to Noah and our guest had a tantrum when we ran out of nuts, but I sent Karl down for reinforcements and immediately the situation was stabilized. And so Noah's sixth birthday passed into history.

July 2, 1972
Karl asked me: "Do you think the Boston Massacre was really a massacre?" I said, "Yes." "But only eight people were

killed there," he argued. "That's still a massacre," I said. "Then what do they call Vietnam?"

July 3, 1972

A gift arrived for Noah's birthday from the high school girls who helped us take care of him in California. It's a sweatshirt with a rainbow, too big to fit even Karl, but it's a lovely present. A nice reminder of our California friends on a sweltering summer day in New York.

July 9, 1972

Bodil, Lovaas's Norwegian student, visited us. She brought with her a fifteen-year-old autistic boy and his mother. The boy, who had beautiful blue eyes, sat in almost a lotus position on our couch. He was completely controlled by the eye movements of his mother. It was an extraordinary thing to see.

The mother had the shrill note of one who has been warring —and wary—far too long, the mark of any autistic child's parent. And the boy, for all his controlled, appropriate behavior, gave me creepy forebodings. These children, no matter how much they seem to progress, are all edging toward the same inhuman back room of a mental institution.

July 17, 1972

Some friends dropped in with their normal three-year-old son. He took one look at Noah, bouncing on the couch, and immediately began to play with Karl. Even a three-year-old could quickly understand that Noah was not for playing.

July 19, 1972

Noah is having some toilet lapses again. But what disturbs me more is the way he eats, filling his mouth as if there is no next bite. Perhaps that's just a side effect of the use of food as reinforcers. But I'm simply afraid that one day he will choke on a piece of meat.

July 20, 1972
We saw a documentary showing some scenes from Willowbrook State Hospital. I could not possibly institutionalize Noah there. I can only hope that when the time comes for me to institutionalize Noah, the institutions will have changed.

July 21, 1972
The dog keeps barking. And we have to right the wrong of the barks. I'm going to take out a summons against our neighbors.

July 22, 1972
Foumi wrote a last-ditch note to our neighbor. And the woman came storming angrily into our house saying she had done all she could do and that her dog did not make as much noise as trains or fire alarms. Foumi pointed out there wasn't much any of us could do about train noises or fire sirens but that we were responsible for our pets. Foumi outargued her with logic, but then later she became so angry thinking about it she could not sleep all night, even though the dog was quiet for a change.

July 23, 1972
I've decided to break away from my pattern of indolence by taking a vacation. Each afternoon I take the boys to the lake and play with them in the water. Noah, though six, is still a baby, jumping up and down and never allowing me to stray out of sight. Karl is at the "Look at me, Daddy" stage, as he splashes about with a surfboard. Foumi remains the resident genius. By steadfastly refusing to buy a bathing suit with such flimsy excuses as "They're too expensive," she gets out of the watering chores as successfully as she manages to avoid driving duties. But, hell, she deserves a vacation in her own fashion too.

July 24, 1972
A cool day at last. I mowed the lawn, I took Foumi to White Plains, shopping, I even worked a little with Noah. And I

talked with Karl as he went to sleep—lying next to him on his double bed. He talked of camp, his friends, of how some of the other kids call him Greenfoot as a joke. And as he talked he gently rubbed his hands over my rough, bearding chin, just as I loved to run my hands as a child across my own father's sandpapery face.

July 25, 1972

The dog barked us awake again this morning but talking to our neighbors is like talking to Noah. And instead of trying to change things, our good neighbors would rather defend themselves. Just like Karl. I'm surrounded by children.

July 26, 1972

This morning Noah urinated on the bathroom floor as he was trying to get his sleeper off. It's so pathetic. He knows he's supposed to go to the bathroom and he tries, but it takes so long for him to pick up his own urinary impulses; it takes so long for him to get through to himself. We just have to make sure he gets as much education as he can possibly get. And yet at the same time I'm sure he'll eventually regress no matter how much education he gets. Especially if we put him into an institutional environment. But perhaps we're better off —and he's better off—if we put him into an institution now so that he can begin to adjust to it.

No matter how much my mind reels I still don't know what to do.

July 27, 1972

I talked to my former good neighbor about his—and our—dog problem. We had been getting along famously for five years until they got this yelping terrier which they chain to a post in their backyard at some times, allow to roam freely at other times, and put out as early as five o'clock every morning. I think if the dog's bark were not so unhappy we would not

69

mind it so. My neighbor said we were "supersensitive" and asked bluntly if we wanted the dog destroyed. I said, no, of course not. I suggested the dog could be kept in the house, could be put out front, could generally be trained better. Otherwise, I would have to sue him. But he wasn't listening to me. He just kept repeating: "Do you want that dog destroyed?"

July 28, 1972

I measured Noah next to Karl. He's just a few inches shorter. And he is still not toilet trained in the sense that he can monitor himself completely. I think he knows this and it frustrates him.

July 30, 1972

I'm a bit saddened seeing Eagleton dropped from the vice-presidential spot on the McGovern ticket. Not because I like the man—I never even heard of him until last week—or because of any political principle, but because of the reason. If he had taken some drug or had received some form of "talking" therapy rather than having once or twice undergone shock treatment, I doubt if quite the same fuss would have been made.

We still function, I'm afraid, in a witchcraft society. Our superstitions and prejudices have not diminished through the years—just transferred.

July 31, 1972

For the past week Noah has had the screaming meemies. When he wants—or does not want—something, he opens his mouth and lets out a blast pitched relentlessly at a single high note.

August 1, 1972

Each night I talk with Karl before he goes to sleep. I lie on his bed beside him and he asks me questions about the American Revolution. I don't always know the answers and I have to be careful how I fake them. He's only a seven-and-a-half-year-old child. Last night he wanted to know why Washington went to Valley Forge for the winter. I said it was because the Bermudas belonged to the British. I shouldn't crack wise so much to the kid.

In addition to the meemies Noah has been tantrumming and pinching again. Yesterday they had to carry him from school to Mr. Rose's cab. And this morning he refused to eat, refused to urinate. One consolation: We're told that before these children start to talk they get this way. I hope so.

I also hope not. The worse Noah behaves the easier it will be to put him in an institution and forget about him.

What a ridiculous situation: to find even a ray of hope . . . blinding.

Karl and Noah had a custard orgy at Carvel's. Karl ate the custard with great boyish enjoyment, dripping the chocolate all over his shirt, his shorts, his knees, and even his sneakers, while I neatly spoon-fed Noah from a cup.

I tried teaching Karl how to ride a two-wheeler. But when I pushed him off to coast by himself he became frightened and hysterically leaped from the bike and fell. I asked him to get back on the bike again but he was too fearful and kept crying, "I don't trust you anymore." I guess he'll have to learn how to master a two-wheeler from someone else.

Foumi and I agree Noah is beginning to exhibit some sort of weird electrical impulses in his brain, perhaps something like epilepsy. He suddenly has these fits in which he is beside himself, crying and scratching and rolling his eyes.

71

August 6, 1972

Our block had a garage sale. I set Karl up with a card table and he had a grand time selling two books and some toys. He also bought at other vendors a necklace for Foumi, and an old football jersey for himself, three sizes too big at the shoulders —"to make room for the plaids"—which he wore to bed.

August 7, 1972

I visited an old friend who lives nearby in a big house and is always trying to impress me. Telling me what a good novelist he is, what a great publisher he is, how rich he is. And one would think with all that money he would be happy. But he isn't. His unhappiness is just more lush. Noah was with me. He began to pinch me and scream and lie down on the floor and kick. My friend asked me about putting Noah in an institution. "I couldn't," I said. "I don't know a place I can trust."

He said: "You have to put him in a place and just forget about him."

"I couldn't," I said.

August 8, 1972

Our neighbors, we've learned, gave their barking dog away. Which accounts for the lovely silence of the past week. It's a shame our relationship with them, five and a half years of good, neighborly friendship, had to be needlessly howled away.

$$\left(\;4\;\right)$$

I looked at Bruno Bettelheim's *The Empty Fortress* again. Bettelheim believes that autism is caused by cold, "refrigerator" parents who so frighten and traumatize the child that he chooses to remain in an arrested state of development. Bettelheim seems to view such family units as mini-concentration camps and takes his analogues from there. I buy neither his jargon nor the idea he seems to encourage of allowing certain autistics to literally play with their own feces. Both are repellent to me.

I also don't like the idea that he draws his generalities from the experience of working with only six or seven autistics at a time, none of whom seem to be suffering from the usual accompanying severe retardations and poor muscular coordination. The children he's talking about at worst seem to have minor brain dysfunction. In addition, I have the disquieting hunch that while he publicly takes credit for whatever good things happen to some of the children he's treated through natural maturation, he also may be burying his mistakes in regard to the bad things simply by not writing about them. There is no hint of any scientific control present in his report.

When Noah pinches and screams it presents a problem in a teaching situation. We just can't send him to his room until he quiets down. Because that way he gets out of doing what he wants to get out of doing.

Trouble with Karl at summer day camp: Karl told his counselor, whose brother is in the hospital because of a weak blood vessel in the brain: "I'm glad your brother is sick." What a weird projection and transposition. I said to Karl: "Would you like it if people went around saying they were glad Noah is autistic?" "I wouldn't mind," he answered. "It's only words. It doesn't hurt my feelings." Oh, how he's begun to insulate his feelings, to protect himself from the possible slings—in words: Jew, Jap, autistic's brother—of others. Anyway, I made him apologize to his counselor.

Otherwise, the camp director told me, Karl's been having a good summer, improving immensely in athletics.

After dinner I pitched the Whiffle Ball to Karl. And I could see that he can really hit them out now. Playing in our backyard, on our acre of land, I felt, too, the pangs of moving. We'll really miss the expanse when we move to L.A. this November.

Noah was terrible yesterday afternoon. Screaming and tantrumming, taking off his clothes and urinating on the floor. Foumi said it was one of the worst hours she's ever spent with him. She had never seen him so inconsolable. It all happened after

I had driven away. Evidently he had wanted to come with me for a car ride.

When I returned home he still wanted that car ride. But I forced him to take a long walk with me to the pedestrian bridge over the highway that leads to the railroad station. He loves to sit there and look through the railings at the cars tunneling through below. It must be for him like a rock-concert light show is for an acidhead. He sat there for twenty happy minutes and then walked home with his hand in mine.

August 13, 1972

Just a few weeks ago Karl was complaining to me that he had no friends at all. This morning he proudly told me he could make friends anywhere—on a plane, a train, in New York, in California.

August 14, 1972

Last night was classic. Noah awoke in a tantrum, hitting at his own head, flailing out at me as I tried to comfort him, employing his new-found screaming-meemie talent. As I restrained him I wondered again what I would do as he became older, bigger, stronger. And I wondered how a Bettelheim would deal with such self-destructive behavior. How would he handle a child who awoke at midnight, striking hard blows at his own head? How would he teach an otherwise passive child whose only activity was rebellion against any innovative activity itself? Finally, Noah's fit mercifully subsided and he became his warm, chirping self. But it was a bad night for sleeping. An even worse night for wondering.

August 16, 1972

Usually, when I take Karl out to breakfast he orders a stack of pancakes, drenches them in syrup and butter, nibbles at about a third of the mess, and pushes the remainder toward me. This

75

morning I wised up. I ordered just one pancake for him.

This evening I hope I learned the secret of dealing—at least sometimes—with Noah's pinch-screaming. Assume his discontents are as basic as a baby's: give him something to eat or to drink or let him sleep.

August 18, 1972

Roberta has gone on to a full-time job and Noah has a new part-time tutor—or therapist. Her name is Marie and I like the way she tries to teach him rather than to control him. Which is, I guess, the secret. But the secret of what?

August 19, 1972

A woman came to our house, a nun who was visiting her father in the next town and had read of Noah. She spoke of perceptional deficiencies in vision and how special training eyeglasses helped. She spoke from personal experience: she had had an eye problem. We certainly should test Noah's eyes. And his hearing. I'm convinced that Noah's hearing is extremely tenuous, the signals fading in and out like a distant radio station late at night.

August 22, 1972

We took a small trip over the weekend, back to Peterborough, New Hampshire, to the MacDowell Colony, the writers' and artists' colony where Foumi and I first met, thirteen summers ago. The days were great, seeing all manner of old friends again. But the nights were torturous, sleep almost impossible. Noah just can't accept a new place. It was funny though: during one of his long wake-up-and-cry periods in the motel he did not quiet down until I put on my eyeglasses. Then finally he began to sleep. And even I was able to doze off. With my glasses on.

My family moved to New York from Malden, Massachusetts, in 1938, when I was ten years old. I grew up in the East Flatbush section of Brooklyn, a step up from the ghettos of Brownsville and Williamsburg for Jews in the 1930s and 1940s. I took Karl with me yesterday to my old block. It is now part of a neighborhood in transition, a step up for blacks out of the Bedford-Stuyvesant and Brownsville and Williamsburg ghettos this time, the old Jews and new blacks coexisting. The nameplates in the apartment house cluster I once lived in were now a commingling of Danielses and Williamses along with Feinsteins and Landaus. The avenue corner featured two real estate offices, where once had stood a delicatessen and a grocery. A kosher butcher shop was a few doors down from a mini-market advertising collard greens. The one remaining delicatessen had two waiters, one black and one white. (Karl and I stopped for lunch there and he was most impressed with how quickly he was served his hot dog, straight from the grill; there was no great wait like at a Howard Johnson's.) Candy stores had all but vanished; yet drugstores and dry-cleaning establishments seemed to endure. The lots that had been vacant along the business-avenue block had developed into buildings but at the same time many of the old storefronts were boarded up. The effect was that of a rotting mouth containing new bridgework. There were other paradoxes: The streets seemed wider, from sidewalk to sidewalk, yet the distances between streets seemed shorter. The schoolyard in which I used to play ball—and shoot craps—looked neglected, grass and weeds had sprung up between the concrete boxes; yet there were nets on the basketball hoops—something we never had. I walked past the local Jewish Center: the huge Honor Roll for those who'd served in World War II was gone, but the same rabbi who presided at my Bar Mitzvah was still in charge. My brief moment of *déjà vu* in front of the Jewish Center was interrupted by a flashing sense of the present—cops frisking a black against the side of a car. When we got back into our car I asked Karl what he thought of my old neighborhood. "It isn't such a slum," he said, "but I'm glad we weren't mugged."

This morning as I looked in the mirror to shave I saw my mother's face. Yesterday as I walked through my old neighborhood with Karl I felt as if my every action, my every gesture, was that of my father. It's amazing how much time does not change, how little places alter, how ineffably we are fated to play familiar roles.

August 24, 1972

Karl and I were speaking of watches. He wanted to know when they were invented. "Long after the clock," I said. "People used to have to come to a clock to tell the time. They couldn't bring it along with them." "Couldn't they have used flies?" Karl said. "You know, time flies. Isn't that how they got their name?"

He was joking, of course, and I loved it. But I wish I was sure he was joking the other day driving back from Brooklyn. I pointed out Grant's Tomb and asked him: "Do you know who's buried there?"

"Tomb?" he replied.

August 25, 1972

I received a letter from a woman who says she had an autistic sister but as a child was never quite aware of all the problems involved. Unfortunately, I don't think Karl has been that fortunate.

August 26, 1972

I took Noah for a quick bathe at the lake. He likes to be in the shallow water, enclosed by my knees, as if we were sitting at home in the tub together.

He also now cannot abide to see me without my eyeglasses on. This distresses him at the beach. Even at home if I take them off he will run across the room from his perch on the couch and put them back on my nose. And if he hears me typing in my studio he will come checking to see if my glasses are still on. The irony is that as I have become older I can see better without them, especially when I'm reading. But Noah is fixed to routine—and to image: the image of me in my eyeglasses.

August 27, 1972

The Croton Volunteer Fire Department was raffling off a Ford station wagon and I was so sure I was going to win it. I even pictured myself driving out to California in it. Because I figured the odds were in my favor. I had bought five dollars' worth of chances; I was told they planned on selling only $10,000 worth of chances, which made the odds 2,000 to 1. The odds on a Jew married to a Japanese having an autistic child have to be a lot greater than that and I brought that long shot in. So this would be an easy winner to bring home, I thought. Wrong.

August 29, 1972

Last night, as Noah was having his third tantrum of the day, and as I held him to the floor, pinning him, Foumi kept saying, "We have to put him away." She was, of course, right. But I just said, "Let's not talk about it now." "If not now," she cried, "when then?"

Pretty soon I will be unable to restrain him physically. And, I guess, ultimately, that's *when*.

August 30, 1972

I told Foumi to go to Japan for a month. She needs to get away in order to retain her sanity. The only problem is that I would go crazy taking care of Karl and Noah during that period.

August 31, 1972

I am convinced that any programs and plans and facilities for special children must be parent-run. We need no paternalistic

79

administrative help, no professional specialists from outside our community. Because once things are in the hands of experts we—just like the poor, just like the blacks—are dead.

September 5, 1972

We went to Washington, D.C., to give Karl a last American hurrah here in the East. He saw all the sights, the Washington Monument and the Lincoln Memorial and, of course, best of all, the Smithsonian Institution. We had a day free of Noah. The parent of an autistic child in Virginia graciously took care of him (though we missed the drone of his presence continually). And I was able to spend some time with my best friend from college. He told me that he was worrying about his twenty-year-old stepson who has petit mal, a type of epilepsy; that another of our college friends was worrying about his teenage daughter who was too thin—over five seven and less than a hundred pounds.

So the parent—or paternity—game hasn't been exactly a complete joy for any of us.

And the autistic home in Virginia was frightening: a shattering glimpse at a future Noah—the autistic boy there was strong and muscular and uncontrollable.

In Washington I also spoke on the phone to a first cousin of mine. He described his grandson's behavior. The kid sounded autistic to me. Coincidence? Or family genes?

September 6, 1972

A lovely, autumnal, I-never-want-to-leave-Croton day. But I called Alys Harris in California and told her we'd be out in California by November 15. I dread packing. Getting settled again holds no allure for me. But it is time to move on and I want to move to California.

September 7, 1972

Noah seems to grow bigger daily and I can begin to discern the face of a man in him. It's terrifying.

September 8, 1972

Noah has been behaving well lately. If he isn't always ready to obey commands, at least I feel he understands them. And he seems to be showing the inkling of a memory. He can be angry with me for something I've done before, which means both his memory and understanding may be as good now as they were before he lost his speech.

September 12, 1972

Every time one feels a breath of hope about Noah, reality perversely intrudes. Last night he was up from 3:30 on, screaming. This morning I can hardly keep my eyes open, let alone get my brain started.

I'm not only disgusted with Noah, but with his school. I don't think they're giving him a full day. He goes from 9:00 to 2:00 but that includes a lunch period, 11:45 to 12:30; a rest hour, 12:30 to 1:30; and departure preparation, 1:30 to 2:00. Which means school stops at 11:45. And who knows how long it takes to get started in the morning.

I've talked with the director about the situation and he's professionally rigid: "We can't listen to twenty-five parents." So my choice is this: Do I keep fighting for change here or save my energies until we get to California?

September 14, 1972

When I look at our land and all the work Foumi has done to landscape and cultivate it I am loath to leave. When I consider winter's coming and the coldness of the climate and my dissatisfaction with Noah's school, I am anxious to get going.

September 17, 1972

I am in the playroom, watching television. I hear Noah crying. I go to the living room. He is banging his hands against his head, crying. I try to comfort him. I bring him to the playroom. He strains to get away, striking out, scratching, pinching, pulling my hair. I restrain him and he inadvertently bangs his head against my elbow. He cries out even more loudly, this time in genuine—or at least justified—pain. And I think: We cannot go on this way. Yet, what other way is there?

I worry about Karl too. He seems unable to tell time no matter how often he's been taught. Won't any of my progeny come through?

September 18, 1972

I started off the day feeling great. The sky was blue, my head was clear, I smelled promise in the air. I would do my work, I would make my money, I would enjoy my life. Then Noah had one of his fits. He hit his head with his hands, stamped on the floor, was utterly uncontrollable. And soon I was down in the dumps. I am an emotional yo-yo at the end of his string.

The fits do more than upset my mood. They disturb me for another reason. They mean Noah's illness is like some weird golf course in which all the holes must be played but in no set or predictable order. Self-destruction—and self-mutilation—is an autistic characteristic that I felt he had been spared. But now I see it coming. It's as if every small gain carries an implicit loss—he begins walking so he stops talking, he finally uses the john so he starts hitting himself in the face.

Soon we simply can no longer deal with him. Soon we have to start protecting ourselves. Soon it will be him against us . . . and I will have no choice.

September 19, 1972

This morning as I tried to dress him, Noah tantrummed again to the point of self-laceration, beating against his face, pinching his thighs, pulling roughly on his penis. To be sure there was a reason: he wanted to go downstairs immediately to eat. He is becoming more willful if less manageable. He is also becoming smarter. Yesterday, Foumi tells me, he was able to match groups of seven objects. Still Noah must go. And we both know it.

September 22, 1972

I've been reading S. N. Behrman's memoir and feel almost nostalgic about the playwriting career I never quite had. I've had fiction and nonfiction books published, I've written for almost every major magazine, but nothing else for me has ever been quite like an opening night in the theater. I remember most vividly the opening of my play *Clandestine on the Morning Line* in Washington fourteen years ago. My mother came down from New York and she was so proud. And for me it was the stuff of drama itself: all my hopes and dreams boiling down to that one performance and the review of it in *The New York Times* the next morning (the *Times* called the play "unsubstantial").

Behrman uses a marvelous phrase about someone's "incessant productivity masking sterility." My sterility is going undisguised these days. I just can't get down to working on anything—let alone a play. And instead of writing I turn to books like the Behrman.

September 24, 1972

I took the boys to a Croton High football game. Oh, how I love the football season, the crisp weather, the intense effort of a high school team on an autumn afternoon. Those are the truly great days. That time of life packs the brain, fills in memory a size all out of proportion. My last twelve years of marriage occupy less space than those few years of high school. How quickly and fully one grows then. And I can watch it happening outside my window now: a new generation passes in review every few months.

September 26, 1972

Politically I just don't know how I feel these days. Capitalism has always been a con, convincing those it robs that it is the fairest way for them to be robbed because otherwise they would be robbed even more unfairly. Socialism, on the other hand, is government committing the biggest crimes of big business as it becomes the biggest business of them all. So what's left? Or right? I just don't know. The key question, I guess, is: Under which regime would a Noah be better off? And the sad answer is: neither.

Society is not responsible for special children. Society is not responsible for normal children. But at least it tries harder to educate them.

September 27, 1972

We have an old friend down the street who is ill. He is over eighty but until a few months ago walked several miles a day. He and I were both born in the same New England town. I went to see him this morning. His face had the yellow pallor of death. He was a bag of thin bones on a small iron-frame bed. He talked with a dry throat, complained that his muscles would not follow orders. He could not turn over. He did not say my name. But he did call me "man." Perhaps he did recognize me.

His wife, in her late seventies herself, was clear-eyed but distressed. She told me she could not get Medicaid until she spent all her savings and went on welfare. And she is much too proud to ever do that.

September 28, 1972

I have been thinking of all the causes that need a writer's help. I remembered the guy I met in the rehabilitation hospital when I was recovering from polio. He was a paraplegic who wanted to write a book so that "the world" would really know about rodeo hands. "The world" must really know, we say constantly; though once "the world" really knows it still does nothing. We refuse to believe that "the world" could know and not care. But so it is: *"The world"* can even make a greater expenditure of effort in not really knowing than in any search for knowledge itself.

84

September 29, 1972

Last night I spanked Karl. He did his arithmetic atrociously. There is no excuse for his not getting eight plus three right at his age.

This morning I kissed Karl. I've often heard stories of children being ashamed of their autistic siblings. But this morning I watched Karl go into Noah's room and lie down beside him and hug him as Noah lay in happy but inert first wakefulness.

September 30, 1972

My old neighbor friend continues to look like Gandhi and his memory is slipping. I worry about him. I worry even more about his wife. She hasn't been sleeping much—"because I have to be awake in case he wants something." She needs help and it's time one of her sons or daughters was forthcoming.

October 1, 1972

Karl accused Foumi of having racial prejudice. "That's ridiculous," said Foumi. "No," said Karl, "you have racial prejudice against kids."

October 3, 1972

It isn't as if Foumi doesn't have enough problems of her own. But every day now she goes to our old neighbor's house and with another neighbor helps bathe him and walk him around. But this is something that really can't go on for too long. Foumi says his mind wanders, he repeats the same stories, and he seems to be losing his bowel control.

October 4, 1972

Though it's really none of my business, I took matters into my own hands. I called one of the old man's sons long distance and told him that he and his brothers better do something soon unless they wanted to lose both their parents. (Then I looked

85

into the two slim books of poetry my old friend had once written and privately published. How young it seemed—an inept poetic voice always sounds eternally youthful.)

October 6, 1972

Foumi is disappointed in the wife of our old friend. She refuses to remove the scatter rugs from the floor that are so easy for her husband to slip on.

October 7, 1972

Noah has a memory, a remarkable memory. I drove him downtown and parked about a block from my office. Then I walked down the street with him. In front of my office building he tugged my hand toward the door.

October 8, 1972

Every afternoon I throw around a football with Karl. He gets upset too easily when he drops a pass he should have caught. Yesterday, after bungling one, he walked away sulking. So I began to throw the ball around with a neighbor's son. This made Karl even more furious. He demanded his ball back and stalked into the house.

When I was young, oh, how I wished I could play football. But I was never a good athlete. So I chose to write about sports, the next best thing to participating. But then the great irony: when athletes get old all they can do is write—or broadcast—about sports, so we all wind up together on the sidelines.

October 9, 1972

I'm impressed with the way Noah can match letters. Maybe a good deal of his problem is hearing after all. I wonder how I could have it tested. Perhaps with a hearing aid he would be able to understand us after all.

But still he would have six years of cold storage to come back from.

Karl has become interested in poetry, the rhyming aspect. I suspect that's because his teacher complimented him on his execution of a simple exercise. A little flattery with him—as with Noah—goes a long way.

Noah, who has a new home tutor beginning tomorrow, seems to understand most commands better now even if he doesn't always want to follow them. Speech still remains his big stumbling block.

I visited Noah's school this morning and was pleasantly surprised: it seems much better than last year; they're doing much more there now than one-on-one teaching. But then places always seem better when one is about to leave them.

Karl had to interview me for a school assignment. I was a little tough. "You have to remember," he said, "this is my first interview." True. But at least he could have been polite enough to thank me when he was through. Or is that expecting too much from your own kid?

The deadline grows nearer. Soon we'll be moving. I treasure each autumn day as if I will never know another. I go to each high school football game as if it is my last. I act as if I am preparing to move to some strange and far-off country.

And it's only California. But could the light ever be so clear, the skies so blue, the foliage so golden, the weather so glorious as here?

October 14, 1972

I've begun to give Noah large doses of niacin. I put it in ice cream and soon he'll be able to tell the taste. If he is thus conditioned not to like ice cream we have nothing to lose; if it improves his awareness and behavior we have everything to gain.

October 16, 1972

I sometimes forget that not all adults regard Noah as an aesthetic experience. We now have a different cab driver taking him to school each day because the town decided that Mr. Rose lacked sufficient insurance. And as I watched Noah depart this morning, doing his curlicue route, slowpoke routine down the stairs, stopping at each landing, I noticed how impatient and restive the cabbie became.

October 17, 1972

Noah had a bad reaction to the niacin. He pulled Foumi's hair until she cried out in pain. And then last night I dreamed of a child like Noah who was a constant burden. I went to the movies with him. But he wouldn't stay seated, disturbed everyone around him. The child, as I say, wasn't Noah precisely, but he was just like Noah in his behavior. Finally, I had to take him from the theater. The meaning of the dream seems so painfully obvious that I shudder. And, of course, meanwhile I've reduced the dosage of Noah's niacin.

October 18, 1972

This morning an early taste of winter came to town: there was a sprinkle of snow, and I loved it.

I've decided not to sell our house. One never knows the future, and this way I have a home to return to in case California pales on us.

October 20, 1972

When I was in the post office this morning, looking at the clerks working there, I recalled the summer I had spent in the General Post Office in New York. After I graduated from high school I thought I would go swaggering into the world. Instead, I was in the subbasement of the post office, in the bag room, checking empty bags under a light-bulb lamp for contents left in by mistake—a kind of lower depths of monotony. For me the summer would end and I would start college but I wondered how the regulars could do it, day after day, without the promise of an end. And they even had had to pass a Civil Service exam to do it.

I have always hated every job I ever had. Money never seemed reward enough for the time spent getting it. I am simply not for working-at-a-job born. But then, who is?

October 22, 1972

Nixon will be in the county today, passing in a motorcade and stopping to speak. Perhaps I should bring Karl to see him. It is a way to spend the afternoon and to pick up a memory for life. But why should I inflict a memory of Nixon on the kid for the rest of his life? Better to spend the afternoon throwing around a football with him.

October 23, 1972

Some friends came over with a three-legged dog, one they had salvaged from a frostbitten litter they had found in a garbage can. As the poor thing gimped his way about the house, Noah seemed far more interested in that dog than he usually is in animals. Perhaps there is a community of kinship among all the maimed.

October 24, 1972

Last night was atavistic. We were about to go to sleep when Foumi heard Noah coughing. Only he wasn't coughing, he

89

was retching. We cleaned him and his bedding and put him back to sleep. Again he vomited. This time we gave him a bath. Then we changed his sheets again and put him back to bed. We finally got to sleep ourselves about 3:30. But when we awoke at 7:30 we found Noah reeking of puke again. Poor kid. Poor six-year-old baby. When he's sick, he's so vulnerable. And so are we.

October 25, 1972

I've been sorting through my papers, my junk, down in the basement. I came across my high school diploma and my University of Michigan diploma. I also came across pictures of old girl friends. One of them was of Cri-cri, the French-Swiss girl I fell in love with when I was in the service. I showed the picture to Foumi and Foumi said she looked very healthy and wondered why I hadn't married her. I wondered, too, for a moment, half forgetting all the reasons—that it was just one of those turning points of my life that did not turn. Oh what memories are evoked by the boxes in the basement! Memories that have reached the point where they mix with old fantasies and desires. Still, she would have been a good childbearer, my Swiss girl friend, Cri-cri.

October 26, 1972

I have tended to ignore Noah lately. Foumi tutors him. I help only in the mechanical aspects of taking care of him. I do not teach, I do not try to engage him. It is too much for me. I look at him and wonder sometimes if I will come to hate him: we eventually hate those we love who are dependent upon us. And in that way certain problems can be resolved. But *resolved* is the wrong word. *Resolved* implies solutions achieved again. I know of no previous solutions for a Noah.

October 29, 1972

I'm enjoying Karl more and more. He likes to laugh, he has a sense of humor, he is becoming—trite as it sounds—a person I like. With Noah there is no "person" to like. I simply continue to love him in almost a completely physical way.

October 30, 1972

How lovely the river looked—quiet, gray ripples beyond golden, wavering trees—while Foumi and I lunched on sandwiches and coffee. Fall is truly beautiful here—but then it's beautiful everywhere.

October 31, 1972

Last night Karl could not find a Halloween costume to his liking in either Croton store so I drove him to the Woolworth's in Ossining. First he wanted a skeleton, but they did not have one in his size. Next, a Frankenstein, but they were all sold out. Finally I switched him to a hideous robot with a light-up mask, in utterly bad taste but no worse than any of the others. He was delighted. As we drove back home, Noah bouncing beside him, I heard Karl's small voice mouthing uncharacteristic words: "Thank you."

November 3, 1972

I saw my old neighbor today. His wife was about to take him for a ride and I helped him into the car. He had slipped on the scatter rugs again, he told me. He doesn't know what he's talking about, his wife said.

November 6, 1972

I've had a row with Foumi about holding a garage sale. Somehow it's a big project to her and I belittle it. I know it isn't worth the effort. I think she's forgotten the purpose is to get rid of stuff. And if it's easier to get rid of stuff another way— for example, by calling the Salvation Army—one should. What really upsets Foumi is the fact that in our country it often makes financial—and common—sense just to throw things away.

Now she's in tears because I put her down. Foumi's tragedy is that she's always right in the long run, but not in the short run—and a lot of short runs never get to be long runs.

November 8, 1972

The elections. My quadrennial reactions:

As I get older, elections mean less; I lose the ability to be disappointed, my energy to care diminishes. I also have the knowledge of experience, I have covered elections, I know neither man is ever wholly angel or sinner. So it's just a question of style and image. George McGovern is in a sense no better representative of me, of my own image, than Nixon. He is pragmatic in a corny way, he has the basic Protestant-Calvinist snobbery even if he's a Methodist. His literacy in style is only a biblical one. Nixon, of course, is America's foremost exemplar of high school. He understands that we are a nation of high school students. When he speaks to us it is almost as if he visualizes all of us sitting in an assembly at the high school auditorium and then knows the appropriate things to say. I wish I had wanted McGovern more, if only because I care for Nixon so much less. His evil is a banal one and he is not so much tricky as murky: he has taught us not to think as he appeals to the worst that is in all of us—and in all of us there is a lot of the worst. Nixon wisely turned the election into a referendum on ourselves and we were not about to go mea culpa to the polls and vote ourselves down as genocidists and racists.

November 9, 1972

Today Foumi held her garage sale and did rather well for the first day, something like seventy-five dollars. I was wrong to belittle her. Even if she had not done two cents' worth I was wrong to belittle her. What an indomitable spirit she has! I could use some of that spirit.

November 10, 1972

My life is still filled with Foumi's garage sale. Pricing and carrying and arguing and mostly refraining from telling Foumi it isn't worth it. But it really isn't worth it financially. A scatter rug goes for five dollars that will cost us fifty dollars to replace. And the bookcases. And the TV set. But I hold my tongue.

November 11, 1972

When I berated Karl for what I consider a lack of reading ability, he turned to Noah and said: "Noah, you're our only hope when it comes to reading."

November 12, 1972

Noah's school called: the school would be closed, the roof is leaking. I called the local school board: Could they furnish facilities if we furnish the teachers? They told me it was out of their hands legally and not a good idea educationally. They would offer no substitute site during the period in which we lacked a school structure. What dismayed me most was the fact that the principal had never even visited Noah's school. Noah's teacher, who is twenty years younger than I, talked to me as if I were a child as she told me that I must accept the conditions of life.

I don't mind accepting the conditions of life. It's just that I resent like hell the disadvantages that are heaped upon the already disadvantaged and then described as "conditions."

November 13, 1972

Karl plays all over town now. He's reached the age where distance is no barrier to friendship. And now, poor kid, he'll move. Those are the conditions of life.

Noah is doing well at matching, at supervised activities. But when left to himself he grinds his teeth and twiddles endlessly with the plastic string of one of his pull toys.

This is our birthday month. In a few days Foumi will be

forty-two. In a couple of weeks Karl will be eight. And then in three months I'll be forty-five. One's own age should be the most difficult to accept, but I find it is Noah's. It's impossible for me to really believe that always-to-be-baby, that forever child is almost six and a half years old.

November 14, 1972

Noah pervades my life. Still I try not to think about him all the time. This morning I saw someone in front of the supermarket soliciting funds for the Knights of Columbus drive for retarded children. And I walked right by. I just did not want to think about the problem at that moment. I even resented being reminded of it. I hope someone is there tomorrow.

November 15, 1972

Foumi's birthday and we spent it teacher visiting.

Karl's teacher, a local housewife who only lately has returned to the teaching ranks, seems to like and enjoy him. Spelling is his weakness, unfamiliar words throw him, but otherwise she thinks he's developing fine. "A strictly nonfiction kid," she described him.

Noah's teacher this year is also of local origin. She is our plumber's daughter. We met with her and the aide who has been working with Noah, another local housewife. They outlined Noah's progress, the puzzles he can do, the tricycle he can now ride with encouragement. The aide, who obviously loves Noah, cried a great deal when she learned we'd be moving. I promised I'd bring Noah to her house on Sunday.

When we got home I began to think of asking her to adopt Noah, to take him in a foster-parent situation. It's something to think about in the last extreme. I can even see myself making a midnight call from California: "Come, take my son."

After dinner, to celebrate Foumi's birthday we had a doughnut-and-milk party. And Noah could say "Do" with surprising ease to get extra nibbles.

November 17, 1972

Foumi's in a postbirthday funk. She wonders about throwing her life away for the kids, throwing her life away for me. She is a woman with enormous talents and wasting her days disturbs her greatly. That disturbs me too. As always, I vow that I will carry more of the domestic load. But as always I know that I won't.

November 18, 1972

Each night Noah can hear me as I talk to Karl before he goes to sleep. So last night I went in and talked to Noah. And then he fell asleep with a smile on his face. I'll make it a point to talk to him every night too.

November 19, 1972

The days have been filled with the traumas of moving, the exhausting activities of relocation: Packing. Bill paying. Errand running. Arrangement making. I have done no work for days and days. I look forward to California. To the heat, to the warmth, to the end of prewinter.

Six years in this house. Six years is a long time in one place. I spent less than six years in high school, in college, in the army, in Japan. So perhaps it really is time to move on.

$$\left(5\right)$$

December 10, 1972
We've been in Los Angeles for two and a half weeks, back at our old apartment hotel in Westwood. But we have rented a house out in the Pacific Palisades. I hope we'll be able to move in by Christmas.

Lovaas has been a disappointment. He once told me there would always be a place for Noah in his autism project at UCLA. Now he tells me, after I had called his office three times before he called back, that they're working only with two- and three-year-olds at UCLA. In this show-business town, academia can drop a young Noah as ungraciously as a studio dumps an aging star. What disturbed me more than the fact that there was no place for Noah at UCLA—I'm not sure what they can do for Noah at this point anyway—was the fact that Lovaas didn't even express—or profess—an interest in seeing Noah now. I hate to think, at this late date, that he was more interested in his data than in the human material it was derived from.

Alys Harris did come through. There was a place for Noah

at his old school. But that school seems shorthanded and over-crowded now.

So the future in sunny California does not seem as bright as it appeared from a dark distance. Coming to a place to live is a lot different—as the saying goes—from just coming to a place for a visit. Los Angeles's wrinkles show more clearly now; the city as a fate is not as attractive as it was as a prospect; one rainy day washes away an awful lot of golden smiles.

Noah remains progress in slow motion. He hears everything but is slow on the uptake to anything and I'm still looking for a place that knows how to test his hearing. He does not talk, plays with his blanket endlessly, and still has little interest in his environment. But moving has been helpful in getting rid of some rutted toilet habits. For example, he no longer has to use a plastic add-on toilet seat.

Karl bears the brunt of our peregrinations. He has already pointed out to me that after we move to the Palisades he will have had three teachers in one year. And the other night when I was reminding him to drink his milk, he charged, "You always pick on me just because I'm the normal kid."

But I mustn't let him get away with poignant rejoinders. When I was a kid, I remember, I would tell my parents: "You always pick on me just because I'm the youngest kid," or "You always pick on me just because I'm the only boy."

The next time he pulls that line on me I'll say, "I was once a kid myself." How's that for a poignant rejoinder?

December 12, 1972

Welcome to California. This morning the L.A. *Times* had a piece telling how terrible a nearby state hospital for the mentally retarded was. Flies all over the place. Inadequate ventilation. Not enough help.

I had to come three thousand miles to read such things at breakfast.

December 13, 1972

Yesterday Noah matched pictures to words. He did it once and that was enough. He wouldn't do it again. But isn't that how it is even with normal kids?

I awoke this morning from a recurring dream: I hear Noah and I go into his room to quiet him down so I can continue sleep. And very casually he begins to talk to me, wondering what we'll have for breakfast, what kind of weather it will be, what the Lakers did last night.

I told a friend about the dream at lunch. He said, "That must be a nightmare." "No," I said, "it's the loveliest dream I have."

December 15, 1972

Noah is beginning to have the definite look of the demented, the drooping eyelids, the unfocused stare.

December 16, 1972

These hectic days I'm thankful I have Foumi's indomitable presence with me. For all her quirks and fears she is a life enhancer, while I tend to gloomily waste my energies being a death fearer.

December 17, 1972

I have made many bad financial moves during the past year. I should have bought a house out here last spring; I should have sold our house back East this fall—I should never have listened to any advice, realized that all the general truths apply only to the typical and the average, and we are neither.

Indeed, what is hardest to learn, most difficult to accept, is that with a Noah you cannot depend on even your wisest friends, your closest family for any kind of valid advice regarding all the usual areas where outside expertise and experience can help. In everything you do you have to be out there alone and without guidance. And that's so hard to get through my thick head. Not only does my son deviate from the rules, but so too must

I accordingly. And the biggest and most costly mistakes I have made have been because of my failure to recognize that.

December 18, 1972

Though it's palm-tree warm, there is a gentle breeze, a lovely reminder that we have managed to escape the worst of winter weather. Yesterday, it was in the twenties in New York and I watched the Jets game on TV, the crowd freezing, shivering, a race apart from the one I now live among.

December 19, 1972

Noah is quick to scream, to clutch, to demand, to be unreasonable. He is a tyranny I will never quite learn to live with. He is an obsession I will never learn to live without.

December 20, 1972

Noah was up for a second straight night. And this morning we explained to Karl that we might be putting Noah in a residential setup soon. No choice.

December 21, 1972

The death of *Life* magazine is a blow. In fact, when I heard the news on the radio I was working on a story for them. I immediately drove to the Beverly Hills office to join the staffers I know. The bottles were out, the liquor was pouring, the fellow victims of a disaster huddling together in a wakelike scene. We went out to lunch and ate and drank and laughed with the usual journalistic bravado but none of us was really merry. In all my coming-to-California plans, for example, I always assumed I could pick up a major parcel of my income through the magazine. And now that source is gone. I guess I will have to go local and begin thinking earnestly about writing movie scripts.

December 22, 1972

Here we go moving again. Last night, before falling asleep, I tried to remember the addresses of all the places Foumi and I had lived in. I couldn't recall the street names and numbers in Japan. But I did remember that we lived at 86 Pierrepont Street in Brooklyn, 92 Revolutionary Road in Scarborough, New York, and, of course, 17 Hillside Avenue in Croton. In Japan there was the house in Kyoto in Matsugasaki, and then the one in Mondoyakugin and the one in Shyukugawa. And out here we've rented houses on Ashton and Thayer avenues in the past two years. All together eight houses in twelve years of marriage. Poor Foumi. No wonder she has decided that we will not move again. That this is it! California for us, and *fini*.

But on this spring day in December I miss New York and the adventure of the weather. And when we buy a house we will have to move again, anyway.

December 26, 1972

Noah baptized our new house, urinating twice in his pants. But that always happens when we move: he backslides in the unfamiliar.

I like our new house, even though it's only a rented one. We have space. And now we only have to fill it productively.

December 28, 1972

I don't know where Christmas went but it's gone. Unless it's in one of the cartons we have yet to unpack. But how I do love to have Foumi's paintings hanging again. To sit among them, to live with them, is a joyous thing for me.

December 29, 1972

This place, the guesthouse in the back where I now work, except for the largeness of the bathroom, reminds me of my first apartment on Sullivan Street in Greenwich Village, the one I've been thinking about lately. I have been trying to recall

100

that period in my life as the basis for a novel or a movie. Is my life following my art around, looking for the same locations?

December 30, 1972
Noah urinated in his pants again. It was the third time he's done that in this house. So I took him to his bathroom and placed him under the shower roughly. Just because I can't understand his behavior doesn't mean I have to condone it either. I just can't afford to let him regress so quickly.

January 1, 1973
Karl spent New Year's Eve at a friend's and this morning at breakfast Noah obviously missed him. When I asked, "Where's Karl?" Noah looked over toward the chair Karl usually occupies and began to cry.

Foumi is also convinced that Noah can now read four words: *Dog. Flowers. Bug.* And one more word to be named at a later date.

January 3, 1973
This morning as I lay awake listening to Noah's morning sounds I thought about the wanderings of my Greenfeld family over the last three generations. My grandfather took the long journey from Russia to Boston. My father took the same journey as a boy and then as a man added the small hop to New York. And now I complete the family pilgrimage to California. I can glimpse the beckoning Pacific from our front porch. Perhaps Karl will take it full circle: back to the Orient, China, and then Mother Russia.

January 4, 1973
Alys Harris advises me that "Noah will reply to the way you come on. So you must come on lightly, low voiced, but firm."

Alys, too, has noticed that I have "a short fuse, a very short fuse."

January 5, 1973

Last night, on a whim, I picked up a box of strawberries at the market even though they're out of season. And when Noah saw them on the table at dessert time he uttered his annual word: "Strawberries."

January 7, 1973

I received a letter from a family in Connecticut who had followed the same terrible master script with their son that we now live out with Noah. When he was eight years old they finally placed their son—brain-injured, autistic, childhood schizophrenic, whatever one wants to call him—into the state institution at Southbury. Now he is twenty-four and they bring him toys and candy and teddy bears whenever they visit him.

Without taking my finger out of the emotional dike, once more I realized the money down the drain, the life downhill, the hopes eternally dashed. But still we've hired another tutor-sitter-chauffeur for Noah. She's a nineteen-year-old, granny-glassed UCLA student who is married and still has braces on her teeth.

January 10, 1973

At his school they're trying to teach Noah some basic academics. Meanwhile he's forgetting how to brush his teeth, something he was learning in self-care in his school back East. So it's win one, lose one.

January 12, 1973

Noah had a laughing fit, beginning at six o'clock and lasting until long past his nine o'clock bedtime. He just kept laughing and laughing.

Noah cannot understand the concept of "wait." Which is something most household pets can do.

I had lunch with a film editor who has a nineteen-year-old daughter who bears the autistic, emotionally disturbed, childhood-schizophrenic label. She has been in and out of institutions. The more he spoke about her the less I listened. I do not even want to begin to imagine Noah at nineteen.

Each day at Noah's school I am greeted with reports of his "progress": "He's making circles." "He's drawing straight lines." I relay them to Foumi. And she says, "Yes, we've been working on that at home."

I still tease Karl too much. The other night Foumi counted his football and baseball cards: there were over one thousand of them. So this morning when he couldn't find his pants belt I told him he'd have to sell his cards—holding his pants up with one hand—to get money for a belt. And he would really be out of luck, I said, if someone bought the cards with a bill requiring change because then his pants would fall down.

This infuriated him and he left the table in a fit of crying. If I keep making the mistake of making jibing entrances into his world and on his level, he'll end up losing all respect for me. Respect is keeping a world apart, staying out of somebody else's world.

There is a boy in Karl's class who called him a "Jap." Karl told me he doesn't feel up to facing a confrontation with the kid.

I said I would speak with the teacher. No, said Karl. He would handle it himself.

Last night Karl and I played Monopoly. Now the green houses are made of plastic rather than of wood but it is still the same game I played as a boy in Brooklyn. I kept wondering, though, whether I should let Karl beat me, he so loves to win at games. But then I thought: What would be best for him in the long run? To conquer me or to be conquered by me? To have his self-image enhanced or to have his respect for me increased? I finally decided I would try to win—and did. I guess, at bottom, I'm so competitive I would even have tried to beat Noah.

I took the boys to the park and Karl performed a lovely brotherly act. Noah had approached the slide, was considering—in his hesitant way—climbing it, when a little kid behind him became a trifle impatient and started to edge in. Noah immediately backed off and walked away. But Karl took Noah back to the slide ladder, and stood protectively behind him—like a blocking back—so that Noah had all the time in the world to slowly climb it. Which he did.

The nights are cool and uncomfortable and I always wake up cold. Is this the winter in sunny California? Then I miss the winter of New York, the snowed-in, gray, warm-with-family days. I also don't like all the driving I have to do. My heart flutters nervously every time I make my way onto a freeway ramp. Driving, I think, will cut several years from my life— no doubt the same several years that abstinence from smoking and the absence of a frigid winter are supposed to add.

January 29, 1973

When I am down—and I am down these days—Noah depresses me even further. He seems worse off to me today than a year ago. Nor do I think any longer that operant conditioning is the answer. I don't think there is any answer—unless it's belated infanticide. And it will come. Eventually there will be euthanasia for children like Noah. After abortions, the killing of the very young, and geronticide, the killing of the very old, it's the next logical step if one believes in a domino theory of societal morality. And I do.

January 31, 1973

This morning I caught Noah raiding the refrigerator, a pile of once- and twice-bitten apples and pears on the kitchen table. He had the proverbial caught-in-the-cookie-jar expression on his face. And when I laughed at him he seemed to laugh back every bit as amused as I was.

I took him off to school still delighting in his company. He was so beautiful to behold in his Karl-hand-me-down blue coat.

February 1, 1973

I've finally read Pearl Buck's book about her own retarded daughter, *A Child Who Never Grew*, and was close to tears. The book is almost fifty years old and it told me nothing new, but at the same time reminded me that there is nothing new, either, when it comes to dealing with children like Noah. We have come no way at all in the past five decades. "A continuing sadness" is the way Pearl Buck describes the parent's plight then. And so it still is now. All any parent can really do for a fellow parent is to offer neither comfort nor inspiration but just the testimony of a companionship.

February 6, 1973

Karl's school psychologist called and asked if we would allow him to be tested for the "gifted children's program." It seems

105

his teacher suggested that be done. I said yes, provided Karl didn't know what he was being tested for and that we would have the choice of not putting him into the program—even if he qualified for it.

Gifted children. I don't like the elitist tag at all. I also don't want him spending less time with his current teacher either. He seems to be thriving with his first male teacher, the first teacher he's had who really has a sense of humor. Karl needs humor more than most.

February 7, 1973

Alys Harris at Noah's school has been sick and Foumi's been going there daily as a volunteer to help out in her absence. She's the only parent doing that. But then she's the only person I know who so quietly and unselfishly does all sorts of uncommonly thoughtful things.

February 8, 1973

At school, Foumi tells me, Noah still won't willingly participate in any activity, that he has to be coaxed gradually into anything.

Why should he be any different at school than he is at home? Because it's a controlled situation, that's why.

February 11, 1973

I spent a hectic weekend in the currency business and within the autism bind. Something new and something permanently blue. The currency business involved exchanging a few thousand dollars into yen because of the impending devaluation of the yen from 305 to 285 to the dollar. I'm such a big speculator I did it at the airport.

The autism bind involved spending a Sunday with the hyperactive family in the valley with whom we had observed Sunday, shitty Sunday, a year ago. Their autistic son seems to have improved in the critical period between four and five. He has more sounds now than Noah had at his age—in fact than Noah

106

has now at seven and a half. His excitable father as always was full of schemes: start a school here, a residence there. And for that purpose he had invited us, along with other parents "to start spinning some wheels."

The man has much energy but little direction and no coherent philosophy. For example, his wife, who is in therapy, had invited her own psychologist, a bearded academic type, who spoke of autistic children being the wave of the future, "angel children," and other such Arthur Clarke sci-fi and R. D. Laing psych-fi sort of drivel. What people will do to hold on to a literary theory of the brain!

But there was a mother of an autistic girl present who told me a heartbreaking tale. Her daughter is academically ahead of the kids in an educationally handicapped class but can't cut it at all in a normal class—and there is no middle ground at all available in the public school system. The woman has no choice but to keep her child in the backward class. At least the teachers treat her better there, she said.

I watched her daughter—so far ahead of Noah—closely. Which means our journey with Noah is just beginning. If the Chinese proverb says that a thousand-mile journey must begin with a single step, then each thousand miles of progression with a Noah is but a single step on an endless journey.

February 12, 1973

With Alys still sick Foumi went off again to volunteer to teach at Noah's school. It is not good, of course, for Noah. He receives the least attention when his parent is in the teaching position. Some of the other mothers, the mothers who gather on the deck and drink coffee before school each morning, should also pitch in during the emergency. But they seem unwilling to work and I've begun to resent them. And who am I to resent them?

February 13, 1973

A typical day: We're up at 8:00 and we breakfast together, Noah being allowed to linger, to come to the table last, because

107

Karl has to be off to school first. Karl is anxious to get to school these days, but he still has to be goosed every step of the way: Did he brush his teeth? Did he take his vitamins? Does he have his homework? He's out the door by 8:50—the last admonition being about not forgetting his lunch money.

Noah's school, of course, has no cafeteria. So while Foumi is preparing his lunch—a sandwich, milk, sliced cucumber, fruit—I take Noah to the bathroom, urge him to urinate, and next suggest that he remove his pajama bottoms and training pants. He wiggles his way over to his bed and somehow manages to step out of them en route. I hand him his underwear, which he wiggles into and then we repeat the process with his pants. I ask him to stand, start the procedure whereby he squirms out of his pajama top, and help him into the sweatshirt he wears these winter days.

I then seat him in his little chair and hand him his socks. He puts them on like a drunk trying to fit on ice skates. Finally, he pokes his feet into his Hush Puppies—and fifty percent of the time he chooses the right shoe—and I buckle them. Then it's off to school—a twenty-minute ride on the Pacific Coast Highway and the Santa Monica Freeway.

Noah's school has fifteen children, three teachers when fully staffed, occasional volunteers, and a very good play yard. But the gingerbread-looking school lacks provisions for any one-on-one teaching, the children being more cramped here than they were in Noah's old school in the bunker outside of Croton back East. The routine involves free play, alternated with attempts at structured teaching of such concepts as numbers and letters. In Noah's group there are two Down's syndrome boys; two girls, one spastic and one with autistic tendencies; and Noah. In terms of ability, Noah is the exact median in the class—between the two boys and two girls.

At 2:30, Susan, our granny-glassed, teeth-wired UCLA student, picks Noah up and brings him home, arriving here about 2:50. Then she tries to work with him matching numbers and objects and letters, takes him for a walk, and generally occupies him until 5:30.

Karl comes home from school at 3:15 and busies himself with

neighborhood friends, television, occasional homework, and his omnipresent football cards.

Dinner is somewhat of a mess, Noah strewing rice all over the table, Karl disgorging himself of the frustrations of the day. Noah, in spite of all the speech therapy poured into him, is silent except for wails of demand. Karl, for all of his moods, is flowering. He's interested in myths, in astronomy, in history —and, a recent announcement, in becoming a sports announcer when he grows up.

Dinner winds down about 6:30. After the dishes are washed and put away, we watch the TV evening news together. And pretty soon it's eight o'clock and time for the kids' baths. We bathe them every other night. But we don't get them into bed until 9:00—Karl watches TV for most of the hour while Noah bounces about on a couch. Noah is a great pain when it comes to brushing his teeth, fighting me every stroke of the way, but neither he nor I have any choice and I'm not giving in.

From 9:00 to 11:00 is our time. Foumi and I read, watch TV, take our own baths, unwind. At 11:00 or so we have a nightcap and a snack, catch the weather report, peek at the beginning of Johnny Carson, and turn out the lights at 12:00.

February 14, 1973

Noah is off niacinamide. The only vitamins we now give him, in addition to the usual children's multivitamin containing minerals, are a 400-mg E, a 500-mg C, a 500-mg pantothenic acid, and a 200-mg B_6. At this point, though, I have no great faith in megavitamin therapy. Not for Noah anyway.

Instead, I do think there is a correlation between my Lithuanian-Jewish genes on my mother's side and Noah's condition. I've heard of too many Jews from Northeast Europe with autistic kids. Perhaps like Tay-Sachs, the genetic disease that strikes Jews, autism is just another form of Jewish losing.

February 15, 1973

Karl keeps insisting he wants to be a sports announcer when he grows up. I had the exact same aspiration as a child. Karl

109

also likes to call me "bum." Which is what my father called me. Somehow it is as if he knows exactly—through his genes—how my father referred to me.

February 16, 1973

Karl, who's now in the third grade, has been tested by the school psychologist. He's on a sixth-grade level in reading, fourth-grade level in everything else. Which shows where our schools are at.

Karl also reported the psychologist's interview with him:

PSYCHOLOGIST: Do you have any brothers or sisters?
KARL: Sort of.
PSYCHOLOGIST: What do you mean, "sort of"?
KARL: I have an autistic brother.
PSYCHOLOGIST: What do you mean?
KARL: He's brain-damaged.
PSYCHOLOGIST: Has he been brain-damaged since birth?
KARL: Yes, of course.

"What did she think," Karl later told us, "Noah came down with brain damage like it's a cold?"

The kid's so far in front of most professionals, it's frightening.

February 17, 1973

We tried taking Noah to a restaurant. He screamed up a storm. I took him outside and bought some nibbles. Finally, he sat at our booth. But when we left the restaurant he was all screams again. Foumi thinks any change in lighting, from outdoor to indoor, for example, upsets him greatly.

February 18, 1973

I took Noah to the beach and he surprised me. I was about to settle back on my blanket when he began to wander away.

I followed him in the direction of the swings. But then he walked right past the swings to a ramp that led to the parking lot. I ran after him. Soon he was turning toward one of those pillbox constructions that house public latrines. And he was walking right toward the door that said MEN. I caught him at the entrance and ushered him to a john, assuming that he wanted to urinate since he already had his b.m. at home. But after I lowered his pants he turned around and deposited himself on the toilet seat and delivered himself of his burdens. I was so proud of him I kissed him profusely.

February 19, 1973
I met a woman who told me of her son, now twenty, "in the booby hatch" (her words). She described the conditions at the local state hospital: the filth, the bugs, the lack of sufficient personnel, the absence of any program—in a way that made me shudder. Then she told me Noah was just like her son as a six-year-old.

February 24, 1973
Foumi is really down: "Noah doesn't let me sleep even on weekends." "He's nothing but a waste of time." "In the end we'll have to institutionalize him anyway." "He's dragging us all down." "We're wasting our lives."

All the old and too familiar songs. But there it is: she feels unrealized, she no longer paints, she has had no career. And last night she said to me: "I'm waiting for nothing."

$$\left(6 \right)$$

February 25, 1973

This morning would have been a good day to sleep late. A Sunday. We didn't get to bed until after one last night. But Noah was up before seven, already whooping it up in the living room, eating the curtains. How can we escape his tyranny and still survive intact as a family?

February 26, 1973

The simple truth: Noah can't take care of himself and we can no longer take care of him. We have to find a place for him soon. I don't want him around anymore. In July it will be seven years that we've put up with him. If Job had seven years of afflictions then seven years of Noah is enough. He has even ceased to be lovely to me. I look into his face and I only see trouble. And more trouble—an endless childhood without a statute of limitations.

Today is my birthday, that seemingly milestone year of forty-five. But it does not seem a milestone at all to me. I see no great dividing line in my life unless it is the day we do the inevitable and send Noah away. The other night I told Karl we might have to find a place for Noah soon. "I like Noah," Karl said. "He can always stay in my room."

Alys Harris, Noah's teacher, is back at school. I mentioned to her that Noah's conduct had degenerated badly these past three weeks while she was out. I hope she can get him back in line.

I signed a permission slip for Karl to participate in the gifted children's program. I'm delighted with how much he's bloomed in the past two months, flowering under the sun of a good teacher. It seems if Karl is treated as a smart kid, he reacts accordingly.

Foumi was at me again. Why hadn't I taken down the living-room curtains? (Noah has eaten and chewed them away.) An argument started and recriminations gave birth to recriminations. Until finally: Why hadn't I put Noah away immediately when we received the first intimations of his condition? The doctors were trying to tell us something. We should have put Noah away and proceeded to forget about him. We've been fighting for a lost cause ever since.

She's right. We have to find a place for Noah. The decision is made. It is a decision I have shied away from, but one that I have also known is coming. Now I have to effect it. I have no choice.

I try to think of work to do, work that will give me money to help meet the additional expense—a private residential facility will cost at least $15,000 a year. I can't think of anything. Noah palls everything, destroys my every idea.

113

My heart breaks for Karl—the conversations he has to hear. For Foumi—the "waiting for nothing" life she has to live. For Noah—his utter defenselessness. And for myself.

March 2, 1973
I called Santa Barbara and set up an appointment to visit a Catholic residential school there. They said they have facilities for eighteen boys, a waiting list of three. I will ask that Noah be put on the waiting list.

I also went with the hyperactive parent from the valley to see a lady from the L.A. County school system who is setting up a program for autistic children. She seemed to understand a great deal about where possible fundings lie and the bureaucratic twists necessary to loosen all manner of financial screws. But she wasn't very clear about where she'd get the proper teachers, the kind and length of the program, and the transportation arrangements.

Foumi and I also visited a special school housed in a nearby church basement. The facilities are fine and the teacher seems nice but I don't think she would know how to deal with a Noah.

March 3, 1973
I have been thinking. Suppose I hired a psychology student full-time to live with us and work with Noah. What would I have? I'm not sure. The fact remains that Noah is, I think, selectively or partially deaf, has poor space perception, and may also tune out certain color waves in terms of vision. And how do you work around that?

March 5, 1973
Last night we had Chinese food. Noah's fortune cookie: "A little conversation can remove great hindrances. Try it."

Karl received a bundle of letters from his old classmates in Croton. I was relieved to see his peers write just about as badly as he does.

Karl has merged his growing interest in sports and geography with the ever present household topic. "I have a good name for a team from Canada," he told me. "The Ottawa Autistics."

A thirteen-and-a-half-year-old boy at Noah's school has been committed to the state hospital on an emergency basis. He's a kid whose behavioral history Noah's most closely resembles. His parents made the same pit stop we did at UCLA with Lovaas; they also tried the megavitamin route. But now he's six feet tall, and with both his older brother and sister out of the house, his parents simply can no longer handle him.

This morning Noah said his word for the month: "Good-bye."

Friends ask me about Noah: "How's he doing?" And I don't know what to say. It's not as if he has the kind of illness that goes away, each day showing marked improvement in his condition until finally he is better. All I can truly say is that he has fewer toilet accidents than he used to. But in all honesty I have less hope in the long run as the long run gets shorter. After all, even Noah's infinite childhood is finite. We keep thinking of finding a place for him. We know we have to start the long weaning process. But how hard it is to wean oneself from a six-and-a-half-year test of love.

We also wonder how it is all affecting Karl. We have no way to judge. I'm not sure how he'll eventually react. I hear that siblings of autistic children become embarrassed by their brother or sister as they approach their own teens. But I don't know. Perhaps it's simply as teens they have the courage to reflect the true parental attitude. But I think Karl knows I'm not ashamed of the genetic rot I've wrought. If anyone should be ashamed it is the society that turns away from Noah.

March 16, 1973

We visited the Catholic residential school in Santa Barbara, but it seems to be for kids far above Noah in skills. Indeed, I think too many facilities are wasted on kids that ordinary public schools should be able to absorb.

We also spoke with a girl in Santa Barbara who wants to start a foster home for special children. But she really didn't seem to understand the parents' position. Parents just can't send a kid away for six months at a time, they need a longer commitment because in any interim they chance losing whatever school placement they already have.

When we returned from Santa Barbara last night Noah looked at us with such genuine love. It will be just as hard to part with him as it is to live with him.

March 17, 1973

The institution we toured yesterday is run by an order of nuns. As we were walking down a corridor I looked in an open door and saw an old woman lying in bed. "That's Sister Theresa's room," said the nun who was guiding us, as she closed the door. "What does she do?" I asked. "Prays for us all," said the nun, "prays for us all."

March 25, 1973

Today Karl wondered: "Maybe Noah can feel things better than other people?"

And yesterday Foumi heard Noah mumble what sounded like a sentence to her. But so what if Noah is an "angel child"? So what if speech comes? He still can't wipe his ass and he'll still have to be put away.

April 2, 1973

Karl told me that if he had three wishes they would be: That he could have all the football cards in the world. That he could have a good job when he grows up. That Noah would be normal.

April 5, 1973

Karl is extremely depressed. Last night I confiscated his baseball and football cards. They were cluttering up his room, his mind, his life. And I don't like his having the same trivial inclinations I had as an eight-year-old. I don't like seeing him do what I did. He should study music, learn Japanese—and then wind up a dropout.

April 13, 1973

Open school night at Karl's school: I liked the atmosphere of the school and I was pleased to find out that his teachers genuinely like him.

At Noah's school yesterday a fifteen-year-old kid I call the "Jolly Green Giant"—he's always eating leaves—came over to me and peered into my face as if it were something else—exactly the way Noah does.

April 14, 1973

I heard that Lovaas at UCLA is getting a grant of $750,000 from the federal government to work with two-year-old autistic kids. What a joke! At the age of two years it is too early to diagnose a developmental lag and to assign a cause. The behavior modification people seem just as irresponsible in their way as every other establishment.

117

To break up the Easter holiday vacation we went to Palm Springs for a weekend. And Noah did well enough. Our first day there he made a scene in the restaurant and was up half the night in the hotel. But the second day he went to restaurants and did finally fall asleep at a reasonable hour.

Karl was eager to see snow so we took the tramway to the top of the mountain. But we had to leave Noah behind in the car; he was just crying too much. Karl and I had our snowball fight, Foumi snapped a few pictures, and we quickly returned to the parking lot to check Noah. Noah was hot—he was in his duffel coat—but not bothered.

April 28, 1973

I don't spend that much time with Noah these days. I leave him mostly to the charge of his school. And unfortunately the school isn't doing that well. They've begun rotating the three teachers from class to class every thirty minutes. To meet the letter of the law. The law requires that all the children be exposed to the single credentialed teacher on their staff. A bad policy. It may sound good on paper but it just doesn't work out in fact. Not with kids like Noah.

April 29, 1973

The family went to a restaurant for lunch. Noah behaved perfectly throughout the meal.

April 30, 1973

Foumi and I met with Karl's teacher. We told him how pleased we were with Karl's progress under his aegis this year. He agreed that Karl was doing well, was above average in every area, academically. If Karl has a wayward tendency, he said, it was to be too smart-alecky. But that's something, he assured us, Karl's peers would soon correct.

May 1, 1973

I've finally found someone who knows how to test Noah's hearing. At the Neuropsychiatric Institute at UCLA there is a woman who has recently developed a way of testing hearing by means of EEG waves.

May 2, 1973

This morning we wouldn't let Noah leave the house to go to school until he said "Bye-bye." He wept, he cried, he tore his own hair. But finally he said "Good-bye."

May 7, 1973

The highlight of our weekend was our second successful trip to a restaurant with Noah. Again there was no untoward incident. I feel good about that. It means Karl can enjoy the experience of eating out with his family. I think what Noah requires of a restaurant is that it be quiet and well lit.

May 8, 1973

Noah lost a tooth yesterday. His mouth was bloody and he was more confused than anything else. And his school has lost the "Jolly Green Giant." At fifteen, almost six feet tall, he simply became too big for the teachers to cope with. His mother has found a place for him in Pasadena for the time being. But that's a daily drive of over an hour each way.

May 9, 1973

I have been thinking all afternoon of my great irony: After living the Bohemian life during my twenties, I decided that perhaps the middle-class way was the way for me; that the realities of its rewards were worth the surrender of my illusions; that it was better to have a family and children than to write seriously and have a life in art. Noah mocks that decision. I

119

have been dealt the joker in the bourgeois deck. And I wonder if it is because I violated a fundamental law: I made a move which was alien to my natural tendencies; I tried to play a game I was not meant to play.

So much for cosmic musings. Now I listen to the Watergate flow on the radio. The testimony, I note, gets more picayune the higher it reaches; and the higher it reaches the more accomplished the lying.

May 11, 1973

I drive Noah to school every morning. I buckle him into the seat beside me. I try to talk to him. I say: "Hello, Noah." "We're going to school, Noah." "It's a nice day, Noah." The rest of the ride is in silence.

May 12, 1973

It was back to the testing grind for Noah. We took him to NPI, the Neuropsychiatric Institute at UCLA, where a technician gave him an EEG for hearing, tacking four spaghetti wires to his head that were linked to a cardiogramlike recorder. She seemed to understand Noah's type pretty well. She put us all in an isolation booth where we diverted Noah by letting him twiddle with Foumi's purse strings and munch on raisins while little sounds issued out of a speaker. Noah scarcely protested while the attached wires were measuring his brain-wave reactions to the sounds. The test seemed to go well and we'll be repeating it next week. But I'm sure it will show, as all tests do, what we already know: that Noah turns off hearing—like everything else—from time to time.

May 16, 1973

As I was preparing breakfast Foumi began to yell at me—she had been trying to talk to me and I wasn't listening to a word. And last night I didn't want to listen to her at all. We both always seem to be picking at each other these days: "Didn't I tell you to get the steaks?" "Do you always have to leave the water running?" "Don't you think somebody else might want to read the newspaper too?" Our marriage seems bogged down with a tired inappreciation of each other.

May 18, 1973

Noah suddenly sat down, joining us in front of the TV in the den, and watched with great interest the performance of the chorus line in a musical. Karl looked up and asked, "Does Noah think they're all 'self-stimming'?"

May 19, 1973

Another wires-connected-to-his-head hearing test for Noah. To keep him still I kept popping raisins into his mouth. And every once in a while after a beeping sound he would turn to me for a raisin, as if that were his reward for having heard it. We'll learn the results of the hearing tests after they're correlated.

May 23, 1973

We've put Noah on the list for a new pilot project L.A. County is hoping to start for autistic children in September. I have some misgivings but it might be the best place for Noah for the time being.

May 28, 1973

We had been hearing about a doctor in San Diego who had cured autistic children. So we went down there and had him conduct some tests on Noah. It turns out that this doctor had had some passing success with one alleged autistic child whom he found suffering from a metabolic disorder called hyperuricemia. "It's all a flier, anyway," he told us flatly. And I can believe him. In a preliminary interview his associate actually asked if Foumi and I were blood relatives. While in San Diego

121

we also met with some other parents of autistic kids to discuss starting a place for our children. But the requirements were too diverse, the children all at different stages, and the scopes and dimensions of the dreams too varying. If I want a proper place for Noah, I'll have to start it myself.

At this point I don't want a place that will study his plight scientifically. I just want a place that will take care of him humanely. And I guess that's really looking for a miracle.

June 5, 1973
Noah's schooling for the fall remains a puzzlement. Alys Harris keeps hinting about how bad it is to change or alter a child's program. We're loath to take Noah out of his present school. But it's also very tempting to try something new such as the county project.

June 6, 1973
We've decided to stop the "ah" and "ee" approach to speech with Noah and go straight into words. We can't do much worse than we've been doing.

June 7, 1973
In quick succession I've learned of two fathers of autistic children who have come down with cancers. The stress of an autistic child can do any big daddy in. I should get rid of Noah before he gets rid of me.

June 18, 1973
The Los Angeles County Autism Project has been funded. And I've been informed they have a place for Noah for next year. And that's how it is. A year at a time. Even a month at a time. So we push on with Noah, beating endlessly against the waves.

June 25, 1973

A paternal weekend. Saturday I took Noah swimming at a friend's pool. I wish there was a way I could teach him how to swim. He does love the water.

Sunday Karl and I went to Dodger Stadium. I remembered my father continually. I wondered if he had been as bored taking me to baseball games as I was taking my kid. But Karl enjoyed himself. And after we came home he got out his bat and ball, insisting I play with him. I remember putting my old man through that too.

June 26, 1973

I looked over the play yard at Noah's school this morning. Two children were climbing the monkey bars; two children were on the swings; another child was balancing himself precariously on top of the ladder bars. And Noah was embracing a tree.

June 27, 1973

The results of the hearing test are in. Noah, we're told, can hear the normal range of sounds. But what does that mean if he can't differentiate among them?

July 3, 1973

We've begun to look for a house to buy in the neighborhood and once again I've had to stop and think how much extra Noah costs us in dollars and cents. Unlike a normal brother, he can't be put in the same room with Karl. And an additional room means additional mortgage payments and taxes.

July 4, 1973

I'm beginning to dream of returning to the East, to a place with the threat of fall, the terror of winter. It's only the Fourth of July and I've had enough of L.A.'s unremitting summer already.

But we did have a good time today at a beach picnic. The loud fireworks, though, did upset Noah.

July 5, 1973

The L.A. County Autism Project is running into an expected snag. They can only hire teachers who have "credentials." The best people I've run across in the field of special education don't have "credentials." They're just too commonsensical to put up with all the classroom nonsense required to get "credentials," having learned all the hard lessons in the field. The whole idea of "credentials" designed to be protecting becomes self-defeating when it prevents the hiring of the best people. My army experience has taught me to suspect anything that is government run—even a special education program.

July 6, 1973

Noah has lately been grinding his teeth excessively. So I'm scheduling an appointment for him with a dentist who I've read has developed a biofeedback way of getting people to stop teeth grinding. I doubt if it will work with Noah—but like anything else, it still might be worth a try.

July 7, 1973

Foumi and I have been talking of a trip to Japan. She hasn't been back there in eight years, Karl left Japan when he was six months old, and I just love the place. It would be both difficult and senseless to take Noah along. So we'll have to begin thinking of arrangements for him. Perhaps Susan, his tutor, can look after him.

July 9, 1973

Karl went to the YMCA day camp for the first time. I asked him how he liked the counselors. "They're nice," he reported. "They're Christians. What are Christians?"

I read in the newspaper this morning about a man who, after seventeen years of blindness, may be able to see again through an eye operation. And I immediately began to daydream again of a miracle for Noah, that he would start talking again just as surprisingly as he had stopped.

July 13, 1973
Noah in his short pants, his shoulders hunched over. He still looks like a baby, feels like a baby, but he's seven years old.

In contrast, I watched Karl leaving day camp, his jacket sleeves tied about his waist, carrying a piece of paper, walking diagonally across the flat dusty fields, taking a shortcut home, a little boy exhilarated at the prospect of freedom for the rest of the day.

July 16, 1973
A note from San Diego saying that the tests showed that Noah suffered from no metabolic disorders. We assumed that anyway. The complete medical report, dated May 25, 1973:

This six-year-old white male was examined to see if he is an example of an autistic child with hyperuricemia.

The child was the product of a normal pregnancy and delivery to a thirty-five-year-old Japanese mother and thirty-eight-year-old American-Jewish father. He had a birth weight of 7 lbs., 11 oz. The mother has miscarried once and also has a normal son, now eight years old. There is obviously no consanguinity.

Since birth Noah was found to have a very poor suck and a weak cry. He had delayed developmental milestones, sitting and smiling at nine months, walked at twenty-three months; according to the family he started talking before he began walking, but after walking he stopped talking and only made sounds. Vision and hearing are normal. The child has been evaluated in several institutions for mental retardation and autism. No specific diagnosis had been made.

125

Physical examination revealed a nice-looking boy, obviously the product of a mixed marriage, with some Oriental stigmata. The boy was sitting in the corner, speechless, playing with his hands and making sounds. He was not interested in his surroundings. He was uncooperative during examination. HEENT were unremarkable. Funduscopy was normal. Chest was clear. Abdomen was soft, no organomegaly. There was no evidence of deformity in the extremities. Neurological examination revealed good muscle tone, no spasticity, and deep tendon reflexes were normal.

IMPRESSION: Severe mental retardation, cause unknown. Autistic child.

PLAN: Blood was drawn for uric acid and twenty-four-hour urine collected for uric acid and creatinine ratio.

RESULT: Serum uric acid was 3.1 mg%. Results of the urine are pending.

ADDENDUM:

Twenty-four hour urine for uric acid and creatinine ratio were reported as: 0.82 mg of uric acid per mg of creatinine—normal for age. Noah does not have hyperuricemia. He is autistic and retarded.

July 17, 1973

Noah has been wearing a hat, a blue-and-white beanie cap, because his dark hair attracts the sun. But Alys Harris is afraid that Noah will become fixed on that hat, insist upon wearing it at all times. So we gave him a little golfing hat which he was willing to wear. One of the Down's syndrome boys noticed the new hat on Noah at school this morning and began to trail after Noah in the play yard, obviously coveting the hat. Noah roamed the school yard with the hat on his head like a crown, until the Down's syndrome boy finally snatched it. Noah surrendered the hat without the slightest struggle. Alys forced the boy to put it back on Noah's head. He did so. And Noah pranced away, the hat still luring the Down's syndrome boy after it. I could see what kind of day was in store for Alys. But she asked for it.

July 18, 1973

Karl left the house bearing his new sleeping bag, his toilet articles, anxiously looking forward to his first camp sleep-over. Noah went to his summer school, still wearing his hat.

July 19, 1973

House hunting reminds me that one is never too far from the movie life here. Each house somehow has a "credit." Even down to "This house belonged to Ronald Colman's secretary." (The house we're renting, for example, was once leased to Carroll O'Connor *before* he became Archie Bunker. Which shows where we fit in.) Anyway, it's all like living in the middle of a page of *Variety*. No wonder I miss the rigors of New York living, the ascetic part of aesthetic values. Here the name of the game is money. And woe unto those for whom money is not enough.

July 20, 1973

Noah can place different size Styrofoam balls into the appropriate buckets. He can also put objects upon the words they symbolize. He can also chew his sleeves and cry for no apparent reason.

July 21, 1973

Does Noah know that we plan to leave him behind for a few weeks when we go to Japan next month? Does he understand the concept of a future point in time? Why does he pull my hand whenever I'm nearby? Is he afraid I am about to desert him forever?

July 23, 1973

We're buying a house. It's small, lacks enough land and sufficient storage space. But it has a lovely view of the ocean and is attractive to us in its other aspects: it's not in the path of much traffic, it's in a good area in which to take Noah on walks, and the backyard is fenced in.

July 25, 1973
After I dropped Noah off at school this morning I spoke with two of his classmates' mothers. We all agreed how hard it is to accept the inevitability of the decision before us. Driving home it was almost a relief listening to the Watergate drone on my car radio. I know that will also inevitably lead to a difficult decision. But that decision will be the nation's—not mine alone.

July 27, 1973
I made one of my increasingly infrequent attempts at teaching Noah and I quickly became impatient and slapped him. He cried. And he wasn't interested in learning anymore. But he hadn't learned very much anyway. I just couldn't get him to pay attention.

Somehow Noah seems to me to be slipping in his toilet habits. He used to put down the toilet seat carefully before sitting. Now, more often than not, he forgets and sits directly on the porcelain rim.

July 28, 1973
Noah likes it whenever Karl comes along on our walks. He knows it means that we'll stop off at the candy store for a supply of nuts.

July 29, 1973
The brain is there, I've decided about Noah, but there is no will, no concentration, as if the chemical that induces the active effort to live and function is missing. This morning he awoke out of a deep sleep in slow stages, and when we finally got him dressed in socks and shorts and T-shirt, he seemed so old. It's still hard for me to accept that he's seven—going on nowhere.

July 31, 1973

Today Noah wore a different hat, a fisherman's hat that Karl had bought in Palm Springs. And I knew that Noah's Down's syndrome classmate would notice it right away at school. The boy did, as soon as Noah entered the play area, and he wrestled Noah to the ground and took the hat away.

August 1, 1973

A gray, heavy day and we visited Camarillo, the nearest state mental hospital. It's located amid flat farm fields, the buildings are coffee-and-cream-colored, with Spanish tile roofs. The streets between them are lined with carob trees and there is dry brush along the sides of the mountains in the distance. There are some new buildings, of salmon-and-red brick, housing administrative personnel who have papers to flash demonstrating that they're running a constructive program. But still it has the air of a Letchworth Village West. The people are simply not cared for because there aren't enough people to care for them. I took special notice of the children's wards, hoping I would like them more, possibly finding a place for Noah there. But there were flies buzzing around, attacking helpless children while a staff psychiatrist obliviously turned the pages of a book in an air-conditioned cubicle. When I complained to the psychiatrist he told me haughtily that he had more important things to do than swat flies. "But there's no one else around that I can talk to about it," I said. "Well, it's certainly not my job," he said, dismissing me. I felt sorry for the children, angry about the situation. An allegedly normal child like Karl could barely survive there. How could I consider it a place for Noah?

We also visited the school there and saw a boy who had once been a classmate of Noah's. The boy did not recognize us but his teacher was interested in knowing more about him. I was shocked to learn that no one from Camarillo had been in touch with the child's school to find out his educational history, what he could and could not do. I gave the teacher Alys's phone number.

Ivar Lovaas, our UCLA behavior modification mentor, has offices in an old building, where he and his students work on some research project or other. But they seemed to me, like the psychiatrist, more interested in writing papers and comparing notes than in the kids themselves.

Upon Ivar's recommendation we dropped in on a "satellite house" that had been set up on the hospital grounds. Here a married graduate couple was serving as foster parents for four "disturbed" children in what could pass as a "typical American home," complete with a kitchen, living room, bedrooms, and a backyard.

The foster parents struck me as being more ambitious professionally in terms of their field, psychology, than in terms of the children themselves. And the one kid we met was more or less normal, he wasn't anywhere near a bottom-liner. For such children satellite homes, I'm sure, are a lot better than the institutional life, several dozen to the ward. But I have great doubts that such foster parents could deal with a Noah.

August 3, 1973
Still another autistic parent down with cancer. I passed the word along to a fellow autistic parent, mentioning somehow that I do have a retirement plan. "Are you kidding?" He laughed. "With a son like Noah you're not going to live that long."

August 4, 1973
A former college housemate called me. He's an endocrinologist who is teaching at a medical school now. We began to talk about megavitamins. He told me he's seen dosages of vitamin C and B$_6$ and niacinamide produce adverse effects on liver functions. I didn't give Noah any vitamins today.

Just as my belief in Ivar Lovaas and operant conditioning is waning, so, too, is my enthusiasm for megavitamins. I guess acupuncture is all that's left. I've reached *that* point. Ugh!

August 7, 1973

The Neuropsychiatric Institute of UCLA accepts autistic children in residence for a year or two for extensive observation and study. Naturally, they have a long waiting list. But the hyperactive parents from the valley managed to place their autistic son there just for the summer so that they could enjoy a respite. Through the politics of power play—the hyperactive father is head of a parents' group—they bumped other children from the waiting list. Not fair.

Their son does come home on weekends, though. And the first thing he does when he enters the house, I've heard, is quickly change into his pajamas—as if to ensure his sleeping at home that night.

August 10, 1973

I'm beginning to get excited about our trip to Japan. It will be hard leaving Noah behind. It would be hard taking him with us. I don't know which is harder. But I do know that with Noah I've learned every decision one makes is the wrong one. There's no way you can win.

Because of the trip, for example, we're finally getting around to making out a will. As always, Noah is a problem. There are several friends we can leave Karl to in the event anything happens to us. But to whom can we leave Noah? Perhaps it's best to leave him as a ward of the state. I do not want in any way to inflict him on Karl—or anyone else I love. It's the only kind thing to do. Poor Noah.

August 12, 1973

Karl is nervous about the trip. But I think it is important for him to go back to his place of birth, to see another culture, to know that America is not necessarily the end of his line—or the end of the line for him.

And, lately, Foumi is always on the brink of tears. She does not like the idea of parting from Noah. This parting, she knows, is only the beginning.

131

I have my moments too. In the early morning hours I wake up with the face of Noah's former schoolmate whom we saw at Camarillo before me. And I try to erase that face and fall asleep again, dreaming of a miracle.

August 13, 1973

We ate dinner out and Noah behaved extremely well. Perhaps we could manage to take him along, after all.

August 14, 1973

Visas, shots, airline tickets, Internal Revenue slips, Noah-sitter and house-sitter briefings. Last night I had a long talk with Karl explaining why Noah couldn't come with us, sympathizing with his problem of having such a brother. But Karl said that he was better off than one of his friends who had two older brothers "who treated him rotten and were so mean to him." "Noah is never mean to me," Karl said, "even though sometimes he can't help himself."

August 15, 1973

Noah has been crying and carrying on unduly. I don't know whether it's because he knows we're going to leave him behind or whether it's because we've recently taken him off B$_6$. But it is breaking my heart. A realization of the ultimate accentuates the immediate. Weaning is not easy for either side. In this sense, the trip will be a kind of basic training for us as a threesome family.

August 16, 1973

My will is done. I am ready to pass on. Foumi and I went to our lawyer's office this morning and affixed our signatures. The important thing was to make sure that our money, what little there is, would go toward Karl's education.

We haven't even left yet and I'm beginning to miss Noah. But it is important for us to get away from the tyranny of his love—or our love for him. His is the absence that has to hurt the most, because he is never really present, but rather always vaguely omnipresent.

Before I drove Noah to school this morning I asked Karl to say good-bye to him, to kiss him. And Karl did, Noah as always burrowing his head into his shoulder, shyly. And I watched Foumi turn away crying. Then Noah went to her. And Foumi breathed out between her tears, "He knows. He knows we're leaving." And I quickly shepherded him out the door.

I don't think Noah knows much cognitively. I do think he senses a great deal instinctively, like an animal, like a subject in a poorly conducted ESP experiment—one that doesn't quite resolve anything. I hope our absence will somehow seem like just one long day to him, interspersed with many meals and naps.

Alys Harris at school has been trying to prepare him—by talking to him about our leave-taking—and so have we, but as I drove Noah to school it was like any other day. At school he did not give me any special good-bye, but just headed straight for the swings in the play yard the way he always does.

What is sad, as I keep saying, is that the parting presages the breakup of our family yet at the same time marks our distinctiveness. We are a family of three, not four, by any realistic reckoning, with Noah irrevocably part of our family-of-three consciousness—and conscience. A difficult concept to grasp—especially for an eight-year-old like Karl. I worry a lot about Karl. It will be the irony of my life if something goes wrong with him while my eye is averted to Noah. The normal kid can inflict the more excruciating pains at any given moment; the special kid arouses the long, dull, aching ones.

I feel old returning to Japan. It is as if I left the last and best part of my youth there and I know I can never recover it. But I also feel the exhilaration of impending change, the sense of adventure that comes with any break in self-protective patterns and routines. And isn't that youth itself?

133

7

August 19, 1973

Honolulu. We love the clear ocean, we're dazzled by the waves, and we find the absence of Noah like "white noise" suddenly ceased—as if we've finally learned to close a window to the sounds of passing traffic.

August 22, 1973

Tokyo. We miss Noah. But it is as if I have been walking for an uncommonly long time hunched over and at last can stand up straight.

August 25, 1973

Kyoto. I am conscious of not being conscious of Noah. I know that if I allow myself to be conscious, the delight would turn to pain. I simply feel so buoyant without the ballast of his presence. Life—even living out of a suitcase—is infinitely easier without him.

August 28, 1973

Kobe. While Foumi was meeting a friend, I took Karl to our old house in Nishinomiya, the one we were living in when he was born. A huge apartment complex was now two doors away, farther up the hill, and our old house seemed abandoned, huge weeds growing in the garden. I walked around the corner to the hidden pond where I used to love to go to meditate in my own fashion. Water lilies still grow near the edges but it is now fenced in, surrounded by new houses. On the whole, though, I sense no great qualitative change in Japan, but rather a quantitative one of degree. More luxuries. More riches. More houses. More cars.

And for all the cars and the traffic jams I've seen I have yet to see the shards of glass on the street, the sparkling residue of a single accident. In Los Angeles I run across them daily. Conclusion: Either the Japanese have fewer accidents or they pick up after them faster.

September 4, 1973

Tottori. We're in the countryside visiting Foumi's grandmother, a ninety-year-old woman who is not always quite with it—she looked at me strangely for a moment last night and said: "You're tall for a Japanese"—but is there enough for Karl to know he is definitely part of another tradition, that America is not his only destiny? What Karl likes best about this place, though, are the carp which are kept in the irrigation channels of the rice fields, to devour the threatening insects. He wants to take one home.

September 10, 1973

We returned home and Noah was so glad to see us he followed me about the house for over an hour. It was as if he were afraid I would disappear if he ever let me out of his sight again—even following when I went to the bathroom. But then he finally returned to his couch-bouncing, finger-twirling ways.

We, of course, were glad to see him again. But we weren't as

135

tearful as I expected. Perhaps we simply were not *that* glad. Because the truth of the matter is that our first separation from him was more relaxing than traumatic. In the land that cherishes serenity, we were quite serene without him. Because we had no image of Noah to really miss. I cannot close my eyes and see him riding a bike, drawing a picture, running down a garden path to greet me. I can only remember a constant concern: Did Noah urinate? Has Noah gone to the bathroom? Is Noah eating the curtain? Where is Noah now?

Our eventual parting from Noah won't be half as traumatic as keeping him. Something, I fear, we've always secretly sensed.

September 11, 1973
For three weeks—except when we willed it—we did not have to think of Noah. We did visit a Japanese hospital, a national hospital that housed some autistic children. We talked to the psychologist in charge, who was more visionary than practical, and we came away feeling it wasn't even remotely a place for Noah.

We also visited some friends who have a fifteen-year-old daughter suffering from cerebral palsy. She can barely move a muscle; her head lobs over to the side; her mother has to drive her to and from a special school; the family has to transport her from room to room. But her cognitive brain functions perfectly; she is an aware and intelligent human being. I couldn't help but wonder who was worse off, she or Noah.

September 12, 1973
I had to take Noah for a "psychiatric interview" for the Los Angeles County Autism Project. The psychiatrist was a small Irishman who puffed away on a big cigar. A researcher did most of the work, asking and recording all the usual questions about Noah and his history. Noah was his old reliable smiling, gurgling self. He's become like an old pro, a veteran, because he's probably been through more such interviews than the interviewers themselves.

We brought Noah to a Mexican restaurant for lunch. He did not eat well there but neither did he cause any disruptive scenes. I think he's beginning to adapt to restaurants. The only problem now is me. As he gets older it's harder for me to adjust to having him with me in a public place such as a restaurant. He becomes more of a curiosity, more of an object for head-turning stares.

Noah has been accepted in the L.A. County Autism Project. But already the project seems to be one in which bureaucratic and professional considerations will override parental needs. They want us to bring him to school for one hour each day for three weeks. Then four hours each day, from 9:00 to 1:00. And it won't be until the end of November that there'll be a 9:00-to-2:00 program. As for the after-hours day-care program once promised, there is still no funding for it. I looked at the scheduled calendar. It seemed one of constant vacations. Public school systems, I'm afraid, just aren't geared for full-day programs, to do full-time jobs.

This morning was Noah's first day in the L.A. County Autism Project. We woke him at 7:15. But he wouldn't get up until 8:15. He needed his usual hour to ease himself up from slumber. Otherwise, he gets the behavioral bends: tantrumming and crying and flailing out. He was due at the school at 9:00 and I didn't get him there until 9:15. No one was very put out about that.

The facilities were modern and spacious—but bare. There was no play equipment in the outdoor area and the toilet–rest room in the rear of the building, reached only by an outside entrance, was behind a heavy door. Which won't make things easy. But there did seem to be sufficient staff about.

I spoke to the bus driver, who'll be picking Noah up each morning at 8:15, giving her explicit routing directions. A chubby, friendly housewife, she seemed to be the warmest person connected with the project.

September 18, 1973

Because of Noah's new program we get up early (6:45) and we get up irritable. We too, I guess, are subject to the behavioral bends. Foumi and I are essentially "late" people.

While Noah naturally—or unnaturally—tends to dominate the family day, there are also returns coming in from Karl's precinct. He is not happy with his new teacher. He is unclear about which work he is supposed to do in class and which he is supposed to do at home. This morning he did not want to go to school. I finally drove him there.

September 20, 1973

A crisis day on the educational front. Karl's teacher called complaining that Karl had arrived at school fifteen minutes late and then proceeded to unleash a stream of obscenities at her. She suggested that she would like to transfer him immediately out of her class. I didn't know quite what Karl had done or why he had done it but I felt that transferring might be actually rewarding him for bad behavior. So I told her to "cool it."

When Karl came home I asked what had happened. All he would say was that he had called her "stupid" because she hadn't made the homework assignment clear. But had he called her anything else? "I don't remember," he sulked.

If she isn't the teacher for him and he senses it, and if she wants him out of her class, then perhaps it's best that in a few days he go into another fourth-grade class. At the same time I don't want him to get what he wants through such tactics either. Something to mull over.

Meanwhile, Noah also had a tantrum today as he was being

138

transported to his old school after his hour at the Autism Project. But that certainly figures.

If Karl is having difficulty adjusting to a new teacher imagine poor Noah having to adjust to two new teachers in two schools. Alys Harris is no longer at his old school because she lacks the special-education credential necessary for the school's eligibility for state funding.

Educational theories may be great for educators and may look great as theories but how valid are they when they do not apply to the particular teachers and the particular children involved? The "special-education" credential, for example, is supposed to protect Noah from being exposed to unqualified teachers. But Alys Harris is the most qualified special-education teacher we've encountered. And the theory behind the one hour a day at the County Autism Project is that the child should be gradually eased into a school situation. But Noah has been going to school for four years now.

It all reminds me of when I used to read the critical theories on how to write a novel. They all sounded plausible, seemed to develop logically. Until I realized that no single theory could apply to the four greatest novels I ever read: *The Tale of Genji, War and Peace, Remembrance of Things Past,* and *Ulysses.*

To compound—or simplify—matters Karl suggested he thinks Noah tantrummed on the bus to his old school because he wants our attention. Which, of course, was Karl's way of saying that he got in trouble in school because he wants our attention—or more of it.

September 21, 1973

We went to see Karl's teacher. She is young and immature, and I see I'll have to worry about her insecurities as much as Karl's. She so wants to be liked by the children, doesn't know how to deal with a rejection of any sort. It seems she was put off by Karl again this morning.

She told us that she announced to the class as she handed

out a form that after it was filled out it meant there would be no more shifting around, the children would be permanently assigned to her room. "Everyone cheered," she proudly told us. "Except Karl. He booed."

Foumi and I looked at each other and did all we could to keep from breaking up. But it really is no funny matter for a teacher to want desperately to receive from—rather than give to—the children.

She was right about Karl's attitude. He never seems to want to work or study. So this evening I had a long talk with him, explaining that unlike his brother Noah he had the gift of a brain that functions so he had the responsibility of putting it to use. "Look how hard Noah has to struggle to accomplish the simplest things," I said. "Imagine how much you could accomplish with that same effort."

I didn't mean to set Karl competing against Noah or to start him feeling guilty, but he did end up in tears.

September 22, 1973

I woke up early to take Karl to the YMCA flag football clinic, an activity he seemed to enjoy enormously. He was complimented for his pass-catching ability and came away very pleased with himself.

Noah, too, is coming along. Foumi awoke after we left to find him proudly urinating by himself in the bathroom. In many ways he's less of a burden than Karl right now.

I think we can have Noah with us for three more years— until he is ten. It is as if I had a kid with a mental form of leukemia. By the time he is ten I have little doubt that his seizures will increase, that I will be searching out drugs to contain them. His brain waves, the electrical connections, the chemical processes, the electronic fields of activity, are all uncontrollable and unchartable.

When the human brain works it is marvelous, when it fails to work it is chaos. We do not understand it, neither in performance nor in breakdown. It is the door to everything but we have been unable to open it more than a crack. All the modish theories of behavior that tend to simplify, to verbalize, to view emotion as the stuff of literature rather than of chemistry and physics are just so much game playing.

Since Karl is still unhappy with his present teacher, I spoke with the teacher he had last year, asking for advice. He said he would talk to the principal about switching Karl. He agrees with me that Karl shouldn't have his way so easily but at the same time he thinks it's foolish for Karl to have to suffer for the whole year. And I think he's right.

I read another book about autism, this one by Carl H. Delacato, the Philadelphia doctor who pioneered *patterning*, the theory that crawling and creeping activate the brain cells responsible for neurological development. Once Delacato gets over the ego-trip part of his writing, he has some interesting things to say. He claims autism is brain injury; that the repetitive acts of the autistic child are attempts at clearing the sensory channels to the brain; that there is no essential difference between the brain injuries of those called retarded and those called autistic; that in the five sensory areas—taste, touch, smell, sight, and hearing—the autistic child is either hyper (extrasensitive), hypo (not sensitive enough), or simply overwhelmed by the "white noise" or hum of the sensory mechanism itself.

It seems to me to make a lot of sense to view Noah as if he were suffering from brain injury and disabled in terms of his senses. But I don't know where to go from there.

Karl has been switched to another fourth-grade class. Which solves the problem from his teacher's point of view at least. Though I wonder: If she was so offended when Karl cussed

141

her out in this affluent precinct, what would she have done in the inner city?

October 1, 1973

I've taken title to our new house. But since Foumi and I are too tired to move again just now, I've rented it out until the first of the year. Which means at this very moment I'm the proud owner of three washing machines and three dryers. I left a dryer and a washer in the house we still own in New York; I bought the washer and dryer from the previous tenant in the house we're renting; I also bought the washer and dryer in our new house. So if things ever get rough I guess I can always open up a Laundromat.

October 2, 1973

Once more the professionals have taken me down a long corridor of promise only to show me the back alley door. I've discovered the L.A. County Autism Project will have no after-school day care, no Saturday, holiday, or summer program, as first promised. And the school day itself will be only four and a half hours. When I called the director to tell her how disappointed I was she informed me that kids up until the third grade were not *mandated* to get a school day longer than that. As for day-care and summer programs, they were not *mandated* either. I wonder: Was I *mandated* to have a kid like Noah?

So, already saddened, I decided to make a call I've been putting off—to a friend back East dying of cancer. Her voice seemed deeper, gruffer than I recalled. She said she did not fear dying but just the pain of it. She recently had an operation which was very painful: they removed all her organs and looked for signs of new cancers on the table. Her pancreatic cancer has not spread but it remains as large as a lemon. They are now giving her chemotherapy to keep it down, injecting something into her bloodstream which they hope will destroy the tumor. We exchanged much black humor until it came time

142

to say good-bye—the one word Noah can say. Then we both lingered with the gnawing sense that it might be the last good-bye we ever say to each other. Death, of course, is the last good-bye. ("Hello," Noah will say. And die.)

October 4, 1973

The director of the Autism Project called me to say that professionals do feel they are responsive to parents. The school day will be extended to five hours. "Three hundred minutes" is the way she put it.

My squawking may have paid off. But oh what energy it takes! The price of vigilance over Noah is eternal struggle. Still, having lost faith in any treatment or educational process, I wonder what I am fighting for. I know Noah's fate is the dim one of a life—or a death—in an institution. I just live from day to day knowing I am dealing with a problem incapable of solution. All I can do is try to delay the inevitable as long as I can. But isn't that one of the basic game plans of life? The only possible miracle I can achieve is a small one, an economic one, and use that money to establish for Noah a private and controlled situation with a continuity. But I've never been one to go after the big bucks. Material considerations have always been the least of my motivations.

Meanwhile, I wean myself away from Noah consciously—and unconsciously. A sense of my own aging process desentimentalizes me. My resolve to make sure the pain he receives is never the result of anyone's personal vindictiveness is what sustains me.

October 5, 1973

Noah's last day at his old school. Next week he begins going full-time at County. I brought apple juice and carrot cakes to school so Noah could have a farewell party. His new teacher told me that Noah has been having a good year there; the director told me there would always be a place for Noah there. But most dramatically I realized what minute progress Noah has made in the three years he'd been going there. He's toilet trained, yes. But he has more tantrums too.

October 7, 1973

We had a family picnic at Will Rogers State Park. While Foumi tried to hold Noah in check, Karl and I played football with another father and son. They beat us. Because Karl and I were constantly arguing with each other. That kid has a big mouth; so have I. We make a bad team.

October 8, 1973

It looks like a movie script I've been working on—about an old man and his cat—will definitely be made. So I'm told. But in this land of make-believe, I'll only believe it when I see it on the screen.

October 11, 1973

Noah is settling in at County. But he does seem to be spending more time on the bus than in school, over an hour each way each day, and he's really tired when he gets home. Karl has been transferred to another teacher's room and already he's unhappy there. Yesterday he had a model military airplane confiscated. Otherwise, I can devote full time to the really pressing issues at hand—the Arab-Israeli war, the agonies of Agnew, and the Mets' chances in the World Series.

October 14, 1973

We don't know what's happening with Noah at the County Project. I do know his speech is nil now. He is generally more tractable but still extremely inscrutable. He can assemble puzzles, group similar objects, broadly mimic certain actions. He can nod yes or shake his head no, but his only sound is "ah." If County can get him past "ah" vocally, they will have accomplished a great deal.

144

October 15, 1973

Some of our friends really bring me down sometimes. They know us, and they know Noah, but after all these years they can still spout Freudian pap at us. It's as if, given a choice between the official reality of pop culture and the evidence of their eyes, they'll always go blindly toward the great white public light. We visited some friends in Santa Monica Sunday and it was disconcerting to discover that they still didn't understand that Noah was not suffering from an emotional disorder but rather from a brain dysfunction.

October 19, 1973

Some notes on the autistic life: Susan, our UCLA ·student helper, took Noah on a bus. The driver, observing Noah, asked her how old he was. Susan didn't want to pay for Noah. "Four or five," she said, "I don't know." The driver studied Noah and decided, "He's older than that. The kid's autistic. I can see that." Then he explained: "My wife's in special education." And allowed Susan to get away without paying.

I read today about an Indian holy man who constantly twiddles his fingers in the air. In that way he claims to send out messages to his followers all over the world. Somewhere Noah must have a million followers to whom he is responsive.

October 22, 1973

Since I can't figure out my own future, I mull over Nixon's a great deal. I think he'll stay on until they are ready to press criminal charges against him. That's the only way he'll go—plea bargaining.

I'm also involved in elective office: I'm running to serve on the Advisory Council of the PTA at Karl's school. One of Karl's friends noticed my name on the ballot. "If your dad doesn't get elected," he said, "he should change his name to Greenfailed." Pretty funny for a fourth-grader.

145

October 25, 1973

Foumi cried at breakfast. Karl told us that the principal came into his room and asked the children who had any brothers or sisters to raise their hands. "I didn't raise my hand," Karl said. "After all, Noah isn't a brother."

November 1, 1973

Notices from Noah's and Karl's schools. A meeting of the parents of the autistic children. A meeting of the parents of the gifted children.

November 5, 1973

Foumi is reading more and more about the bilateral functions of the brain, about which hemisphere governs which activity. For example, she tells me, the left side of the brain governs speech, for the most part; the right side of the brain is in charge of visual activities. I can't keep up with her. I just think if we can hang in with Noah for three more years, it will be something.

November 17, 1973

Susan, Noah's after-school tutor-companion, went to see the County school. She found the air generally permissive, the program almost completely unstructured.

November 19, 1973

Not one of our better mornings—or nights. Noah tantrummed before going to sleep. And this morning he defecated all over his room. But it was not his fault. Evidently he was unable to open the door to his bathroom and I had latched his bedroom door so that he could not come to our room. After cleaning up the mess I tried to relax with the morning newspaper. But there was a piece by a woman telling how enriched her life was because of having a handicapped child who died. My cup must be running over: I have a handicapped child who lives and breathes—and defecates.

November 23, 1973

Thanksgiving. Foumi prepared a fine turkey. And we had no intrusions, no visitors, no guests, no helpers, just us, together as we are, our small, fragile, tenuous, incomplete nuclear family.

November 26, 1973

Today is Karl's ninth birthday. The celebration was yesterday. I picked up five of his friends and took them to Will Rogers Park to play football. They were funny as they bounced out of the car and ran onto the field, announcing to each other how great they were. I had forgotten a nine-year-old's immodesty and I couldn't stand them. I'd also forgotten their appetites. After the football game I drove them to Santa Monica for an ice cream orgy and today Karl is sick, lying in bed, complaining of a bellyache. But I did delight in seeing him in the quilted blue brocade bathrobe Foumi made for him for his birthday. Unlike his slovenly old man, Karl enjoys clothes and soon he'll be strutting about the house in it like a fashion peacock.

December 1, 1973

We're losing Noah's transportation to the L.A. County Autism Project—unless we can pay five dollars per day for it. I wouldn't mind paying the five dollars if I didn't feel sold out. The director claims she has to backtrack on her promise of transportation because the cost has been much higher than her budget. At the same time I've learned that the hyperactive parent from the valley, who lives some twenty miles farther from the school site than we do, will not have to pay transportation charges for his kid. He has somehow appointed himself leader of the parents and negotiated his own deal while letting the rest of us down. The politics of autism.

But the really bad news is the project itself. Foumi and I

147

visited it yesterday and our worst fears were confirmed. There is enough staff but the teachers simply don't know what they're doing—or even what they're supposed to do. In their insecurity they sales-pitched to us rather than taught the kids. They came on like acts doing Vegas turns.

The schedule itself was a scam, ending for all intents and purposes at 11:40. After that was recess, lunch, rest, and good-bye time. A nursery school program—at a cost to taxpayers of something like $275,000 per year. A cruel and criminal joke.

What hurt the most, of course, was watching the treatment of Noah. They were having him do tasks much simpler than he can do. I mentioned this to the teacher who seemed to be spending the most time with him. She said the reason they were having him do such simple tasks was to build up his confidence for independent activity. But a moment later I observed the music period. He was supposed to follow the instructions of a record that went at breakneck pace. When I complained to her how impossible it was for him, she said flatly, "Noah has to learn to keep up. He's such a slowpoke anyway." She then proceeded to mime Noah, not without comedy, but not with affection either, slowly going to the bathroom.

That did it for me.

Then she told Foumi she wasn't going to listen to any "lousy parents" when it came to handling these children.

That did it for Foumi.

Once more our instincts have been confirmed: you simply can't trust the establishment.

December 3, 1973

When Foumi spoke to the director of the L.A. County Autism Project today, Foumi reminded her that she had promised us transportation for Noah. "I promised you transportation," the director replied like a Philadelphia lawyer, "but I didn't promise you wouldn't have to pay for it."

148

December 4, 1973

Each morning I get a great pang as I watch kids walk by my house on their way to school. I know their parents have such great dreams for these kids. And my dream is that someday my kid will be able to walk to school by himself.

December 6, 1973

Last night I was utterly depressed. Finally, at one point, I took Noah in my arms and while he giggled remotely I asked him, "What am I going to do about you? Nobody gives a damn about you but us, you know."

And while he laughed, I cried.

December 8, 1973

I spoke to Noah's old school. They will let me know if and when they can take him back. Meanwhile, each day I've been driving him twenty miles each way to the County Project, on general principles.

December 11, 1973

This morning I had a long talk with an animal trainer. She told me she rarely worked with kittens because she didn't like to condition with food when health was in question; she said she generally waited until cats were at least a year old before trying to train them. "Kittens like to play too much anyway," she said.

I couldn't help but think that the behavior modifiers of animals were not only more advanced but also more humane than those who worked with people.

December 14, 1973

I went on a Tom Snyder "Tomorrow" TV show devoted to the question of medical infanticide and played the hard guy, advocating the mercy killing of children like Noah. Then af-

149

ter the taping I raced home and gave him aspirin and helped Foumi get some juice down his throat to try to help alleviate the fever he had.

I have taken that extreme position in order to dramatize the plight of autistic children. At the same time I wonder about the result. It helps get money, and money can help. But, unfortunately, the administration of money can fall into the wrong hands. Look at the County Autism Project and all that public money set to go down the drain.

December 18, 1973
I stayed up to watch myself on the tube last night: I was furtive-eyed and sloppy-looking; my turtleneck sweater looked like a whiplash collar; my face was too stiff and my lips half-curled into a snarl whenever I spoke. And since I knew what I had to say it was not worth staying up to see myself.

December 19, 1973
The proposed Christmas vacation recreation program of Noah's County school, like everything else about it, is a joke. I spoke with the girl from the Department of Recreation who will be running it. She said that she wanted to use a recreation site, a park. But the school insisted that she use the school facilities "because the kids are used to it." Which would make sense if the school had a good recreational setup to begin with. But it doesn't.

December 27, 1973
To my great confusion Noah's transportation has been restored. And now if something can only be done about his education. He still has to be taught the fundamentals—to eat, to dress himself, to wipe his ass, and to control his latest habit, teething. This morning we awoke to find that he had chewed down the sleeve of his new sleeper—our Christmas gift to him.

And last week when Foumi tried teaching him sign language

—the theory being, once he learns to communicate in one way, the floodgates will open in other ways—his coordination was too poor. Noah just couldn't make the fine finger movements necessary for signing.

I'm beginning to suspect there really isn't much point in worrying about his education beyond the fundamentals. There really isn't any way to take care of him other than to take care of him. That is not throwing in the towel; but simply clinging to it all the more tightly.

December 29, 1973

We finally went to a holiday party. It was a good evening with interesting people. At one point we were all discussing what our reactions would be in finding ourselves on the same plane with Richard Nixon. Foumi said she wouldn't talk to him. A TV director said he'd find himself saying hello in spite of himself. The crusty grande dame, Janet Flanner, said she'd spit at him.

Except for the fact that I heard Foumi say to someone that we have an autistic child, I forgot about that fact entirely. But such respites are brief—and rare.

January 8, 1974

We spent the New Year's holiday season moving into our new house. I was afraid it didn't have enough storage space; we have plenty. I was afraid I couldn't find privacy here, but our room is staunchly independent. The living room tends to get dark easily, but otherwise we're delighted to be in a house we own again. Even Noah. He knows his room, he knows the bathrooms, and he's found his routes to twiddle-hop through the house.

If we're settling in here, we still haven't resolved Noah's school question. We've merely put it off, trying to handle one problem at a time. Perhaps, if only because they don't know what they're doing at the Autism Project, I'm determined to know exactly what I'm doing in transferring Noah out of there.

Noah came home from school wet, having urinated in his pants. That's the first time that's happened in a long time. And the teacher didn't even notice it.

Another accident. Noah came home from school with soiled pants. Whether it was because he had loose bowels or because he didn't know where the bathroom was, or because they don't know how to read his toilet-intention signals is unimportant. We just can't let him backslide in his toilet training. We're taking Noah out of the Autism Project.

Karl was annoyed with Foumi for making him do his math homework and called her a "dumb Jap." "Okay," she said and started to walk out of his room. "Get the smart Jew to help you."

I drove by while Susan was taking Noah on his walk. I waved to them. They waved back. Then Susan tried something. She waved at each succeeding car. But Noah did not wave at any of them.

When they returned home Noah was furious with me. It was as if he remembered that my car had gone somewhere without him. I took him for a short ride and he was tickled. If we cannot have a normal father-son relationship at least we can enjoy a chauffeur-passenger one.

I love the view from my window, past the palm fronds and over the cliff down to the Pacific. On a clear day I can see Catalina. I can't quite see, though, what to do about Noah's school situation. Suddenly, his old school is making it difficult for us to accept a placement there, insisting we clear his after-school educational activities with them. It's as if they want to make us eat some sort of educational crow for having strayed away from there. I said, point-blank, we couldn't do that, we would still hire whomever we wanted to work with Noah in our home.

January 27, 1974

I brought Noah to the park and he played in the sandbox. A little boy came over to him and asked, "Do you want to play with me?" Noah ignored him. The little kid persisted with the question, "Do you want to play with me?" Noah left the sandbox and ran to the swings. The little boy was confused. "He doesn't talk," I finally told the child.

February 2, 1974

Last night Karl and I decided to go to the Palisades High School basketball game. Foumi suggested we take Noah along. We did.

We came in during the B basketball game, that of the tenth-graders. The game went into two overtimes. Noah loved it all —sitting on bleachers, hearing the kids pound the bleacher floors in their cheering, watching the players "self-stim," poking his neck about, ducking his head against mine. He loved the idea of being able to stand and sit and move and squirm around and make noise without any chastisement. He kept looking around and smiling at me. During halftime of the varsity game I sent Karl for popcorn and Noah nibbled on it throughout the second half. We returned home at 9:30, Noah having been in a public place for over two and a half hours without creating a scene.

Karl was delighted with Noah's behavior. He had been afraid we would have to leave early if Noah acted up. He was so proud as he recounted the tale of Noah's exemplary behavior to Foumi.

Karl has become most professional in describing—and explaining—Noah to his friends. He does it very matter-of-factly: "Noah is not deaf and he's not blind even though he can't see or hear perfectly," he says. "He has a behavior problem because his brain does not function properly." And then he answers any questions asked by his friends as if he were conducting a seminar.

Some of his friends, with incipient male chauvinism, think Noah is a girl and call him *she* since he's obviously a lower species apart. Others simply think that because he looks so Japanese it's logical that he can't speak English. But Karl always offers a step-by-step explanation.

In the basketball game the tallest player on the court was a Japanese center from University High, which also had a small playmaker who was Chinese. On the way home, Karl said, "I might want to go to Uni."

February 5, 1974

The weekend was fraught with decision—and indecision. We had all but decided to keep Noah at the L.A. County Project because we could not let him go back to his old school under the terms and conditions they had laid down to us. But then the old school called and said they hadn't meant to appear so absolute, that we certainly could have outside therapists and teachers.

Foumi and I talked it over. It meant Noah could go back there and we could retain our dignity. It's amazing how professionals automatically assume that having to bear a burden somehow lessens you, that they can just push you around. So I called Noah's old school and said he would be back this week.

February 6, 1974

I overheard Karl playing with a friend of his when suddenly they had an argument. Karl exploded: "Go home. I don't want to play with you anymore." He has a short fuse, my son, just like his father.

But Noah, too, is just like his father. I was watching television and I put my hands behind my head. Noah did the same.

154

I lifted my legs. Noah did the same. He imitates, he's aware, and the County school was not offering him enough models. I'm not sure all autistic kids should be in the same school. I know autistic parents don't belong together. Or at least I don't belong with them. I cannot lie; I cannot play political games; I know that if I lose my moral edge in fighting for a better world for children like Noah, then I have lost everything.

$$\textbf{8}$$

February 7, 1974
Noah cried when I delivered him up to his old school this morning. I don't know if we've done the right thing in transferring him again. But I'm just sick of autism and autism people.

February 8, 1974
A friend called. She heard of a place in Canada that might provide permanent residence for Noah. Do I want to move to Canada? Should I check it out? Meanwhile I exhaust my energies piddling around with local day schools.

February 9, 1974
Noah seems happier than he was—at least he knows where the john is at his old school. And the County school has not yet called to discover why he's been absent.

February 10, 1974

Karl asked us, in all seriousness, if he could bring Noah to school for his science project. We didn't know whether to laugh —or cry.

February 11, 1974

One of my oldest friends was in town for some meetings. He's the head of the psychology department at a midwestern university. When he was over at our house Saturday night he offered some smart advice about Noah at this point: "Send him to the school that can do the least harm."

February 16, 1974

Noah seems to be more himself. Whatever *self* means. The County school was killing the joy, the fun, the humor, the delight in Noah. And if he loses that he loses his basic survival tool.

February 17, 1974

A friend who is teaching a creative-writing class at UCLA this semester reminded us of the California mentality. He said that if he says he doesn't really like a student's story, the student blinks unbelievingly with a dazed smile, showing more surprise than hurt. The student just doesn't expect not to be liked. Which made Foumi and me think of the administration of the L.A. County Autism school. They expected parents to smile charmingly at any faults, rather than attempt to overwhelm them with truthful criticisms.

February 20, 1974

I called the L.A. County Autism Project to say that we were officially withdrawing Noah. The secretary was sweet. "I don't know if you can do that," she said. "We don't have a withdrawal form yet."

I feel relieved that Noah is out of there. And so is he. When I took him to his old school this morning he leapt from the car and ran happily to a swing in the play yard. For someone who does not know how to communicate, he communicated to me very well.

I realize now, as with any normal child, his happiness always has to be my prime consideration. I'm glad we've walked away from the County program. Perhaps we can begin walking now toward some program that is in our control as parents.

February 21, 1974
Noah continues to be easier to live with, he follows directions with a smile. I think at the County school he was bored, harassed, and confused. This morning in the school play yard another boy came up to him and hugged him. Noah turned away, as he always does, but he was smiling.

Whenever people ask about Noah's schooling, the question usually is: "Is he making progress?" But whenever they ask me about Karl's schooling the question is: "Is he happy in school?" It seems to me now that they may be asking the wrong question about the wrong kid. It's perhaps more important for a child like Noah to be happy—if hence more manageable—than anything else.

February 24, 1974
Foumi laughed when I asked her if there was any mail this afternoon. She mentioned a package of books, some bills, and a letter from Japan saying that her grandmother had died. Only once before had I seen a similar reaction to news of a death—Foumi's father giggling when he learned that his best friend had died. The Japanese way of viewing death must be genetic. Karl just kind of shrugged when we told him that his great-grandmother had died. But Noah, standing nearby, positively grinned.

158

February 25, 1974

Noah enjoys our rides to school each morning. And so, I must confess, do I. I'm glad to be free of the County setup. They meant no harm to us but only good for themselves—which produced harm for us. A lesson.

But what a short school-life expectancy these kids have. Aside from two other children, Noah has been at his old school altogether—he first started there over three years ago— longer than anyone else.

February 28, 1974

Yesterday, my forty-sixth birthday, went unobserved. The family did not gather about my chair at breakfast and sing a joyous hymn, no special dinner was served, and I went to bed giftless —except for the warmth of Foumi's company, the joy in watching Karl grow, and the pure delight in Noah's intransigent beauty.

March 4, 1974

Over the weekend a thirteen-year-old autistic girl was raped in Camarillo State Hospital by two fellow patients, deaf retarded adults in their twenties. An attendant saw the second incident, catching it *in flagrante delicto.*

The social worker who notified the mother of the girl told her, "You shouldn't think your daughter is a bad girl." And then she suggested that the girl be put on the pill.

March 11, 1974

We were at a brunch in Beverly Hills yesterday. Mostly movie people. The host, an old friend, had told us to bring Noah, saying that he is used to him and that his other guests would not mind. But as Noah pranced about the garden, picking at the grass, squealing to the trees, hooting to the skies through twirling fingers, I overheard a couple at the buffet table on the patio talking.

"Whose child is *that?*" a tall, bronzed woman in her forties, dressed for tennis, asked her shorter and younger male partner. "I don't know," he shrugged, and picked at his mustache. "A child like that belongs in an institution." "You can say that again." I could not help but interject. "Excuse me," I said. "That child is my son. And I know of no institution where I'd care to put him right now." "Oh, pardon me," the man said. "But there must be a place for a child like that," the woman persisted. "There is," I said. "In my home. With our family." They quickly picked up their food and hurried away.

March 12, 1974
A letter came from the County Autism Project acknowledging Noah's withdrawal—but not asking for the reasons. A good deal of their funding came because they were a research project. It strikes me as some research project if the folks in charge don't want to know why their students drop out.

March 13, 1974
We went to a movie, leaving Noah with a new baby-sitter. When we came home we discovered that she had been unable to deal with a Noah tantrum and was very upset. I told her that we can't deal with his tantrums either.

March 15, 1974
Noah seems hyperactive lately. Whether it's the medication we've been giving him to counteract a skin rash he's developed or the return to a more satisfactory regime at his old school that has given him the energy of liberation, I don't know. But he gets up before seven each morning these days and then proceeds to hoot and howl. And this afternoon, in the supermarket,

when I deposited him in a shopping cart and began to load up, he blithely began to throw out all the food.

March 16, 1974

Foumi reports that Noah can now match a real banana with a picture of a banana. Which is an important step. It means he can discern relationships between three dimensions and two dimensions. At the same time, though, he's developed a new fetish: whenever he sees me wearing my slippers, he insists on removing them.

March 17, 1974

At this point I don't know what I believe can be most helpful to Noah. I began in confusion and I will end in confusion and the only thing I will have gained is the sure knowledge that there is nothing in between. I no longer firmly believe in behavior modification or megavitamin therapy. I only believe in good teaching—which is patience and fortitude and tender firmness.

March 19, 1974

Karl is dreaming of achieving a great height so that he can be a basketball player. I've told the kid that he comes from a long line of short people, that he doesn't have a Japaneseman's chance, but still he dreams on. If Noah were to become a six-footer, though, I wouldn't be the least surprised.

March 26, 1974

Noah still has a rash, no matter how many pills we give him, no matter what salve we try. He scratches himself until he is full of welts and there is no way to stop him. Unless we were to keep his hands encased in mittens.

March 27, 1974
Karl's teacher has asked me to talk to his class about being a writer. But Karl says he doesn't want me to because he's embarrassed by the fact that I'm bald and can't sing. I can't follow his logic but I will obey his wish.

April 1, 1974
Am I an April fool or is Noah beginning to talk? His verbal behavior is more imitative and his sounds seem to be growing out of situations. His teacher at school told me that the other day she was asking another child to say "potato chip," when all of a sudden from behind her back she heard Noah definitely say "potato chip." Last night when I asked him to eat his roast beef he said something that sounded very much like "I don't want to eat." And this morning while I was playing with him, I put his arms around my neck and I clearly heard him say "Hug."

April 3, 1974
I think Noah's big breakthrough is over. But Foumi keeps looking for signs. He's begun to spit a great deal and she compares that to the drool of a baby, as an action preparatory to speech. Even if he were to begin to speak, his behavior would still be bizarre, to say the least.

April 4, 1974
California has a program of regional centers, set up to deal with the handicapped. We've registered Noah with the one in our area and took Noah there for our interview. He sat still for the long hour session. He liked the social worker and so did we. She's young, intelligent, understanding, not yet overwhelmed and defeated by the reality of her job.

April 15, 1974

We took a holiday trip up to Carmel and back, Howard John-soning and Holiday Inning it. Noah had his moments but, by and large, behaved well. He did act up at San Simeon so I never did get to see the interior there, but Foumi and Karl described it to me in sufficient detail. And I can always watch *Citizen Kane* on "The Late Late Show."

April 19, 1974

I've begun to car-pool a teenage girl to school with Noah each morning. She talks too much, often repeating the same sentence over and over again as if it were a mantra. For the past two mornings she has mumbled "I love Jesus, Noah Greenfeld." Noah just gurgled and continued to bounce in the back seat.

April 21, 1974

The raccoons are out to get us. They tear at the shakes of our roof and are trying to burrow their way into our bedroom. So I borrowed a Havahart trap from the Bureau of Animal Control and baited it with some pet food. This morning I checked the trap. Two luminous eyes peered out at me. I had caught a black cat.

April 22, 1974

I overheard a parent at Noah's school discussing the movie *The Exorcist*: "That kid didn't seem so bad off to me," she said. "I wish my kid could say those words. I wish my kid could say anything."

April 24, 1974

The annual home visit of the teachers from Noah's school. They came along with the school social worker. We served them cake and coffee and they were impressed with our regal ocean view. I was impressed with Noah's teacher, the young girl

163

who replaced Alys Harris. She seemed both concerned and sure of herself.

April 26, 1974

I was back on television again. Another insomniac special on the "Tomorrow" show. This time on autism. There were all sorts of people from the autism establishment, educators and organization people, and the hyperactive parents from the valley who brought their son with them. When interviewed the hyperactive parents mentioned the County Autism Project and how much they had fought for it and how greatly their son had improved since going there. When my turn came I said that we have taken Noah out of the County Autism Project because it was not very good—in fact, downright lousy. I also said I wasn't even sure there was such a thing as autism anyway; that as a writer I have great doubts about words that cannot be precisely defined or clearly communicated.

The hyperactive parents and the autism educators and autism organization people were all furious with me. But don't those people realize that ultimately none of us can ever afford to be less than honest about the problem that confronts us?

April 29, 1974

One rat. Two cats. A bird. And finally yesterday I captured the raccoon, a graying grandfather, grumpily accepting his entrapment. I read him the Miranda decision and called the Bureau of Animal Control and they came and picked up him and the trap. They also promised me they would do him no harm; they will take him to the mountains and release him.

April 30, 1974

This morning one of Noah's former classmates, a twelve-year-old who is currently in a state hospital ward, visited the school. He has lost some weight and his lovely, curl-framed face had a black eye. "This is his fifth black eye," his father told me.

"Who does it?" I asked. "The delinquent kids," his father said. "I'm going to have to go over there and rap somebody myself."

May 1, 1974

Noah was up at 5:30 this morning. So this afternoon I took him to the beach to let him burn off some of his energy. He went bounding across the beach, swooping down upon the sand, looking for all the world like some strange bird.

May 2, 1974

The whole *autism* thing brings me down. The word *autism* invites the presence of psychiatrists and psychologists who are of no use at all. I don't know how much more helpful neurologists would be, but at least theoretically they have some knowledge as to how the human brain functions in physical rather than metaphysical terms.

May 3, 1974

The raccoons came back, perhaps looking for their grandfather. This time they really savaged the roof. I'll have to call a roofer —and pick up another trap.

May 4, 1974

I had a doctor's appointment for myself but brought Noah with me. When the doctor was treating me, putting medication on the wart on the sole of my foot, Noah cried as if it were he who was being treated. The normal reaction of a two-year-old. Noah is almost eight.

May 6, 1974

The mother of an eleven-year-old boy in Noah's school arrived there this morning. Her arms were black and blue, scratched and bitten. Her son had had a fit—or tantrum—over the weekend. She doesn't know how much longer she can keep him at home. Nor where she can place him, either.

May 9, 1974

I caught another raccoon, a huge one, whose hissing awoke me from a dream involving Richard Nixon. I wonder how much more evidence has to be gathered before Nixon gives up the ghost. I wonder how many more furry ones I have to catch before they leave us alone.

May 12, 1974

From the weekly TV program listing in the L.A. *Times*:

TOMORROW: Tom Snyder.
Autistic children will participate in the program. Guests will be three families who raised autistic children (children absorbed in fantasy to the exclusion of reality), including author Josh Greenfeld who believes such children should not be allowed to live and cause grief for themselves and others.

I can't count how many errors there are in those few lines. In addition to the meaningless Freudian definition of the term *autism*, I am dangerously misrepresented. My point has been that had I known at his birth the extent of the brain-damaged condition Noah suffers, and therefore the quality of life in store for him, I certainly would have preferred his not living. And even now, I must honestly admit, I find his death a valid solution to the problems posed by his existence. I mean that if a society does not care it might as well kill, directly and swiftly and kindly, rather than indirectly and slowly and cruelly.

May 13, 1974

There was an interview with an animal trainer on the TV news. "The trainer and the animal have to get to know each other," she said. "The rewards and reprimands have to be done within the framework of the personality of the animal."

Noah has been doing better at speech since we stopped the "oohs" and "ahs" and "mmms" of operant conditioning. Yesterday I distinctly heard him greet me: "Hi daddy" (Hi da-di), and the other night he announced to Foumi: "I want to eat."

I didn't stay up to watch the "Tomorrow" show. But evidently the part in which I said that the County school was lousy was deleted. It seems the hyperactive parents had called the network complaining that I had made a controversial statement and the NBC people, of course, panicked.

The cowardice of the network, which is proverbial, doesn't surprise me. But the utter immorality of the hyperactive parents disturbs me. They would deny me my free speech to suit their own purposes. Don't they realize all we have as parents is our free speech?

This has been a bad school year for Karl. But he'll survive it. Just as I did. In fact, when I look back I can recall a lot of bad school years. It's the nature of the educational beast in this country. It doesn't destroy us, it just lays us out. And since it does nothing thoroughly, somehow we all get up and lumber on.

The mother of one of Noah's schoolmates tells me she has to defend me before people who saw the "Tomorrow" show. They think I'm a terrible person, "the man who wants to kill

167

kids." So much for my TV life. I'm through being an alter-ogre.

June 4, 1974
We again have "gifted children" problems with Karl. A note came from the principal saying Karl would be in a combined fourth-, fifth-, and sixth-grade class for gifted children next year. The idea naturally appeals to his ego and Karl says he wants to be in that class. But Foumi and I sense disaster. Having been through a similar experience with the open-school class back East, we feel like miners with black lung getting ready to go back into the pits. We told Karl to think it over very carefully. Foumi pointed out that a history teacher she had in an early grade—who had taught her the difference between an objective and a subjective point of view—affected her whole life.

June 5, 1974
Karl acted very disturbed all day. At dinner I asked him what's the matter. "It's not easy," he said. "I have to make a decision which might affect my whole life."

After dinner he and I took a walk along the bluff. We looked down at the firefly lights of the Pacific Coast Highway, the brown blanket of beach sand, the rolling waves of the ocean, the necklace bend of the Santa Monica Bay, the Chinese Garden lantern lights of Palos Verdes, and I recalled my own boyhood in Brooklyn, walking down Church Avenue with my father to the candy store for an egg cream, the trolleys clanging past us, on a spring evening.

June 6, 1974
Noah murders sleep. He was up at 5:30 yesterday, 6:00 this morning, singsonging us awake. I feel as if I've been on a plane all night, catnapping between snacks. And here it is

9:30 P.M. and Noah is still full of energy, bouncing on our living-room couch.

June 7, 1974

We visited the Spastic Children's Foundation in the inner city. The facilities seemed excellent, they have a five-day live-in program, and the kids go home on weekends. More important, there is an air of care and concern that we did not sense in any state institution. We're not sure it's the right place for Noah—his physical condition is too sound and at the same time his behavior is too errant—but it does reinforce my growing belief that in this country the private places are the best places for someone like Noah.

June 10, 1974

A weekend of TV watching. The local six o'clock news had a report on the County Autism Project. It gave the impression that the project was the epitome in the education of "autistic children." I'm not going to do anything about it. I'm sick and tired of fighting the self-serving hyperactive parents and the insensitive directors and bureaucrats. It just takes up too much energy. I'm also convinced that, since they're on the wrong track, they'll soon derail themselves anyway.

I also watched the cerebral palsy telethon. I learned that cerebral palsy funds were being used to research speech, and that already successes had been achieved in motor movement through the insertion of pacemakerlike mechanisms into the brain. And I realized again that whatever help Noah ultimately can get will come from neurologists, that once psychogenic professionals—and psychologists—are involved it all comes to naught in terms of productive research. To divide one function of brain activity from another—as they separate "emotional" and behavior problems from sensory and perceptual disorders—is as absurd as having right ventricle and left auricle specialists of the heart. We have to steer clear of these hustlers.

They strive to maintain a status quo, a lock on their franchises, no matter how little they actually know. To deal with them willingly would be an act of brain dysfunction on our part.

June 12, 1974
Last night I trapped another raccoon. But when I flashed a light I saw his buddy scampering away over the fence. I felt sorry for the animal I had caught and put some bread into the cage. In the morning my prisoner was gone, evidently freed by his friend, who might have been attracted by my post-bait. I have a growing admiration for the intelligence of raccoons.

June 13, 1974
Karl was playing with a friend, spelling out "expletives" with his magnetic letters on the refrigerator door. I asked them what they were doing. "We're making a presidential refrigerator," they giggled.

June 15, 1974
Noah did not seem keen on taking a walk with me after dinner. But I forced him. He protested, crying all the way. When we got home I removed his sneaker. There was a pebble lodged in it, and he had developed a blister. I keep forgetting that crying is often communication, even if imprecise.

June 16, 1974
Father's Day and my annual heartbreak: Noah brought home from school his gift, a folder with a silver top hat pasted on its cover and inscribed, *Happy Birthday to the greatest dad in the world. My work.* Within the folder were some of his better line scrawls.

June 17, 1974

Karl went sailing with a friend and when he didn't come home by 10:30 P.M. we began to worry. A boating accident? A traffic mishap? I kept looking out the window, thinking of life's grim jokes, the irony of how a Noah might survive and a Karl go under prematurely. Karl finally came home a little after 11:00, moody and sleepy. They had been caught in traffic. I went to bed, too, tired and relieved.

June 22, 1974

I've had an office here at Twentieth Century-Fox for the past few months. I love a movie studio on a Saturday. I look out my office window at the turn-of-the-century *Hello, Dolly!* El still standing here. There is a complete otherworldly, time-stand-still silence. I could be anywhere. I could do anything. Except write a few pages.

June 24, 1974

The mini-event of the weekend: Karl's friend slept over and in the morning after they had cleaned Karl's room I gave them a few dollars. They went off to the toy store to buy magic tricks. An hour later they reappeared at the door, crying. Karl's friend had been caught stealing, and the clerk had taken both their names and phone numbers. Karl's friend called his mother: "Mom, promise you won't be angry. But I got caught ripping off something."

Karl said he had not stolen anything. But he did admit that his friend had told him that "he would rip off something." I told Karl that he should have talked his friend out of stealing; that would have been a real act of friendship. And I had both kids write "I'll never steal again" one hundred times and then drove them back to the shop to apologize. That was the hardest for me. It was really difficult for me to keep a stern face as I listened to them rehearse their apology speeches in the back of the car.

The one who was most upset by the incident was Foumi. She never heard of such dishonesty in Japan, because no child there would ever dream of stealing.

Two definitions of a family:
A family is a place where you worry as much about another person's problems as you do about your own.
A family is a place where you talk endlessly about trivial things you'd never talk about anywhere else.

Last night I came home ready for an ordinary weekday evening. Then Foumi reminded me that it was Noah's birthday. I rushed out and bought a carrot cake and candles. After dinner we lit the candles and sang "Happy Birthday" to Noah. He was afraid of the fire, shied away from blowing out the candles. But he thoroughly enjoyed the cake.

Karl was a little amazed, his own development having its uneven pockets. "Doesn't Noah know it's his birthday?" he kept asking. And I had to say, "Of course not."

Next week we'll be going to New York for the press previews of my movie, *Harry and Tonto*—the whole family, except for Noah. There would be a problem in taking him. There is a problem in leaving him here. The problem is us: we have such ambivalence.

Foumi is in the next room typing up instructions for Mary, a special-education teacher's aide, who will be taking care of Noah. Noah, meanwhile, knows we're going, doesn't like it, and shows it—tantrumming.

172

In New York we saw old friends, ate well, had a very good time. Karl, at first, was a problem. But then we sent him off to stay with Robe, his best friend in Westchester County, and he was happy there. And then Robe came to New York City and spent a night in the hotel with us. It all worked out.

The movie, too, went very well. The critics liked it. That means there will be offers for me to write other pictures. I won't have any money worries for a while. And what a relief that is.

So it was a heady week for me, full of the highs of anticipation and the exuberances of fulfillment. But this morning it was back to reality. When I drove Noah to school he tantrummed and refused to get out of the car. I guess he was afraid I was about to desert him again.

There was a meeting at Noah's school at which the director handed down an executive decree: All parents would *have* to undergo counseling. Foumi and I blew up. We couldn't stand the idea of having come all this way to have to go back so far. The assumption that any family who has a child like Noah must need counseling is abhorrent to us. It places the burden of responsibility—read, the assignation of guilt—back upon the parents. If a child has a crippled leg one would never dream of demanding that the child's parents consent to *mandatory* counseling before the leg is treated or the child educated.

As always there is the temptation to accept such a mandate with a loyalty-oath shrug. Especially when it comes from the only school for Noah with which we've been reasonably comfortable. I would still find such an action on my part positively repellent. Even more so, since, in a sense, Noah is being held hostage.

I once wrote that many people wanted a piece of Noah, like James Mason, the dying man, in *Odd Man Out*, for their own special reasons. I overlooked that many people wanted to use Noah to get a piece of us, for their own base reasons.

173

I'll have to fight the director at every turn. I can't lose my dignity piece by piece.

August 7, 1974

This morning, driving the kids to school, I berated my car-pool passenger for jumping in the seat behind me. Noah thought I was yelling at him. He began to cry and held out his hand toward me as if to ward off the words.

August 8, 1974

Foumi went to Noah's school yesterday and was dismayed to find no toilet paper in the latrine and a general lack of assistants and volunteers. The school seems to have run downhill as the school year has rolled to an end.

August 9, 1974

I spoke with the state special-education official who is in charge of regulating private schools about the mandatory counseling policy the director wants to start at Noah's school. He told me that as a private institution Noah's school was entitled to make its own rules, to set its own requirements. I then asked him if I had any recourse. "Well," he said, "I guess you can always take your kid out of there."

I'm angry. And even if I have no other option at the moment, I'm determined to act as if I do. It's my only option as a human being.

August 10, 1974

We finally sold our house back in Croton. Immediately I feel relief, regret, and nostalgia. All the hopes we put into that place, the first house we owned! All the dreams that were dashed there by Noah's brain damage! For better or for worse we'd still be there if it weren't for Noah. My memories at the moment are a Currier and Ives blur of the walks I took with Noah and Karl in all seasons: down to the firehouse, up to the railroad station, out to the dam, over to the duck pond.

And I remember, too, how I used to love Saturday mornings, the small-town preparations for football games, the *Our Town*-ness of my office atop the drugstore looking down at the biggest traffic light in town. But my most vivid memory of all is one of Karl, in his blue snowsuit and red stocking hat, whirling down our slope of snow on his shining aluminum saucer. Yes, I look at the checks and signed contracts that came in the mail and I wish I still had the house rather than the money.

August 11, 1974

When I watch Nixon on television I witness my own paranoia writ large. I'm even having that old recurring dream in which I find myself somehow having vaguely murdered someone in my past and afraid that the old forgotten murder will be uncovered at any moment.

August 14, 1974

Noah hasn't been behaving very well these past few days. He refuses to sit down at the dinner table and he's generally irritable. It's almost as if whenever we're wondering where to send him for the immediate short run he somehow has to call attention to the imminence of a long-term—or final—solution.

And whenever that happens, to deepen my funk, Karl, sensing it all, is not exactly a Mr. Wonderful. He refuses to do his chores, talks back at every turn. But he did write a lovely poem yesterday:

> *Noah Noah everywhere*
> *he goes around just like air.*
> *And when you hear his sacred tune*
> *you know he'll come around the room.*
> *And when he comes to stay*
> *he will stay his way.*

August 16, 1974

I spoke with the director of Noah's school again. She's backing down, softening her position. She hints that she won't force the mandatory counseling issue.

August 19, 1974

Karl has been a beehive of imaginative activity, busying himself in fantasy these days. He's either a sheriff posting Reward and Wanted posters about the house, or he's an editor "printing" a newspaper on the typewriter. And sometimes he's both at the same time. Over the weekend he issued the first two editions of his newspaper:

THE   GREENFELD   NEWS   AUG. 17, 1974
JOSH TOOK A BATH THIS MORNING. WE HAD EGGS FOR BREAK-
FAST. NOAH HAS BEEN ACTING UP THIS MORNING BUT HE'LL
COOL OF LATER ON. JOSH IS TYPING A INTERVIEW FOR SOME-
BODY. AND NOW FOR THE WORLD OF SPORTS. ANGELS LOSE TO
MILWAUKEE. DODGERS DROP 5TH IN A ROW 4–3. AND THATS
THE WORLD OF SPORTS. FOSSIL DATING TOOL DISCOVERED. A
SALE IS GOING ON AT LEVITZ ALL THROUGH AUGUST. AND NOW
FOR THE WEATHER IT WILL BE IN THE LOW 60TIES.

2ND COPY

THE   GREENFELD   NEWS   AUG. 18, 1974
BIG BLAST IN DOWNTWON LA. METEROLOGIST EXPECTS END OF
AFRICA DROUGHT. PREMED STUDENT PUTS TOGETHER CANCER
TEACHING PROGRAM. LOST COST OF CALIFORNIA IS THREATENED
WITH DISCOVERY PRIMITIVE REGION TO BE SET ASIDE FOR CON-
SERVATION. I TOOK A BATH LAST NIGHT. NOAH IS WANTED BY
THE GREENFELD & FOUMI COUNTY POLICE DEPT. JOSH IS TOO.
I HAVE $4.02. NOAH IS NORMAL. A SALE IN KARL'S ROOM. A
DESK IS FOR SALE.

August 21, 1974

Karl still wants to learn to ride a two-wheeler. At the same time he's afraid to be seen by other kids learning something

176

they all know. A problem. It gets him very upset. Me too. I wish I could be a pipe-smoking father of endless patience, always calmly ready to teach his son. But I'm not.

August 24, 1974
Karl was complaining to me last night. He wants to be adopted into another family. He wishes he had a *real* brother. And how many times do I wish Noah was a *real* son.

August 27, 1974
Harry and Tonto has opened in New York to good business, lines all the way around the block. And now Karl is making a movie with a friend involving three characters: The Sun Dance Kid. The Sun Burned Kid. And the Sun Tanned Kid. They plan to take some slides and use the *Blazing Saddles* record as their sound track. They also have a third friend, Karl tells me, "who will be the critic because we need him to give us reviews."

August 28, 1974
Karl is still involved in his movie but much of his enthusiasm appears to have left the "project." It seems his friend's mother has volunteered to shoot the film for the children. "That means," Karl tells me, "we can't use the swear words that were in the script—and they were the best words in the picture."

He's also asked me to volunteer to coach in the Y football league this fall. The reason: He wants to play a backfield or end position. He says the coach's kids always get the best positions. Which says a lot about kids and sports and parents in this country.

I told Karl if I were his coach he would definitely have to play the line. Because I would want to be sure everyone thought I was fair. Karl did not repeat his request that I become his coach.

August 31, 1974
We've been sending Noah, these past few weeks, to a special between-school-sessions program run in a church by a mod young man who had been teaching in the County Autism Project and hated it there.

September 4, 1974
Noah has definite ideas about the foods he wants to eat, the clothing he wants to wear. He has strong likes and dislikes when it comes to people too. When we go for walks he does not like me to hold his hand. He wants to be free to go off in his own directions. Often there is simply no way for him to communicate these desires—except when they are thwarted. And then only by tantrums. But the worst thing is when you know what he wants, when he has succeeded in getting through to you, and you have to tell him: No, he can't have it. Or can't do it. This throws him into a mad frenzy. It's as if the whole process of communication—not only a particular application of it—has rejected him.

September 5, 1974
Susan, who has been Noah's after-school sitter and tutor for almost a year and a half, is going to work for Sears full-time.

September 11, 1974
Our problems with Noah have reached crisis proportions. He tantrums when he comes home from school each afternoon, he tantrums at bedtime each night; he tantrums whenever we run out of a food he likes.

To break the pattern we tried taking a trip to Catalina. It was a disaster. The pitch of the boat unnerved him; the tackiness of the hotel upset him. We had a sleepless night, Noah wailing unreasonably, to the point where I felt it was cruel to poor Karl, having to stay awake because of his noisy brother.

The decision has been reached. It is only a matter of carrying it out. The time for us to subject ourselves to Noah's tyrannies is over. I filled out an application for the Spastic Children's Foundation, which seems like the best place for him.

I've always said I keep Noah because we can do a better job with him, provide a better place for him, than any other person or institution. But now I don't think he's happy with us; nor is there much more that we can do for him. So it's time to scrap the project.

$$\textcircled{9}$$

When Noah came home from school yesterday he ran out into the middle of the street and lay down. Foumi tried to drag him back onto the sidewalk. He kicked her in the stomach so hard that she doubled over in pain. She has been in tears all evening, not only from the physical hurt but also from the spiritual one.

Yes, the time has come to separate Noah from us. Oh that we could part from him irrevocably.

I think I will have to send Foumi to Japan. Or up to San Francisco. Anywhere. While I dispose of our poor child.

I have to perform the same role with my son as I did with my father. That was in the winter of 1953, when I was twenty-five and living in a fifteen-dollar-a-month cold-water apartment in Greenwich Village. I had been trying to tear myself away from my family—and my family away from me—so that I could become my own man, and, perhaps more important, my own image of a writer—free, independent, and broke. My father was ill. And as he became sicker he became more irritable. He could barely walk. My mother had hired a male nurse to be with him during the day.

I came home to their apartment in Brooklyn one night to find my father bitterly cursing my mother. My mother was in tears, my sister was in hysterics. I could see they were all near the end of the line together. I called my father's doctor and he said there was nothing he could do. He would not come over.

I told my sister to go into town and register at a hotel. I phoned my aunt, my mother's sister, and told her my mother would be spending the night there. Once both my mother and sister were gone, I called the police. I said it was an emergency, that my father was dying, we needed an ambulance immediately.

The police came and they helped my father into the ambulance. My father was dazed, he did not quite understand what was happening, but when he saw me sitting next to him in the ambulance he was reassured. He said aloud in Yiddish, a language he never spoke to me, "*Wir bader zuzammen*" ("We're both together")—in a tone he might have used to a maitre d' or a headwaiter about to seat us in a restaurant.

My father never came back from the hospital. He died there two weeks later. He was just fifty-four years old. I had thought his deteriorating condition was partially due to a poor "mental" attitude. It turned out his diabetes induced arteriosclerosis, which had affected his brain.

Noah and I, too, are *zuzammen*. I'll have to make the arrangements for him too. And I'll have to do it soon. I'll have to put him in a place where he will face the least bodily danger —and such a place will be hard to find.

The only solace I will have in putting Noah is some institutional residence is removing myself from the clutches—and the whims—of these "special school" and "special program" directors. There is nothing special about them. They expect you to humiliate yourself for the sake of your child, which is much like all schools. It will be satisfying to place Noah beyond their special cruelty.

I'm beginning to feel a Noah pre-partum. Yesterday I came home early to await his return from school. And true to recent form, when Julie, our motor-pool partner, let him out of her car, he darted away from Foumi and down the street. He was lying on the ground, Foumi unable to lift him, when I took matters in hand. Literally. I dragged him onto his feet and pulled his screaming body into the house. Then he ran to the back door and tried to open it. I locked both doors and sent him bawling to his room. A few moments later he came out, laughing and cuddly, his cheery, abnormal self.

I've bought Karl a bike but I shall enlist the son of a friend to teach him how to ride it. So simple a paternal task is beyond me. I think I would rather teach Foumi, with her morbid fear of machines, how to drive a car than teach Karl how to ride a bike.

At breakfast Karl asked me if this would be a good idea for a movie: a father running against his son for President. I said yes, and was frightened. I don't want him turning into a Hollywood kid who thinks the world begins and ends with the movie business.

It took two of us, Foumi and me, to cut Noah's toenails. What happens in six months? I know in my heart of hearts it's better to put Noah away now. But where? The Spastic Children's Foundation has neither a school on its facilities nor a day-care program.

September 20, 1974

I've spent my love on Noah. I know it's an existential situation, that I should enjoy him as long as I can, but I've turned the corner. I dread the future more than any pleasures I can possibly derive from the present.

September 22, 1974

Another bloody weekend. On Saturday I tried to go shopping with Noah. He sat himself down in the middle of the street and would not move. On Sunday we took him to the cat show. Again the same thing: he would sit down and not move whenever the whim hit him. He is harder for me to handle physically, impossible for me to deal with any longer spiritually.

September 23, 1974

Sunday morning I took Karl to a friend's house. He walked into the house slouching, he walked away ten feet tall. Because within twenty minutes my friend's college-age son taught him how to ride a bike.

Karl proceeded to ride the bike the rest of the day. Got himself all sweated up and then drank cold lemonade. The result: Today he's home from school with a sore throat but he's still the happiest boy in the world.

September 24, 1974

Noah refused to eat last night, was up again at an ungodly hour this morning. I've lost my patience with him, I'm beginning to hate him. He ruins my weekends, spoils my days, ravages my sleep, consumes my freedom.

September 26, 1974

A note came in the mail about the twenty-fifth anniversary reunion of my class at the University of Michigan. I should like to go, to get away. Fat chance.

September 28, 1974

Karl is more complicated than I ever intended him to be. Last night he was complaining that he didn't like being Japanese, that he wished he did not have Noah for a brother.

Foumi is depressed. She complains to me that she cannot sleep, that she never has time to do her own writing.

October 1, 1974

The calendar says autumn, the weather says spring. In California, where the seasons lack punctuation, my memory has become soft and blurry and I truly cannot tell the time—or day—of year. Last night, until I was in the bathtub, getting ready for bed, I had forgotten it was our fourteenth anniversary. And afterward, when I reminded Foumi of it, we celebrated very matter-of-factly but appropriately. I still love Foumi.

October 3, 1974

Last night I had a terrible row with Karl over his homework. He said he couldn't do it. And I said it was because of his lack of trying. He then said that he was brain-damaged and that got me furious. We yelled at each other and he said that he wanted to kill himself. Finally he left the house to run away to "join the circus."

He came back a few minutes later because it was too dark to run away. Meanwhile, Noah was bouncing on the couch. And Foumi just pointed at the door and laughed: "There's no circus out there. The circus is here."

October 5, 1974

We went to the parents' "back-to-school night" at Karl's school. He's in an open classroom again. His choice. Our mistake. The teacher seemed too impressed with "learning experiences" to do much teaching, I think. And Karl is someone who can B.S.

his way through "learning experiences," past education, straight into illiteracy.

October 8, 1974

We have a kitten. She belonged to a teenage girl we were trying to use as a Noah-sitter. The kitten is a black-striped, gray-and-brown female who had been named Wilhelmina until Karl rechristened her TeeGee, or T.G. (short for Tiger Greenfeld).

October 9, 1974

The kitten is a joy and a bother at the same time. On the whole her markings aren't as beautiful as those of Brodsky (my previous cat), but her underside, striped in black and brown and white, is lovely. Noah is afraid of T.G. When I say "Touch her," he pokes a single finger toward her. I'm not sure whether having a cat and Noah is a little too much. But after Noah goes I guess we'll have to get Karl a dog too.

October 10, 1974

Karl upsets me. Whenever he is down and out he uses the "I'm different" crutch. Last night he began to moan: "I hate myself. Nobody likes me."

"Why?" I asked.

"Because I'm Japanese. Oh, why do I have to be Japanese?"

"Because your mother is Japanese."

"But I don't want to be Japanese."

"Why?"

"The other kids aren't Japanese. They're American."

"You're American."

"I don't look American. I look Japanese."

And on it went until inevitably it became funny. I was trying to tell him that it was good that he had a Japanese heritage.

"What's so good about it?" he wanted to know.

"Well, you were in Japan," I said. "You liked it there. Remember the trains? Such great trains, you remember?"

185

"The Americans make cars," said Karl.

"The Japanese make cars too," I said. "I have a Japanese car."

"It doesn't run so good," sniveled Karl.

Anyway, it's a problem. Everything's a problem—even the kitten. She's climbing the drapes and scratching us all too much. Still she's easier to take than Karl's insecurity, or Noah's school situation. We've even been talking about starting a school with the mod young male teacher who was in the County Autism Project.

October 14, 1974

We went out to Riverside County to see the site of a new residential facility for retarded children. It had begun in a parent's home, but now was being expanded into a complete compound across the street from a hospital. The children would be housed there and go to a public school that has a special education program. We visited the public school and it is not bad at all, most of the children there were on the trainable mentally retarded level. But the air, the smog, the Southern California desolation that oozes through the area is depressing.

Meanwhile, Foumi is looking for a possible day-school site in our area; perhaps we could get a school started here.

October 16, 1974

Noah lately has been more docile. We have no outsiders helping to take care of him after school. Foumi works with him, I walk with him, and the absence of any other person in the house is nice.

October 18, 1974

I get annoyed with myself: I continually put off finding a place for Noah. The problem is no more resolved now than it was three years ago.

186

October 21, 1974

I spent the weekend going to football games. On Sunday Karl and I went to the Coliseum to see the Rams play. I enjoyed the first few minutes: the walk to the crowded stadium, the vendors and the hawkers, the appearance of the gladiators (who looked less massive and more human as the afternoon wore on). But gradually my interest waned. I don't think Karl was ever interested in anything but the ancillaries—the peanuts and the hot dogs and the soda and the peer-group éclat that having gone to the game would bring him.

On Friday night I had sauntered down the street and walked into the local high school football game. It was more exciting for me as an ambience than the pro game: the pubescent cheerleaders, the gangling ends, the kids in the stands who spend more time waving to each other than observing the action on the field. Anyway, there is something about high school that beckons to me repeatedly. Perhaps it is the memory of my promise.

October 24, 1974

Foumi has found a site for a school in a nearby church. And we'll start our school with the mod young male teacher.

October 31, 1974

Halloween. And I feel sorry for Karl. He was so looking forward to it. And it's raining.

November 4, 1974

Noah uttered a clear "Good-bye" when he left the house this morning. And I hope he'll be able to say good-bye to his present school soon. We'll be transferring him to the new school we're starting as soon as we can get it approved by the district.

November 6, 1974

I came home late into a lovely evening. I took Noah walking into the dusk, silhouettes together, looking up at a maroon sky. Other people were walking their dogs; I walked my son.

To look at Noah sometimes, his fingers fidgeting, his feet skip-jumping, is to see all the chemistry and the electrical activity of the human brain untranslated and unregulated. The process of communication has to begin with order and control first imposed upon oneself. Expression then is the antithesis, rather than the wellspring, of communication. Which means art, like everything else, has been sorely served by the Freudian ethic.

November 7, 1974

Noah was jolly and happy yesterday as I drove him to school in the morning and walked with him along the bluff in the evening. Each day with him is either a blessing or a curse. But I guess that's the way it is with all kids—although the grace of blessing or the state of curse seems less obvious, more definitions and judgments to be deferred.

November 8, 1974

I took T.G. to the vet's for her shots. In a month or so I'll have her spayed. Poor sweet thing. Foumi calls her my daughter. I'll settle for Life, with a capital *L*, being a furry trickster rather than a symbolic fountain anytime.

November 12, 1974

At his school this morning Noah pulled another student off a swing. Then he got on the swing himself. I was pleased by his rare assertion of will—or self. But I was also frightened. What if it means his demands can no longer be assuaged that easily?

November 13, 1974

Karl is now building model rockets. He's also trying out new words. This morning I heard him call T.G. a "tyrant."

November 14, 1974

Foumi and I saw *Pete and Tillie*, a good movie about a couple whose son dies of cancer. Afterward I told Foumi: "At least, they're lucky. They had a normal child who dies young. We have an abnormal child who might live forever."

November 15, 1974

There are only two more major bureaucratic obstacles to overcome before we establish a school of our own with our mod young teacher. The city fire department has to inspect the church premises and then the county education office has to give its approval. After that, we'll try to work out some sort of transportation arrangement. And, of course, recruit some kids.

November 16, 1974

Yesterday was Foumi's birthday. We celebrated it by going to the Bureau of Motor Vehicles, where she passed the written test for a driver's license without a single error. Then we lunched at a French restaurant, and picked up a turquoise pendant for the birthday lady.

November 21, 1974

We met with Karl's teacher and she told us how creative he is and how good-looking he is and how much she is enjoying him. The fact that his spelling and math are almost nonexistent didn't seem to worry her at all. Karl is having a good time in school this year, no doubt about that. But he isn't learning anything, no doubt about that either. Perhaps in this mecca of entertainment it's too much to ask for an education too.

189

November 22, 1974
It rained last night and today is glorious: the sky is clear and blue and the wind carries the hint of winter rather than the smell of smog. Karl, who's going to a science fair tomorrow, is feeling good. Noah, who was swinging giddily aloft when I left him at school, is happy. And our cat, T.G., is a bundle of energy—and fleas. Still I think it is good that we have the cat. Karl should go through the experience of living with a pet —other than his brother.

November 23, 1974
The start of the new school is still bogged down in red tape. I doubt if we can get it going before the first of the year.

November 24, 1974
It's two years since we moved to California. Before that we spent two long winters here. That's four years. Yet I still have a hard time finding points of reference for my memory, getting my bearings in terms of time. If once my year—and my life— was divided by semesters, and later by summer vacations, and then by events such as army service and marriage and births, and finally by geography, I don't quite know what defines— and delimits—my time now.

November 26, 1974
Karl's tenth birthday. Saturday I got the gift he wanted— Motorcross handlebars for his bike. Sunday I gathered his friends and took them to the pizza joint for lunch, to the high school field to play football, and then to Baskin-Robbins for ice cream. Last night his friend Erich took him out to dinner. And tonight Foumi is preparing his favorite dish, tacos.

I remember the Thanksgiving Day he was born in Japan, a blotch of red with some kind of yellow grease on him when the nurse held him up to show me. And now he's a kid who knows how to ride a bike, swim, and is even beginning to learn how to play the piano. He had his first lesson today, Noah observing from across the room, shyly and with a trace of jealousy. But when the music teacher tried to get Noah to play some simple rhythm instruments, he ran off to his room.

November 29, 1974

We visited the area's biggest school for children with learning disabilities. Nice bricks, lovely facilities. But few children seemed that badly off and none of the teachers was that exceptional. We lunched with the director, who volunteered to help us get our school started by referring students.

November 30, 1974

Noah is a pain. I cannot take long trips or even go off on short vacations. I have to drive him to school in the morning, I have to return from work early because of him. I have to walk him, I have to bathe him, I have to wipe his ass, I have to attend to so many ridiculous chores because of him. And yet . . . I do not look forward to the day when he leaves our lives. And I will not decide that day. I place that responsibility squarely on his frail shoulders. He will decide that day when his actions become more than we can endure.

December 1, 1974

Yesterday morning I went rocket launching with Karl and his friend Erich, and Erich's kid brother, Maxie, and their father. We enjoyed ourselves. What spectacular toys the kids have these days. The electrically ignited spark can send a rocket up several thousand feet.

But whenever I watch Karl playing with a friend like Erich who has a younger brother Noah's age, like Maxie, my heart twitches.

December 2, 1974

Noah has diarrhea. So Foumi is busy at the washing machine.

December 3, 1974

Noah is still ill, home from school, and I feel sorry for Foumi, stuck in the house. I also feel sorry for myself. I am as cold and depressed as if I were still in New York. This is always a bad time of year for me, a kind of *mal de fête* between Thanksgiving and New Year's, the days short, the afternoons dark, everyone prey to colds and chills.

Right now I feel that frightened warmth that I confuse with love. I want to huddle with my family, to hug them, happy to be a part of the warm core we have together. All I really care for is Karl and Foumi and Noah—my world has become that small. Or that big.

December 4, 1974

It looked as if it would rain this morning and Foumi wasn't sure whether or not Noah still had his cold, so we're keeping him home from school another day. And I'm staying home too. But I can't write. I can hear Noah whenever he gives a yelp and it cuts through me. Foumi says I have no power of concentration. I think I have too great a power of imagination. Anyway, good-bye to my resolve to help Foumi. I'm getting out of here, running to my office for refuge.

December 5, 1974

Every once in a while the absurdity of our situation hits me. At best we're involved in a holding pattern over an airstrip we don't want to land on: the institution. Today, for example, we heard from two mothers who have children in two different privately funded residences. One would like her son to get some massive dosages of vitamins; the other does not like her daughter being drugged on Mellaril. In both cases, however, the child is in the impersonal hands of the doctors and directors of the institutions, who make the parents feel helpless. Are we willing to give up our say in Noah's fate?

Who said Southern California has only one season? It has four seasons. The trouble is they're all on the same day. Lately, the morning is springlike, noontime is summer, the afternoon is autumnal, and then the night is cold and wintry.

December 7, 1974
Our prospective school was dealt a blow. The fire department inspector said we couldn't have children under seven years of age in a second-floor classroom. And we were counting on two or three such youngsters. So we'll try to borrow a first-floor classroom from the church; or convince the fire inspector that age is absurd when it comes to special children; or see if buying additional fire extinguishers will suffice.

December 10, 1974
I bought a scratch post for the cat. Noah went over to it and looped himself around it. Immediately, T.G. exercised her proprietary rights.

December 11, 1974
Good news. The school has passed the fire department inspection because the church will let us use a first-floor room too.

December 12, 1974
Karl and Noah and I walked downtown to the Hobby Shop last night. I ordered a rocket kit for Karl for Christmas. And he was one happy kid on the way back. And Noah was one affectionate kid. In the dark he stuck close to me, reaching up for my hand and pressing it, and trying to walk more at my pace than his own.

December 13, 1974
The news on the school front isn't so good today. The mod young teacher plans to have two classes, one for the younger kids and one for the older children, a floor apart. Foumi worries about who will get his pedagogical attention. I worry about the disjointedness of such an operation. I'm also beginning to be disturbed by his attitude. Our letting him do all the legal paperwork in setting up the school was a mistake. He has, in effect, shut us out of control, telling us decisions rather than consulting with us before making them. Which, as parents, leaves us back in the same box where we began.

December 15, 1974
We set up our Christmas tree last night but didn't decorate it. We're afraid the cat will tear down all the silver tinsel. And that Noah will mouth it.

December 17, 1974
Now that the school is almost a reality we have misgivings about it. We spoke with the teacher yesterday. Suddenly the scheduled school day was a half hour shorter than we had assumed in the planning. He was exceedingly vague about the curriculum. And he also seemed intent on accepting a child who we know is given to great violence.

December 19, 1974
We're confused. Here we've helped start a school and I'm not sure about sending Noah there. I want to do what's best for him.

December 20, 1974
Yesterday Noah had a terrible tantrum when he came home from school. And I made it even worse. I became angry. Foumi wisely ignores Noah at such times.
Noah's tantrums can be funny, though. He'll take everything

off a table first, before upending it. And he always looks for a rug-cushioned wood floor to beat his head against. And when he notices that no one is watching he begins to make the beating sound with his foot—like a pro wrestler feigning action. And then suddenly it is all reassuring: he does not want to hurt himself.

December 21, 1974

A lovely pre-Christmasy day, chilly but not cold, wintry without shivers. We finished our Christmas shopping yesterday afternoon. Karl bought gifts for Noah (some rubbery Disney figures) and me (a pair of socks). In the haberdashery store at first he was downhearted when he saw cashmere socks for $5.50 a pair. But I worked him down the racks to the dollar ones. Still he had only fifty cents budgeted, which he had saved from the extra nickels I give him with his lunch money. I told him that I wanted those dollar socks so badly because they were nylon and machine washable that I would put up the extra fifty cents. "You really want those socks?" he asked me in utter amazement. I assured him I did. "Because I could get you a copy of *Time* magazine for fifty cents," he said. I told him I preferred the socks. And that wrapped it up.

December 23, 1974

I continue to enjoy the warmth and *gemütlichkeit* of the season. I like being with Karl and Noah and Foumi, simply watching football on television and eating and drinking too much, or taking pleasant walks, and not being too harried, and generally feeling a sense of well-being without too much justification.

December 28, 1974

Last night we were planning to enjoy our big Christmas holiday season social evening. There would be a dinner party at a friend's house, and afterward a big brawl of a party at another friend's. And our special baby-sitter, Mary Albrecht, was coming all the way in from the valley to watch Noah. But before we left the house we noticed Noah's lack of appetite.

Still, we decided to go out. And dinner was a joy, good food and great company, and we were really having fun when the phone rang, around dessert time. It was Mary. Noah was vomiting.

So we didn't get to the big party, we came straight home. Noah vomited once more. We gave him some Congespirin and tried to go to sleep ourselves. I could; Foumi couldn't. She always worries more than I do.

This morning Noah doesn't seem quite right, but he isn't vomiting either. And a friend has already called to tell us that the party we missed was one of the best he'd been to in years.

December 29, 1974

Karl has been busy all day assembling his Christmas rockets and now he's decided he wants to give *me* piano lessons, twenty-five cents per lesson.

December 30, 1974

Foumi heard that one of Noah's former classmates seems to be doing well in a residential school near Fresno. I'll have to call that boy's father to check out the place. Because whenever Noah is home for more than a week—as he's been during this vacation period—it always occurs to me that the day is soon coming when he can't be home at all.

December 31, 1974

I've just taken my second piano lesson from Karl. I'm a lousy pupil. But he's a great teacher. I just love the way he assumes an authoritarian tone, an expert's pose. Foumi says that manner is an exact duplication of his own music teacher.

I must exude a "daddy" smell. In the morning, of a Saturday or Sunday, Karl likes to topple into my bed and roll around with me. Noah comes too. But only at my beckoning. He plops his body, limp and lifeless, across mine, and it feels incredibly heavy. But he does like it when I rub his head.

At dinner tonight Karl repeated that sometimes he's glad Noah isn't normal, that it means he doesn't have to fight with him the way some of his friends are always fighting with their kid brothers.

I wonder if I can accept at face value what Karl says. I wonder if he isn't saying that because he knows it's something we'd like to hear. What guilt I have when I consider the burden Noah must be for him!

10

After all the time we spent helping start a school with the mod young teacher, I'll be taking Noah back to his old school. The mod teacher's school has no schedule, no fixed routine for the kids, and he hasn't hired any help at all. We don't see how he can run one classroom—let alone two. (Foumi asked him what he'd do if he had to go to the bathroom, would he leave the children unattended? No, he brightly replied, he would take the children to the bathroom with him.) We just can't send Noah to a place that seems so formless, so unstructured. Because if we know one thing it's that special children need a structured day, a set pattern they can fall into comfortably. And, come to think of it, who doesn't?

January 5, 1975

This evening we were sitting around the table, Foumi and Karl and I—Noah was lying on the love seat in the living room with

Leroy, his stuffed lion—when Karl wondered what our lives would have been like without Noah. We decided that we wouldn't be living in Los Angeles now, that we probably would have returned to Japan to live for a long spell at one time or another, that certainly Foumi would have been more productive as a painter, that perhaps there would have been another child in our family.

But then I explained to Karl that every family has its "would-have-beens" and "could-have-beens," "might-have-beens" and "should-have-beens." "Only ours," I said, "shows."

January 6, 1975

On my walks with Noah I've begun to jog more and more. He moves so slowly that I can jog ahead one hundred yards and then circle back ninety-five yards. And if I do that enough times I guess I'm a jogger, and Noah may yet prove to be beneficial to my health.

January 7, 1975

At this point let me be honest with myself: What is my attitude toward Noah? How do I view him? I think, put simply, I view him as a responsibility, someone I have to take care of —almost like a job that has to be done. Because if we don't do the job, who will? It's our job by elimination. And I mean job, just a job. I am no Job and Noah is no great affliction and neither of us is part of any cosmic test—or otherworldly joke.

January 8, 1975

Karl mentioned at dinner that one of his friends had suddenly become very moody; his parents were divorcing. "No kid likes that," Karl said, "for his parents to divorce." The one thing I think Karl is secure about is our marriage. For all our family situation has taken from him at least we've given him that.

199

January 9, 1975

I have a theory about dentists: Always get a dentist who has no hygienist and whose office has no view. I hadn't gone to a dentist since moving out here. Finally, the other day, I decided it was about time. I went to a dentist in Beverly Hills who had antique furniture in the waiting room, a spectacular-looking hygienist, and whose offices afforded a thrilling view of the mountains. He told me I needed a new bridge, eight caps, and that it would cost me $2,500.

I decided to get another estimate. I visited a local dentist here in the Palisades. He had a smaller office and his view of the mountains wasn't that sensational. He said my bridges were okay, but he estimated it would cost $1,500 to fix the rest of my mouth.

I tried one more dentist. In a working-class neighborhood in Venice. His office shared a waiting room of Naugahyde furniture with six other professionals and the view from his window was of a brick wall. But he spoke of only two teeth that definitely needed caps and said it might run me a couple of hundred. They're the same teeth, just different offices with different views.

January 10, 1975

Last night it was quite late when I got to take Noah for his walk along the bluff. While I jogged I noticed that he walks much faster in the dark when I'm flickering out of sight.

January 11, 1975

I called the father of a fourteen-year-old boy who is in the residential school near Fresno. The boy has been at the school for three months now. "They're tough," says the father. "They pull hair, they slap hands, they make sure the kid acts his age."

For the first three months the parent could not see the child. After that it was only on alternate weekends. The children go to school from 9:30 to 2:30. They live in foster homes, rented furnished houses in which young couples act as their parents, four children to a house. The atmosphere is generally small town, the stress in school is on academics.

How would they, Foumi and I asked ourselves, treat a Noah? Who can't talk. Who can barely learn. Who has no academic knowledge or skills. And how would Noah react to their methods? Not too well, we decided. Noah does not exactly respond well to pressure situations, to force and violence.

January 12, 1975

This morning at breakfast Noah wouldn't eat his egg. "You eat your egg," I said, and thumped my chest. "You listen to me. I'm the boss around here." In imitative reply Noah thumped his own chest. But he still wouldn't eat his egg.

January 13, 1975

Noah isn't well again, lacks energy, has a slight fever, won't eat. When he is sick he's literally like a sick animal. Like a cat he refuses to eat. Like a dog he follows you slowly around the house. Like a baby he whimpers quietly.

January 14, 1975

I took Noah to the doctor this morning. He gave him a shot of antibiotics and tested him for what he suspects: a strep throat. In the car Noah's face looked long and thin, like that of a DP, like Ludwig Donath in an old movie, like someone who is living through a holocaust. Which, of course, he is.

January 15, 1975

I took the cat to the vet. *She* was supposed to be spayed. Instead, *he*'s being altered. We discovered *she*'s a *he*, something Foumi has suspected for quite a while. And now Karl is terribly worried that T.G. won't be able to "talk" after his operation.

201

Foumi and I have decided adverse treatment—or negative conditioning—simply does not work with Noah. It can have an adverse effect, turning him, as it would an animal, into a meanie. So we've come sort of half circle: Operant conditioning gives us, as parents, something to do, but we must be discreet in what we choose to do. We must never treat Noah with any less compassion than we would treat Karl. Just as we must sometimes instill fear in him, we must at most times refrain from using punishments. But we must still be able to use punishments —as deterrents—when necessary.

January 19, 1975
Karl gave me another piano lesson yesterday. I love the way he mouths his teacher's every platitude. "Review," he informed me categorically, "is part of every lesson."

January 20, 1975
Noah is better now, happy and healthy again. He eats normally and doesn't just lie on the love seat, cowering in illness. Foumi has her five-hour break during the day while he's off at school. So our house is a more pleasant place.

January 21, 1975
Foumi has finally done it. She's actually taking driving lessons. It will be nice to have her able to flit about—slowly.

January 22, 1975
Foumi spoke to the mother of a teenage boy who once went to Noah's school. The mother told of putting the boy in Camarillo, the state hospital, where he was continually drugged and left for the most part in the corner. Now she's casting about for another place for him.

January 23, 1975

The cat can't figure out Noah. He's only a kitten, always playful, and tries to get Noah to respond to his attacks. But Noah only backs off and withdraws.

January 24, 1975

On TV last night I saw one of those chimps who can play a musical instrument. Again I asked myself the question: How can he be trained to do things Noah hasn't been trained to do? Obviously, our training programs for special humans lag behind those for animals.

We, of course, have had our fill of behaviorism or operant conditioning. It is a starting point, a step, but not the whole journey. We are dealing with physical incapacities. It is no accident that Noah's teeth are oddly spaced, that his body is completely lacking in muscle tone, that his coordination varies from poor to nonexistent. And no educational approach or psychological technique can have any more effect than a cosmetic once-over. So why do I concern myself so about schools and teachers and treatments for him? Because if I were to say there is no hope for Noah I would be saying there is no hope for any of us.

January 25, 1975

Foumi visited Noah's school yesterday. She had many complaints. He is still getting no more than a steady nursery school diet. There is not enough emphasis on self-care; there is little in the way of vocational training. But one thing was obvious. Noah is happy there.

January 26, 1975

I ran into a psychologist in a friend's office this afternoon. He spoke about "rage repression," how such therapy has helped "autistic" children. I had to repress my rage as I tried to make

203

him understand that in "autistic" children we are dealing with organic failings, that "rage repression" could no more affect an "autistic" child than it could alter the genetic makeup of a Down's syndrome child.

Every time I get down on behaviorism, which at least has its commonsensical elements, I meet someone from the establishment psychogenic community, purveying a literary theory of disease, and I grow livid.

January 27, 1975

Karl was giving me another piano lesson last night. I kept making dumb mistakes and he kept shouting at me. I don't know what frustrated him more, my lack of musical talent or the fact that I was making it difficult for him to earn his twenty-five-cent teaching fee.

January 28, 1975

The kitten now constantly watches Karl. When he dresses. When he takes a bath. When he plays the piano. A true disciple.

Noah now has the habit of putting everything in its place. If he sees me reading a magazine, he snatches it out of my hands and puts it on the end-table shelf. If he sees mail or paper clutter on the breakfast-room table, he immediately removes it. And he's awfully fast at putting things into the trash. Spoons and forks have a way of disappearing whenever he takes it upon himself to clear the table.

He makes time disappear too. Also dreams. We could move about, live in France one year, Japan the next, if not for him —or so I would like to dream. The fact that—with or without Noah—we probably couldn't, doesn't matter. The function of dreams is not to produce reality—but relief.

I am thankful though that Noah is not hyperactive. A teenage boy, brain-damaged because of encephalitis, was here yesterday with his mother. In fifteen minutes he tore all the lemons off our tree, scattered our garden tools about the backyard, broke the hinge on our gate. A blond tornado had visited us.

January 30, 1975

While we were all at the supermarket shopping this afternoon, Karl decided he wanted to eat Mexican food for dinner. I gave him money to get two takeout orders of taquitos at the Mexican cafeteria. He came back with the change and handed it to me; there was too much money. He had been charged for only one order of taquitos.

"I didn't cheat them," he told me. "I said two orders at the register."

"Go back," I said, "and tell them they made a mistake."

"I'm not going back," Karl said. "It's their fault. I told them two orders."

"Look, you did nothing wrong," I reassured him. "But you don't want to rip off their money. You know, sometimes I've given a ten-dollar bill instead of a one-dollar bill and the cashier has pointed out my mistake. It's good if we're all honest. It protects us."

Still he refused to budge. I went back to the Mexican cafeteria myself and told the cashier she had forgotten to charge my son for two orders of taquitos and paid her the difference. As I walked back to the car I wondered if I would have been as honest if Karl had not been audience to my act.

January 31, 1975

At lunch a friend asked me: "What do you ultimately plan to do with Noah?" I shrugged. "We just play it from day to day as if we are living with someone who has a terminal illness, enjoying the good days and abiding the bad days as best we can."

But now I feel like crying. With all my acceptance of Noah's fate—theoretically, logically, intellectually, verbally—I still do not like to picture him in a setting unhappier for him than our

205

home. A child should not have to leave home just because his continued presence makes his parents tired and unhappy.

February 3, 1975

On Saturday I took Noah to a recreation program for special children sponsored by the L.A. Department of Parks at our local park. And Noah, surprisingly, got along well there. The teacher seemed to know how to handle him.

February 7, 1975

A supervisor from the Department of Parks phoned: Noah cannot go to the Saturday class at the park. They want to work with higher-level kids. They would let me know when —and if—they would have a program for Noah.

I became angry. Again, it was a question of taking care first of those who need help comparatively the least; while those who need help the most—such as Noah—were cared for last. (Somehow I put it all much better to the supervisor.)

February 10, 1975

Mary baby-sat with Noah and we took Karl to the Magic Castle where he enjoyed the grand buffet, the fine magic shows. We so seldom spend a day away from Noah with Karl. But when we came home there were recriminations. Not from Noah. But from Karl. He refused point-blank to practice his piano. And I think the reason he made a scene about it was a kind of guilt about his normalcy, the fact that he too had left Noah behind.

February 13, 1975

Noah continues to be compulsive, putting everything in the place he assigns to it. Newspapers here, for example, clothing there. At this point, the more he can do, the more trouble he can cause. I know of an "autistic" little girl just like Noah who can wiggle out of car safety belts, "escape" from closed car doors, and go charging away in search of some want. Fortunately, Noah can't do such things yet.

February 14, 1975

St. Valentine's Day. Our love must do for Noah what we cannot do.

February 15, 1975

The politics of "autism" can get me down as much as the malady itself. For just as "autism" doesn't really exist—as a unique and disparate distinct form of brain damage—the game some people are playing with it is real enough. I mean those who have a vested interest in the continuance of the designation. Those who have the clout that comes through the perpetuation of their organization and their positions in it. Those who have the professional authority to trade on the power inherent in their own esoteric expertise. Those who want to play games, pull quid pro quo tricks, look for easy deals.

I just want to be as honest as possible with myself. It seems to me that the moment I become dishonest about Noah's condition or my estimation of the efficacy of any of the proffered treatments, I'm finished. All I have going for me in dealing with Noah's condition is a basic belief in my ability to judge the reality of what I am doing and the morality of what I am asking.

February 17, 1975

The trouble with most institutions is that they have no programs after 3:00 P.M. They have a school of their own—or a liaison with a school—and after that it is flop-around time for a Noah. With even less supervision than he gets at home.

February 19, 1975

Noah has been speaking a little lately. His rash is back and the night before last Foumi said, "It looks like an allergy." "Allergy," Noah repeated in his way. And then this morning when he was in a hurry to leave the house he distinctly said, "Come on, my dear." Evidently repeating something that his teacher, Adele Morton, might have said.

February 20, 1975

Foumi and I have begun to talk of establishing a day-care center to fill those after-school hours for Noah—and kids like him. Since they just don't go outside and play when they come home, they face an awful void when school is out. And school is out an awful lot: Saturdays, Sundays, holidays, summers.

February 22, 1975

Last night Karl's friends, Erich and Maxie, slept over. This morning as Karl, Erich, and Maxie played together in their "normal" way, Noah flopped across the yellow beanbag watching them. Then, without warning, Noah blew, tantrumming hysterically. It was as if suddenly he could tell the difference between himself and the others and was protesting against it. Or am I reading too much into a mindless action? Am I forgetting too easily that Noah is essentially brainless?

February 23, 1975

Foumi looked at the nursery school site at the nearby Episcopal Church. She thinks it could be an ideal facility for an after-school day-care center for special children. Perhaps we can get one going with the help of the local Regional Center. The Regional Centers are supposed to help fund programs for the handicapped and the one in our area is encouraging us. I would provide the day-care center with the finances necessary to get started. And this time, having learned from past experience, we would maintain control.

February 24, 1975

This morning I heard over the radio that Art Carney was nominated for an Academy Award for his performance in *Harry and Tonto*. I immediately called him in New York to congratulate him. "Congratulations yourself," he said. And told me that I had been nominated for Best Original Screenplay.

February 26, 1975

Noah woke up vomiting and with diarrhea. There were seven loads for the washing machine. I stayed home—otherwise I would not have had a home. Foumi was ready to leave, ready to put Noah away. Anywhere. Even Camarillo looked good.

And suddenly I had a premonition of the inevitable scenario: How we'll eventually decide to put Noah away. Without thinking. Reacting quickly. Just to save ourselves.

And then I asked myself the question I'm always trying to avoid: Is "eventually" almost here?

February 27, 1975

This morning we slept late because we knew Noah would not be going to school. When we finally did get up we had to rush Karl and he resented it. "Why do we always have trouble because of Noah?" he complained.

I'm staying home, too, because of Noah's sickness. And I'm not feeling that well myself—because today I am forty-seven. I remember when I used to look at book flaps just to see how many more years I had to go before I would be as old as a published writer, an established writer. Well, I am *that* old now.

And I seem to have come full circle—or gone nowhere at all. Today again—or still—I am a bedroom writer, looking at my cat as he stares out through the palm fronds at the bend of the gray ocean, while I cough these pages in an effort to clear my throat before I try to start a working day.

February 28, 1975

Last night I cooked my own birthday dinner. I made Hungarian goulash for the first time in years. And Karl liked it. There must be something wrong with my cooking if it appeals to a child's taste.

March 4, 1975

I wish I did not have to spend so much time considering the problems of disabled children. But Foumi is an activist, a purist, and a zealot. Yesterday we had a meeting at the Regional Center about the establishment of a day-care center for developmentally disabled children. So here we go again, except this time with parents in control: us. And we will not make immoral compromises of any kind nor favor our own kid in any way. And we will trust no one. Neither doctors, nor psychologists, nor educators, nor teachers. Because every time we start trusting—or entrusting—some person or some authority we end up in disappointment as they go off on their own trips.

March 5, 1975

I picked up a copy of *Psychology Today* and there were some of the UCLA disciples who had worked with Noah still peddling operant conditioning as the ultimate cure for "autistic" children. And I guess it is—for them. It gets them grants, it gets them academic positions, it gets them degrees.

March 6, 1975

Foumi is blooming these days: she's actually learning how to drive. But not without complaining. She keeps informing me that it would be cheaper for her to take cabs than to take driving lessons.

March 7, 1975

Noah woke me up around 5:00 this morning—he had to urinate. Then he awoke me at 6:00: he was hungry. I managed to sleep—drift—until 7:50, but thinking constantly of Noah. Almost nine years old but still a baby. How long could I appear with him in public and not be completely embarrassed by him? The answer, I hope, is forever.

March 9, 1975

Sometimes when Karl does not practice his piano, do his spelling, bring home his math book, I explode in a manner I hate, making him cower in fear. And then his fear scares me back.

March 10, 1975

Outside of these pages rarely do I bemoan Noah's condition or let his fate get to me. But every once in a while I break down completely. It happened last night. I was watching television, of all things a Barbra Streisand program, promoting her new picture. For some reason they showed some shots of the Special Olympics—retarded children, much more advanced than Noah, struggling so hard to run, to jump, to win, to do all the normal things. I broke down and cried as I haven't cried in years, tears cascading down my face. Noah, of course, couldn't care less, his head buried in the pillows of the love seat. But Karl was frightened. He had never seen me cry like that before. I left the den and busied myself about the house, making Noah's bed, preparing his bath, putting away the pots on the kitchen-sink drainboard. Anything to keep from watching the TV screen.

Every once in a while it just hits me.

March 11, 1975

Today I'm useless. Just too sleepy. Noah woke in the middle of the night. I lay in bed trying to wait him out. A mistake. I should have taken him to the bathroom, given him something to eat, tucked him in. But I was determined to wait him out. Especially since Foumi was sleeping blissfully beside me. But I had forgotten a cardinal rule. Never enter into a competition with Noah. He'll always beat you, because he has nothing to lose.

March 12, 1975

Noah and I resumed our twilight walk schedule this evening. He was laughing and smiling and eating his jacket lapel all the way. Karl, who joined us, noticed Noah's lapel-chewing and decided to try his own. "These do taste good," he said.

March 15, 1975

Noah has had a prodigious appetite lately: he ate four slices of toast at breakfast. He's also had prodigious discomforts—or wants—that have caused him to rage and tantrum out of control.

March 17, 1975

The weekend passed in a rush of lovely weather that left me depressed. My patience with Noah is wearing thin. I no longer derive that much pleasure from him. I don't like having to drive him to school every morning and having to pick him up every afternoon. I don't like his yelping and screeching in the middle of the night. I don't like having to clean up after his toilet accidents. I don't like having to explain his condition to strangers anymore. I'm no longer proud of his good looks. I'm simply sick of the tyranny of his inhuman—or all too human—condition.

I don't expect anyone else to care about him. I know that as a society our compassion is as seasonable as a fashion—this year blacks, last year junkies. Next year alcoholics. But the year for the Noahs will never come.

March 19, 1975

Maybe it's good that I have the burden of driving Noah to and from school every day. It means that I just can't walk away from my responsibilities, that there is no way I can sweep him under the carpet of my life, that he remains an integral part of every day I wake up to.

March 20, 1975

I'm picking Karl up after school today because I want him to practice piano before he is free to pursue his normal boyish activities. "Why do I have to practice piano every day?" he asks me. "Because I had to go to Hebrew school every day," I tell him. It may make no sense to him, but it makes a lot of sense to me.

March 22, 1975

Foumi bought her dress for the Academy Awards, a lovely lavender one. More important, we've arranged for Noah to go to a special camp for handicapped children during the Easter holiday vacation next week. On Tuesday, Wednesday, and Thursday he'll be picked up in the morning and brought back home in the evening. That should make it both a holiday and a vacation for us too.

March 25, 1975

It always happens. Every vacation. Noah was sick last night, his bowels running, and he did not fall asleep until 4:00 A.M. So this morning we've kept him home, and had our usual recriminatory arguments. Foumi said it was time to find a place for Noah, any place, it did not matter, he would forget us in a few days, and we would have to forget him. Karl chimed in with the intelligence that he was no longer friends with a certain classmate because that boy had said that Karl was dumb and stupid just like his brother. Meanwhile, Noah slept on, oblivious to the fact that he was giving us all a hard time.

March 26, 1975

Noah was up at 4:00 A.M. this morning yelping, but he seemed happy and healthy, so we sent him off to the special

213

camp. We hope the day will prove some sort of respite for us. We need it. Karl has bloodshot eyes from conjunctivitis; Foumi and I have bloodshot eyes from lack of sleep.

March 27, 1975
Foumi looked at St. Matthew's, the local Episcopal Church, as the site for a day-care center. There are some problems there —but she's sure they can be worked out.

March 29, 1975
Noah's continuing his pattern of early rising—even on weekends. I told Foumi maybe he's beginning to make an adjustment to an institution—on his own schedule. They always do get up awfully early in those places.

April 2, 1975
I know I don't have a chance for the Academy Award— *Chinatown* will get it for the best original script—but still I woke up in the middle of the night changing my acceptance speech, the one I had written in my head yesterday afternoon while driving Noah home from school.

April 3, 1975
Noah is very exuberant these days. Too exuberant. He whoops about the house in constant delight. Does he know something about the Academy Awards that I don't?

April 6, 1975
Last night at dinner Foumi and I were discussing adopting a Vietnamese war orphan, a girl. After all, ours would be the perfect family for such a child—if we didn't have a Noah. But finally Foumi shook her head: "We do have a Noah."
"I'd like to do it anyway," I said.

214

"And what will we do with Noah?" Karl piped in. "Throw him away?"

April 7, 1975

Thankfully, the Academy Award hullabaloo will be over tonight and I'll get back to being a normal human being. I don't think I'd be going if Foumi hadn't bought the dress. I know I don't have a chance to win. I know it really doesn't matter very much in the scheme of things even if I were to win. I am angry at the base element in myself for getting caught up in the sweepstakelike excitement of the whole thing. I like to think I am above and beyond such nonsense. But obviously I'm not. I want to win.

11

Needless to say, I did not win. That was expected. But I was
also bored. And that was unexpected. I rented a tuxedo and
rode a Cadillac limousine downtown just to be part of the
studio audience of a TV show. In the rain. During the dinner
hour. Next time I'll just watch the show in my bathrobe. How's
that for being a sore loser?

But Art Carney did win Best Actor for the picture.

And I did enjoy Karl's proudly snapping a picture of Foumi
and me with his Polaroid before we left the house and the way
Noah looked up from his bouncing on the love seat, either
blinking reflexively at the flash or incredulously at our evening
wear. And this morning at breakfast out of the mouth of my
own babe came the reassuring Hollywood cliché. Said Karl:
"I think just to be nominated was a big honor." And he told
me he was proud of me.

April 11, 1975

I haven't written—other than here—for over a week. And whenever I haven't written I become very irritable. And I scratch the sore spot: Noah. I mention how much trouble he is and how hard it is to make a decision about him. But any decision we make about Noah is not irrevocable. If we put him in an institution we can take him out any time we want; and we can visit with him weekends; and we can have him home on holidays. But it is hard to say good-bye to our youngest son and our aging dreams for him—in spite of all the facts.

April 12, 1975

A Friday night at home. A haircut and bath night. Foumi has cut the kids' hair. And now I will take a bath with Noah so that we can wash his hair. Showers terrify him.

April 23, 1975

Again Foumi and I looked over the Spastic Children's Foundation facility and were impressed. Their workers seem to care, there were sufficient personnel about the ward. The social worker suggested that we might want to put Noah there on a respite basis during the summer as a sort of trial period for all of us.

April 25, 1975

Karl's open school night: His class display was an exercise in chaos and disorder. I came away convinced that he hasn't learned anything this year. But then, what is there to learn in the fifth grade anyway? He did write a good poem, the best in his class. It has substance and, I think, even some sprung rhythm. And when Karl comes into a room these days, he looks for the piano, and sits down and begins to play. It's always the same song, "The Sting." Still I like that.

217

May 1, 1975
Noah has a rash again. All the poor kid needs now is to have an allergy.

May 6, 1975
I took Noah to the Spastic Children's Foundation for a physical and an "interview," to complete our application for respite care for him. He passed both.

May 7, 1975
At breakfast I was wondering aloud whether to take on a certain movie-writing assignment that had been offered to me. Finally I shrugged, "Maybe I should just take the money and run." "No," Karl piped up, "take the money and argue."

May 8, 1975
Because I do wish Karl would learn something definite in school, I've asked that he be placed in a structured class next year. (He loves his classroom and the freedom he finds in it. But he's simply too young to handle that freedom.)

I think we demand that he progress educationally not because of Noah, but because of Foumi's Japanese study-a-lot background and my Jewish learning-is-holy tradition. Karl should not feel in any way that he has to make up in expectations the quantum that has not been assigned to Noah. He has to fulfill himself, not two people. All of this is easy for me to state but very difficult for Karl to understand—or to accept. As children we are one with siblings against our parents within the house, and against the great world without.

Karl has problems and we must be sensitive to them. But we cannot allow him to use Noah as a crutch, to blame his own failings on his brother's flaws. If he can manage to emerge from a family that includes Noah he'll certainly be a better person. But oh what a price to pay for virtue.

Meanwhile, these days Karl is keeping a diary. Every evening as he sits down to write in it, he asks me, "What did we have for breakfast?" So I'm not holding my breath to find out what he's written. But he has hinted that besides the menus he has written some very "bad things" about me. I told him I didn't care what the "bad things" were so long as he spelled them correctly.

May 9, 1975

One of Noah's classmates spent last weekend in respite in a place out in the San Fernando Valley. But his mother told me she did not sleep a wink while he was gone, worrying constantly about him. I asked about her husband. "Oh, he enjoyed the weekend. He slept all the time."

It is the women who have the most difficult time when it comes to parting with children. Men can walk—or sleepwalk —away.

May 10, 1975

Last night when I was brushing Noah's teeth he began pinching me. I slapped him. Afterward, he just lay in bed crying. Then he got up, left his room, went straight to the kitchen, opened the refrigerator, and removed a container of milk. All along he must have been trying to tell me that he was thirsty or hungry. So this morning I'm not without guilt.

May 11, 1975

Mother's Day: I took Karl for a ride to buy some meal worms for his new lizard. I took Noah for a ride to get him out of the house and let Foumi have some rest.

May 12, 1975

A local newspaper had an article about a sixteen-year-old still in diapers. His family spoke about how much their lives had been enhanced by having a special child. I had to laugh. It was like saying the Jewish people are better for having under-gone Dachau, the Japanese enhanced by Hiroshima.

May 13, 1975

The tragedies children are heir—or prone—to: I was speaking with a friend on the phone today when suddenly her voice cracked and she began to cry. It seems her sixteen-year-old daughter had a nervous breakdown two weeks ago—and wouldn't be coming home for a while.

I called Foumi to tell her about it. And she in turn told me about her morning, working as a volunteer in the school library. One of the volunteers she works with is the mother of a boy with a degenerative disease. The other volunteer is a woman who suddenly had to depart early. Her sixth-grade son was having an epileptic fit.

Last night Foumi and I talked of the fact that this country had better begin paying attention to bloodlines and to genetic backgrounds. The traditional liberal revulsion to the extremes of Hitlerian eugenics should no longer influence the acceptance of certain biochemical genetic realities. Just as surely as parents look like children and children look like grandparents super-ficially, deeper similarities flow down through inner channels. Ironically, in trying to use a political ethic—in this case that of laissez-faire democracy—as the basis for formulating a scien-tific principle, we may be unwittingly committing the typical Soviet State crime.

May 14, 1975

I'm thinking about a TV special on "autism" that was on the other night. It gave the impression that behavior modification solved everything. It doesn't. And I know with Noah it may have even caused him to lose some of the little speech he had because he would choke up at the prospect of giving an in-correct response.

There was a party at Noah's school today, one of his classmates was leaving to live in the residence in Riverside County that could be a potential haven for Noah. But the obdurate Foumi finds fault with that place. I found fault with that place too. But she finds fault with every institution—either the staff or the location or the bricks themselves. Sure, they have faults. But neither is our home perfect. It's so easy for her to argue against a situation that is obviously less than ideal.

Paternity is a losing proposition. With a Noah obviously. With a Karl inevitably. Last night we went to his school for a meeting to discuss the gifted children's program. The meeting broke down into two factions: those who were happy with the laissez-faire quality of the program; those who wanted more structure and more fundamentals taught. I, of course, was in the forefront of the second group.

As we were leaving the meeting, Karl's teacher buttonholed us and made an emotional pitch, telling us how creative Karl was, how she did not want to stymie that creativity, how she felt his sloppiness was but a sign of his skills and talents. She was impressive, she was earnest; she really wants us to keep Karl in her class next year. We came home confused—a teacher who teaches nothing is still better than one who might be harmful to a child. And we were convinced, whatever else, she wasn't being harmful.

Okay, as we say in California. But then this morning I asked Karl how much one-half and one-eighth were, how much one-sixteenth and two-thirds were. And he couldn't do such simple fractions. I wrote a note to his teacher telling her that. And Karl, who had to bear the note, was very unhappy. He cried in the car that now she would think he was stupid.

But what can I do? How can we get his teacher to teach him anything? Must we do everything at home? Must I hurt the poor child in order to set up a situation in school in which he will begin to learn and his teacher will begin to teach?

Modern education avoids the work, the drudgery of paper, the boredom of fundamentals. I realize that in the great hustle of education no one knows what really works and what should be emphasized. In special education the problem just seems more dramatic and the deceptions are easier to perceive. But no matter what kind of kid, the problem is basically the same: How do we educate our individual child within an establishment that cares more about its own perpetuation than in the education of any particular child?

May 18, 1975

I asked T.G. in jest to "attack Noah." I shouldn't have. Because T.G., no longer afraid of Noah, proceeded to "attack" him, inflicting a small scratch. Mea culpa. I then tried to teach Noah how to frighten T.G. away with a newspaper. But Noah just waved it lazily—not enough to upset T.G. in the slightest.

May 19, 1975

I quizzed one of Karl's friends who is in a "regular" class on fractions and he did as poorly as Karl. So the gifted children are being treated just like the other kids. No elitism there. No one is being taught anything anywhere.

Education, I think, is an even bigger hype than the movie business.

May 20, 1975

Karl is now talking of going into track when he gets older. It seems he has endurance as a runner—or so he says. As for his education, he still practices the piano under duress at home, while in school, I have decided, he is learning the good social life.

May 21, 1975

Yesterday we had lunch with some parents and special educators who want to start a new "autistic" school and perhaps even form another national "autistic" organization. Just hearing the word *autistic* was enough to cost me a night's sleep. Maybe I couldn't have slept much anyway, since Noah was up half the night. But that was because of his brain damage.

May 22, 1975

What I always dreaded might happen did happen yesterday afternoon. I was driving Noah home from school along the Pacific Coast Highway. At the Santa Monica red light, when I pressed down on the gas pedal, instead of the car starting forward there was an explosion out of my exhaust. This happened repeatedly. The car would not start. Finally, I gave up and turned on the emergency flasher.

Of course I was worried more about Noah than about the car. He was chirping away behind me, rocking to supply the motion the car was no longer furnishing. Some teenagers hitching on the side of the highway were kind enough to give me a push past the light and to the side, out of the mainstream of traffic.

I waited there. A highway patrol car came by going the other way, an Out of Service sign on its window. And the uniformed occupant ignored my frantic pantomime and moved on. So did all the other traffic past my car until a yellow Capri stopped, a teenager hopped out, said he had good bumpers and offered to give me a push down to the service station at the next light.

I made it to the service station, waving profuse thanks to the kid as he roared off. But the mechanic at the station, checking my hood, could only come up with a shrug rather than a diagnosis.

I called Foumi, I called for a tow truck, I called for a rental car, while Noah, protesting and restless, cast his socks, his shoes, and jacket out the window. I replaced the clothing and bought Noah a soft drink. And waited.

The rental car came first. I drove the driver back to his office, then rushed Noah home to a nervously awaiting Foumi and Karl.

223

It all could have been so much worse. But thanks to the kindness of the teenagers, it wasn't.

May 23, 1975

Karl, who's now completing the fifth grade, came home from school with a note: He could be placed in one of three classes next year. A gifted combined fifth and sixth grade. A gifted combined fourth, fifth, and sixth. A regular sixth-grade class. We'll opt for the regular sixth-grade class—no matter what Karl wants.

May 24, 1975

My Aunt Jessie was in town and I brought her to the house for tea. (I couldn't invite her for dinner: she would never dream of eating an unkosher meal.) She talked mostly of how much she missed my mother. "It's thirteen years since she died," she said. "And I still expect to be talking to her every day." Her own idiom, her rhythms and cadences, were so much like my mother's, it was eerie.

I loved the way she reacted to Noah in the back seat of the car, though. Noah, not used to someone sitting next to him, began to pinch Jessie. No, she kept telling him quietly, firmly. Which, of course, is just the way to do it. Without any ego involvement. And, of course, he stopped.

May 25, 1975

Karl's open-school teacher will teach a regular sixth-grade class next year. Since he likes her so much we'll ask that he be put in it.

May 26, 1975

Karl's teacher wept when he told her we would like him to be in her regular sixth-grade class next year. "But your parents were so against the open school," she said, unable to understand.

I don't know how thorough she will be in teaching him even in a regular class but she is responsive to him and genuinely likes him.

May 27, 1975

Karl and I went to see a double bill at the local movie house. I so like going to the movies with him, watching him deep in his seat dipping into his popcorn larder, laughing at jokes, or cringing in suspense. Afterward, we had a crummy Mexican dinner which he loved.

Father and son is an inarticulate love story. But perhaps all love stories are too deep for words.

May 29, 1975

It's all been arranged. Noah will spend three weeks at the Spastic Children's Foundation in August, from Monday to Friday. I look forward to the separations from him. But I also wince in fear. Is it the beginning of our final solution?

May 31, 1975

Foumi has been reading more brain books. And she is more convinced than ever that the main problem with Noah's vision is that of a narrowed field. Which is similar to a problem that occurs after strokes.

June 2, 1975

Yesterday I cut down a small orange tree that was rotting in our backyard. In the East I had so many more trees to care for. I would spend long autumnal Sunday afternoons trimming branches, gathering leaves and dead wood, and then delivering the brush to the lot behind our house. I miss that house, all that space and the inexhaustible supply of light. But then I always miss the past. Someday I might even become sentimental about a movie studio.

225

June 4, 1975
Noah still cannot accept the fact that if we have doughnuts for breakfast he cannot eat them endlessly, that he will receive just one doughnut, and no more. Which means that we can't —and shouldn't—give him any sweet stuff at all.

June 5, 1975
Foumi is proceeding on the day-care center. But now we have to go through all the red tape of becoming a nonprofit, tax-exempt corporation.

She's also begun making Chinese ideograph cards and she's going to try to teach them to Noah. In this way—unlike most American sign languages—he would be learning symbols that could be understood by 700 million ordinary people, not just specialists.

June 6, 1975
Last night I saw Karl poring over a book as he was working on his history report. I looked at the book: I knew the writer. I read Karl's report: "The harsh reactions of the British all but made the start of hostilities a virtual certainty." Scarcely the language of a ten-year-old. I bawled Karl out for copying words from a book, for stealing someone else's writing. He said: "All the kids did that." And, of course, he was right. Still I made him begin to write about the revolution in his own words, painfully extracting three sentences from him. They weren't very good sentences, but they were his.

June 9, 1975
I still wish I had a place back East. Because I want to go home again. Because the passage of time is unreal here. Because our long, many-wintered summer vacation in California is over. But Foumi likes it here, Noah requires a monoseason, and at the root of family life is compromise.

Yet I dread the day we will have to compromise on the best

place for Noah in terms of our own happiness as a family. For if the best place for a normal child is in the home, how can the best place for a less-than-normal child be in any place but in the home? Except by compromise.

The mother of one of Noah's schoolmates told me that the IRS had called her in for an audit, questioning her medical deductions. She did not have all of her receipts so she brought her son along. He proceeded to run amok all over the Internal Revenue office. The auditor kept ordering him to sit down but he would bounce up and be off and running again. Finally, the auditor told her to forget about the income tax matter but just get her son out of his office, the boy was driving him crazy.

I've been looking through some of Foumi's brain books. I've always known there are things that Noah understands verbally but cannot say.

But I did not know that the primary function of speech—or the cognitive recognition of a word—was for the working of one's own information retrieval system, not for expression— or communication—to others. Nor did I know that the area of the brain that deals with ideographs and symbols might be better protected from the ravages of stroke than the area that deals with phonetic languages.

Yesterday I had lunch with this year's movie millionaire. Like me, he grew up in Brooklyn. He boastfully complained to me that his new million dollars had not really affected his life: "It only means that if I see a new pair of tennis sneakers in the window I can buy them without thinking," he said. Then he asked me what I would do if I suddenly had a million dollars.

227

I began to talk about Noah. I told him in a rush how I would get a residence going, start a day-care center, pump money into worthwhile research projects. He was silent for a moment, and then changed the subject.

June 13, 1975

The last day of school for Karl. And I notice that he and his friends are tense about the coming of summer: the possibility of inactivity, the responsibility of decision. Normal education gives the kids too much free time just when they have too much energy.

June 14, 1975

Foumi and I have decided that instead of finding psychologists and psychiatrists who label syndromes, we have to look for people who can match up areas of the brain with the failings involved, who can understand which parts of the brain are still functioning and can thus pick up the slack—or act as a compensatory crutch. Vision, for example, is a function of the right hemisphere of the brain. And Noah is beginning to recognize Chinese characters comparatively quickly because that is the hemisphere of his brain which seems the least impaired.

June 16, 1975

I took the boys to a picnic which featured one of those "jump up" tents with an air-blown, pillowy floor for children to jump up and down on. Noah bounced in it for three "rides," perhaps enjoying the fact that he was like the rest of the kids even though he was oblivious to them at the same time.

June 17, 1975

Another altercation with the L.A. Department of Parks. They're having a two-week summer camp for special children. I brought Noah there. They said Noah was "too special." I insisted that they accept him. They threatened to call the police. I spoke to the director, the director's superior, and the superior's superior. Finally, they agreed to let Noah stay on a trial basis. And when I picked him up at noon they all agreed that he had had "a good day."

June 18, 1975

I took Noah to the park again this morning and was pleased to see that the volunteer assigned to him seems to like him a lot.

June 19, 1975

Noah was up at seven this morning. I think he was looking forward to camp. Karl was up early too. But he was very unhappy. It seems his frog had died. I didn't take the news too badly. I didn't know he had a frog.

June 21, 1975

The volunteer counselor who is working with Noah at the park came to the house. She brought a flute along and proudly showed us how she had taught Noah to blow on it. She's just sixteen years old but understands the secret of "handling Noah": simply not being afraid of him. He is at bottom so helpless, so defenseless, so guileless. Imagine, for example, not being able to express one's dislikes in terms of food. Noah's has to be the world's slowest form of communication: not accepting a type of food is the only way he can avoid being served that food at a subsequent meal. And even then we have to guess his positive wants by elimination.

June 22, 1975

We attended the California tryouts for the Special Olympics. As usual the organizational abilities involved in staging such an event overwhelmed me. As usual, when I looked at the older "children," I wept.

229

June 23, 1975

We were over at a friend's house yesterday. Noah kept taking off his pants. And I could tell that some of the people there were wondering why we still keep Noah. Why we put up with him. Why we haven't consigned him to a residence or institution. Social workers and psychologists and psychiatrists always recommend institutions. But then, they are in the institution business themselves, drawing their salaries in part from its base. If we could put Noah in an institution knowing he would be happier there—and why can't his life be based on the happiness ethic just like everyone else's?—we would be happier too. But it just ain't so.

I really get furious with people who see as the solution to our problem the dehumanizing of Noah, who would have us give him the kind of shabby treatment they would not wish on either their own normal youngsters or themselves when they become older.

June 24, 1975

I went to see a lawyer today about doing some of the ever burgeoning paperwork involved in setting up the day-care center. But when I came home Foumi shrugged: "Noah will end up in Camarillo anyway." "Of course he will," I said, "but we'll all end up dead too." And I sat down and made out checks to cover the incorporation fees for the day-care center.

June 25, 1975

I'm sleepy. Noah's been up most of the night for two nights running. But at least we know why. Or think we do.

Last night as we were going to sleep I noticed more than the usual amount of light streaming in through our bedroom drapes. I pushed the drapes open. A full moon. "Of course," Foumi said. "That's why Noah was up all night. Don't you remember he's always up when there's a full moon?" I had forgotten that. And the fact that two other parents had

230

told us the same thing happens with their brain-damaged children.

Now I'm not about to go psychic but perhaps there is some sort of physical phenomenon, like the gravitational force exerted on tides, that a Noah feels when there is a full moon. Perhaps there is some basis to the ancient superstition after all.

June 26, 1975

I had lunch with a guy I hadn't seen for years, someone I went to school with at Michigan. He is now a fat, old, hard-drinking cynic who has had three marriages, two heart attacks, and a fifteen-year-old daughter who has disappeared, literally disappeared. When I came home Noah was tantrumming and Karl was complaining that Foumi wouldn't let his friend sleep over and Foumi let me know how sick she was of both of them —and I didn't mind any of it at all.

June 29, 1975

Noah continues to whoop and holler and do nothing. I give him one more year. Until he is ten. That's a good figure with which to round off his life with us.

(12)

We never all quite had breakfast together this morning. But a moment came when Noah, draped over the golden love seat in his color-coordinating yellow Charlie Brown pajamas, listened to us sing "Happy Birthday" to him. He shyly rose when we reached "Stand up. Stand up. Stand up and show us your face," and ran into Foumi's arms. So it was tear time again at the sentimental Greenfelds'.

July 2, 1975
Noah's ninth birthday was also duly celebrated at his school. I brought a jug of apple cider and two dozen doughnuts for the occasion.

Noah's music teacher, though, somehow thought he was eleven. So ageless, so timeless, I guess, is he.

July 3, 1975

Last night was a lie-around-the-den night. And Noah took part in it. He just loves it when the rest of us are also not doing anything. After all, not doing anything is his "thing."

July 5, 1975

Last night we saw a film showing how behavior modification had been applied successfully to some brain-damaged children at a school in Rhode Island. The film was impressive. But, unfortunately, all brain-damaged children are not alike—just as all normal children are not the same—and should not be cast into stereotypes. In this case, the children to whom the behavior-mod techniques were applied were much further advanced than Noah to begin with.

At this point I think the most important thing we can do with Noah is to get him to understand that he can communicate. But how to do that? And how to make him want to do that?

I question the entire behavior-modification etiology that refuses to take into account the way the brain works mechanically, that in fact proceeds from the premise that the process is irrelevant. I remember the way Sister Kenny's hot-pack polio treatments, though alleviating the victims therapeutically, denied the actual viral base of the disease. However, it was the isolation of the polio virus that led to the ultimate discovery of a vaccine.

July 6, 1975

This afternoon while shopping with Noah in the supermarket I ran into a pediatrician whose son is a friend of Karl's. He asked me if we would be going on a vacation. "We can't," I said, patting Noah on the head, "not with this kid." "Why don't you take him along?" he suggested. "Then it wouldn't be a vacation," I said. When I told Foumi about the incident she said, "Good, let the professionals know."

Some friends were over for dinner and Karl was pontificating. "Thirteen pistachio nutshells can kill you," I heard him say. "They're poisonous." At moments like that I want to strangle him for being so full of himself, and embrace him for being so much a kid.

Our evenings at home are given up to paperwork, the filling out of forms in order to get a license for a day-care facility. Foumi is doggedly seeing it through, getting things done. She is a much more effective person than I ever imagined her to be. Which means I have not been without my prejudices, both nationalist and sexist, in spite of myself.

An occupational therapist came to our house to work with Noah. She left behind a rug-covered platform on wheels for him to belly-whop–crawl about the house on. He needs such exercise to improve his coordination. I like the woman. When Noah pinched her she told him, "Lay off, buster," and he did.

Last night Noah mumbled "Good night" to me. And this morning when Foumi greeted T.G. with a "Good morning," Noah repeated something like "Dood morning T.G."

Last night I atavistically read the original *Tarzan*. I had forgotten—or never really noticed before—that Tarzan had first learned to read in English and speak in French. I related these facts to my own nature boy. Noah does seem able to understand a great deal of speech in certain contexts, though he can use very little speech in any context. So our problem is to get him to understand that he can communicate visually—with cards and signs and whatever—instead of vocally. Like Tarzan, in a sense, he has to learn two different languages, one in which to receive and one in which to send, utilizing different aspects of the brain.

July 15, 1975

We suffered two setbacks today in our day-care plans: (1) It seems the woman who runs the nursery school program at the Episcopal Church objects to our use of the facilities before 3:15 P.M. But if we were to start that late the whole purpose of day care would be subverted. Because it would mean the parents would have the children on their hands between 2:30 P.M.—the end of the regular school day—and the beginning of day care. (2) We're no longer sure the state might fund most of it.

July 21, 1975

Noah now loves the water. This afternoon I took him and Karl over to a friend's pool. I put a small life preserver around Noah's chest and a large tube around his neck. And aside from trying to drink up the pool he was a joy to behold. And hold. I got into the water with him and hugged and tugged him about. When I thought he had had enough I took him out of the water and toweled him off. But he headed right back toward the pool steps. I let him go in again. But this time Karl played with him while I lay back on a recliner, letting the summer sun shine down on me.

July 22, 1975

Another of Noah's former classmates is going into Camarillo today. "Committed at thirteen," as the newscasts might say. He is a boy who can talk, who can read, who can write, who is far more academically educable than Noah, but who is also given to far more violent tantrums and self-destructive acts. I once saw him bite deeply into his own arm, for example, and chew on his own flesh. Noah was afraid of him.

I feel sorry for the boy, I feel sorry for the boy's parents, the inevitable happening to them as it will happen to us.

July 25, 1975

Last night after dinner I suddenly realized there was a gap in my day. I had forgotten to take Noah for a walk. And it was only after Noah and I began to promenade along the darkening cliff—Noah a silhouette walking ahead, perilously close to the edge of the precipice, in his vague but surefooted way —that everything seemed right and orderly again and I felt ready to resume my normal routine.

July 28, 1975

I took Noah swimming again, this time allowing him to go into the pool by himself. He hugged the lip of the pool, chirping half-nervously, half-gleefully, but with complete pride.

August 2, 1975

Noah's school will be closed for the next six weeks. For the first two weeks we've arranged to send him to a private foundation's day camp for crippled children. Then for the next two weeks he'll be at the Spastic Children's Foundation except for weekends at home. In both cases we're putting him in with those who are labeled *physically disabled.*

His stay at the Spastic Children's Foundation will be our first parting from him in an institutional setup. I know I should view it as a hospital experience for him and let it go at that. But still I have Jewish-mother visions of Noah's not eating for a week and getting skinnier and skinnier.

He also might become very angry with us. Because he does have a memory. Wednesday night we went out for dinner, not returning home until after he was asleep. Karl, too, was gone, tenting overnight at Y camp. And in the middle of the night

Noah did a curious thing, something he'd never done before: he came into our bedroom to check on us.

So he knows things, he perceives things; he takes in more than he can let out.

The day-care center produces a daily argument with Foumi. I thought I would have nothing to do. It turns out I have a lot to do: forms and forms and forms.

The "autism" tag can be destructive. The volunteer assigned to Noah at the crippled-children's day camp told me: "When I heard he was autistic I was frightened. But now I see you just have to treat him as any brain-damaged kid who is way behind his age in certain ways."

The teenage girl I used to car-pool with Noah was placed in an institution during the spring. But she ran away from there and is back with her family. And it seems now she won't even get into a car anymore, afraid she'll be whisked away from home. Perhaps she was too old to be placed in an institution? Perhaps institutional placement can never be more than a prolonged respite anyway?

I noticed when I take Noah swimming that his legs have filled out and though he is still skinny he seems to be acquiring muscle tone.

We'll ease Noah into life at the Spastic Children's Foundation gradually: a half day; a whole day; and then an overnight.

237

We're nervous and unsure, certain only that our anxiety is a cliché.

But it's tough for anybody to go into a hospital or an institution. I didn't have my first hospital stint until I came down with polio when I was twenty. Noah, as always, is precocious. He got to UCLA when he was just four; now he'll get hospital experience at nine.

August 18, 1975

We dropped Noah off at the Spastic Children's Foundation this morning at 9:30 and picked him up at 1:45. He was obviously glad to see us as he came down the hall accompanied by an aide. She told us that Noah ate very little lunch. And Noah added one long word: "Iwannaeat."

August 20, 1975

This morning Foumi cried when she came to the door to watch me load the car with Karl and Noah and a suitcase. I dropped off Karl at the Y day camp, then Noah and the suitcase at the Spastic Children's Foundation.

The social worker there showed me the bed in the ward where Noah would be sleeping. I watched Noah wander about among the kids at occupational therapy, as always the little king lost. I was asked if it was all right to restrain Noah in case he did not sleep. I said it wasn't a very good idea, that I would rather come and pick him up in the middle of the night than have him restrained in bed.

I could see they were a little nervous. But then so are we. It's nervous, glimpsing into Noah's future. On the one hand he is still literally a baby at nine years; on the other hand he is taking his first tentative steps in leaving our hearth.

August 21, 1975

Last night I kept trying to reach the ward at the Spastic Children's Foundation. The line was constantly busy. Finally,

I had the operator break through for an emergency. A girl answered me, a sweet black voice: Noah was sleeping, he had had a bath, and "everything was just fine." I hung up enormously relieved.

This morning, as she leisurely sipped her coffee, Foumi said: "This is the first time I've digested a breakfast in a year."

August 22, 1975

Last night we went out to dinner. There is that feeling we have when we're together, just the three of us, Foumi and Karl and myself: I think it's called ordinary family.

August 23, 1975

I picked Noah up yesterday afternoon at the Spastic Children's Foundation. He was sitting beside a TV set in the dayroom while the other children were clustered before it, in their wheelchairs and braces. Noah was very quiet, abstracted, and at first didn't seem to recognize me. But then he tugged at my hair while I laced his untied sneakers.

I took his laundry bag from his bed, his suitcase from his locker, said good-bye to the ward nurse, and brought him out to the car. He still was quiet and stayed quiet all the way home. I studied him in the rear-view mirror. He looked bigger to me, more mature than a two-day absence should warrant.

August 24, 1975

Our nuclear family's fission continues. Yesterday's sputter was Karl's departure for a week of sleep-over camp. When it came time for him to say good-bye to me at the Y there was an awkward moment between us: We were standing in front of his counselor and his group. I reached out to kiss him; he held out his hand to shake mine.

August 25, 1975

I took Noah back to Spastics. Not even the slightest protest on his part. He was happy to dance away in the care of an older ambulatory patient. These separations are harder on us than on him.

Indeed, the thing that is most difficult to accept is that Noah does belong in a place like Spastics, among the crutches and braces and kids with helmets and tilted heads. Noah's brain is as injured as theirs. The injury—or dysfunction—shows in a different way.

This evening I wrote to Karl. I think it's the first time I've ever written to him. I didn't know what to say. Or how to end the letter. I finally just ended: *Love, Dad.*

I will never write to Noah.

August 26, 1975

For the first time since Karl was born: twenty-four hours without a kid in the house. Heaven! And hell!

August 27, 1975

I called Spastics last night, talked to the woman on the dorm —or ward. She said in a soft drawl, Noah was fine. He obeyed her fine. He was just fine.

And a postcard came from Karl. It looked as if it had traveled through mud:

Dear mom and dad:

I am having a lot of fun at camp. Yesterday we took our swimming test and I made advanced swimming. We have a lame LIT. But Robert my counselor is nice. Well I guess I better sine off now. But remember,

DONT WORRY

August 29, 1975

We've had a glorious honeymoon of a week in our own home. We've slept late, dined late, and Foumi even passed her driving

240

test. It certainly has been a lot easier to live without Noah than it is to live with him.

August 30, 1975

Noah's home. This morning I was up at the crack of dawn, awakened by his yelping.

August 31, 1975

We are a family again. Karl is back. He slumped into the house carrying his camping gear like a young Bill Mauldin GI, battle-worn and weary.

Noah began to bubble happiness the moment he saw Karl.

September 1, 1975

Noah's mind may be almost a total blank but his face is still an aesthetic experience. When he is clinging to me in the pool, his face up close against mine, I perceive him as a lover—or, more clearly, as a loved one. Which he is. No matter what else he isn't, that he is.

September 2, 1975

This morning Foumi was crying. Because Noah was crying. She felt that he did not want to go back to Spastics. But when Karl and I got him there he didn't seem to be too annoyed with the idea. At least he waved a docile good-bye to us. Karl was impressed with the Spastic Children's Foundation—especially the fact that every room had a TV set.

On the way back I tried to explain again to Karl that if sometimes I seemed to give Noah more time and attention than I was giving to him, it was because the day would come when Noah would have to leave us. So I wanted to enjoy him—and have him enjoy me—while we could.

Karl said he understood, which was nice of him to say. But how can he? I can't even understand myself.

September 6, 1975
We took a mini-trip to Santa Barbara, Foumi and Karl and I. With Noah I have to guess but seldom hear his every want. Karl was a constant stream of articulated desires: "I want a Coke." "I want a drink." "I want an ice cream." "I want a minibike." After a while I just wanted him to shut up.

September 7, 1975
Noah is back home and we are delighted with him—and with ourselves. He was able to accept the separation from us and we were able to endure a separation from him—or vice versa.

The moment he entered the house he headed straight for the refrigerator, saying "Iwannaeat"—just like any kid returning home after an absence.

September 10, 1975
Back-to-school day. And not a moment too soon. But it has been a good summer—for us and the kids. They've both learned they can manage in environments outside of our home.

September 14, 1975
The studio will send me to Japan next month to do some missionary work for *Harry and Tonto*. We'll take Karl with us. It's very important that we shore up his pride in his Japanese heritage before he runs into the severe anti-Japanese prejudice that abounds here. Foumi has always had to exert double energy to avoid being treated completely as a nonperson. For example, in starting the day-care center the Health Department people gave her a hard time because she's not a smooth-talking Caucasian. One of the officials even suggested that we get another director.

This official came on as a well-meaning liberal, but she actually didn't even recognize her own prejudice. Which, of course, is the worst prejudice of all. Give me the old-fashioned

242

bigot anytime. At least then everyone knows precisely where he stands.

The trip to Japan will be good for Foumi, allowing her to touch base with her sense of self-esteem again. There's an irony there. She left Japan because as a woman she wasn't treated as *somebody*. But in going back, I suspect, she knows she'll never be treated as a complete *nobody* there either.

September 22, 1975

An actor friend was at the house yesterday, with his American Indian girl friend. "The Indians believe children like Noah are inspired," she said. "Ugh!" I replied.

September 23, 1975

I watched Foumi working with Noah. She had him arranging three objects from memory. She placed a pencil, an eraser, and a block in one line. Then she put a cardboard screen in front of it. Noah had a matching pencil, eraser, and block before him, which he would try to line up in the same order as the model's. When he couldn't get them quite right Foumi let him peek at the model objects by dropping her cardboard screen. After a while Noah was matching a set of three objects quite well. But when Foumi added a fourth object, a small ball, Noah became very confused and upset. Which was distressing. Until we recalled that he had approached the matching of three objects with the same confusion and frustration just a few months ago.

Foumi had not worked on this particular exercise with Noah for a few weeks. And yet he did well. Perhaps Noah does need a rest period between learning processes? Perhaps the static repetition of a lesson bores him—just as it bores any normal child? We are not about to reject everything we've learned from the behaviorists, but there are certain aspects of teaching and learning that they can't understand either.

September 25, 1975

This morning I heard Karl wailing: "Noah, stop eating up my room!"

Noah eats up our room too. Even the Indian bedspread we thought was "eatproof" because it is of such heavy material is pretty much chewed away at the frills. "Who else," said Foumi, "has to ask a salesperson about a bedspread, 'Is it edible?'."

September 26, 1975

The State Regional Center people told Foumi how impressed they are with our projected day-care center's statement of purpose:

> The developmentally disabled child is also usually an educationally disadvantaged child. Because of his malady he requires more education than the normal child; instead, ironically, more often he receives less—the victim of a foreshortened school day. This places an additional burden on both the child and his parents. The child, without peers, has long afternoons to fill; the parent has the fruitless task of serving as custodian to this vacuum. The child, lacking social graces, cannot even play with siblings; may even further sense his own alienation. The parent, without the grace of respite, often feels too keenly his own bondage; reaches too quickly his own breaking point. To service the need of both the developmentally disabled child and his beleaguered parent the Palisades Day Care Center for Developmentally Disabled Children has been formed. The center proposes to provide an extended day of supervised training and activity for children suffering from Down's syndrome, brain damage, autism, and other severe neurological impairments. A nonprofit corporation, the Palisades Day Care Center for Developmentally Disabled Children represents a unique parent-conceived, community-supported, child-oriented pilot day-care program. A parent-professional advisory board will guide the center; every member of the board of directors will serve without salary.

September 27, 1975

Foumi wrote a letter to a prominent neuropsychologist describing Noah's history and suggesting that he may actually have

244

suffered a stroke. The good doctor replied that if Noah lost his speech gradually—as he did—then it could not have been a stroke.

But what is a stroke anyway? *Stroke* is short for "stroke of God," hardly a scientific term of pinpoint precision. In fact, *stroke* is one of those basket catchalls like *autism* and *schizophrenia* and *heart attack* and *hepatitis*, encircling much generally but identifying little specifically.

To me, whether Noah's brain suffered a slow deterioration or a sudden destruction is not so important as it is to treat whatever did happen as the ravages of neurological events rather than psychogenic incidents.

September 28, 1975

Noah now removes his pants when he has to go to the bathroom and then replaces them with a different pair from his bureau drawer. And the pair he has taken off he either hides or throws in the trash basket.

October 2, 1975

When I took Noah swimming yesterday I realized anew that he goes through normal stages in terms of certain developments. Last year, at the age of nine, Karl enjoyed swimming for the first time. This year, at the age of nine, Noah likes the water for the first time. So somewhere something within him is ticking on schedule.

October 4, 1975

Foumi met with the canon, the administrator, the day-school principal, and the nursery school director of the Episcopal church. She tells me it was like an exercise in fascism. They summarily withdrew their prior permission to rent their facilities on Saturdays, holidays, and at any time other than between 3:15 and 5:15 on weekdays. They refused to discuss the matter further. They warned her not to contact any other members of the vestry in appeal. The principal of the day school even had the insensitivity to say to Foumi's face that he did not want his school's normal children to even have to look at our handicapped children.

Foumi has been in tears ever since. I'm torn between the impulse to wreak vengeance immediately and the knowledge that I have to apply our energy constructively. We want a site. We don't want to lose what we have there, imperfect as it is. And the fact that they don't want us there is an even bigger reason not to leave. But we could never have a worthwhile program there on their terms.

October 6, 1975

Foumi is still depressed over the day-care setback. She is so idealistic that she is continually surprised by how gratuitously mean and cruel some people can be.

October 7, 1975

Noah still keeps taking off his pants, chewing on his shirt, and generally not acting very much older than a one-and-a-half-year-old. But the occupational therapist we now have coming to the house on Saturdays is trying to teach him weaving. And Foumi still works with him on Chinese characters.

October 8, 1975

The mother of a child in Noah's school has had a nervous breakdown. It happened the same day the church told us it was no good for normal children to look upon our children.

October 10, 1975

Today a friend asked me, how do other countries handle the problem of brain-damaged children? I really didn't know the answer. I assume a lot depends upon the question of national belief as to who "owns" the child. In America, the state "owns"

246

the human being only when it becomes time to ask—or rather demand—that he die for the nation in a war. At all other times, however, responsibility is disclaimed—or Christ is asked to render it.

October 12, 1975

I've been up since four o'clock, listening to Noah's singsong, wondering if he knows we're leaving for Japan. The one thing I do know is that after we drop him off at the Spastic Children's Foundation, Foumi will be crying.

$$\boxed{13}$$

October 27, 1975

We came back from Japan Saturday afternoon, Foumi's mother returning with us. Noah seems to remember Grandma—or at least takes her presence matter-of-factly. He was glad to see us, yelped joyously and continually, and hasn't tantrummed yet even though we all stayed in bed till noon yesterday, trying to catch up on jet-lost sleep. But Noah waited patiently, merely eating his pajama top instead of breakfast.

In Japan Foumi visited two special schools, one in the Osaka area, the other in Tokyo. She was especially impressed with the one in Tokyo. The teachers she saw there seemed to know what they were doing. The daily program was structured, there was a stress on physical activities, there were sleep-overs, there was constant supervision. If less than ideal in some other respects, it still sounded better than anything I know of around here.

I should have known the obvious: if a country has a good normal-education system—and Japan has a superb one—then it also must have something decent in terms of special education. The normal-education system is the basis of any special-education program. Here, in Los Angeles, special education —like normal education—is offered only 175 days a year. In Japan the school year is almost one hundred days longer: the summer vacation is but six weeks; the regular school week includes half days on Saturdays; and even the normal school day is at least six hours long.

With Noah, I know, there can never be a solution; but if there is a place for Noah in Tokyo then I do have another option.

I have long promised myself a year or two in Tokyo and I could have that year yet. I mentioned the prospect to Karl and he didn't like the idea at all. But I think it might be good for him, too, in the long run. Anyway, as a family we now have another option to consider—and *option*, though not quite another word for *hope*, does contain the same root as *optimism*.

October 28, 1975

This morning, while Noah yelped me awake, I thought of the mechanics of getting Noah to Japan. Difficult. A ten-and-a-half-hour flight. Or a five-hour flight—to Hawaii—and then another eight-hour flight. Anyway, this is all down the line. But then what isn't?

October 29, 1975

Foumi had written a letter to Governor Jerry Brown, complaining about the hard time she was having getting a license from the Health Department.

This morning the Health Department called. It seems the governor's office was finally acting on Foumi's letter. And now the Health Department was checking to see how our day-care center was going. Foumi told the Health Department official the day-care center was not going at all since we had lost our site. And the official promised to expedite matters completely if we found another site.

October 30, 1975
The quest for a place for Noah continues to unravel. We received a letter from Foumi's aunt who is on the Board of Education in Nagoya. In her official capacity she is working to start a school there for the retarded and brain-damaged. Unofficially, she wonders if Foumi might be interested in going back to Japan to head it. Foumi's aunt also owns an empty house in Nagoya in which we could live. We discussed the matter at dinner. Karl was adamant: he does not want to leave America.

November 2, 1975
The Spastic Children's Foundation, it seems, lost a pair of Noah's trousers during his respite there. This is not a matter Foumi regards lightly. She works hard sewing special rubber-belted cling pants for Noah, who cannot master a buckle. And it struck her that if Spastics can't take care of clothing perhaps they can't take care of Noah. In Japan, even in the paper-walled, windswept buildings that were below par in terms of housing accommodations, she noticed that all the clothing of the children was neatly marked and precisely stacked. Carelessness and sloppiness is threatening to children like Noah.

November 4, 1975
Last night, sitting around the den, Grandma and Foumi on the couch, Karl on the beanbag, watching *Airport*, of all things, it was good to have an extended-family get-together. Noah even joined the family ensemble for a while.

November 6, 1975
Karl got into a fight at school. He and another kid were discussing human biology. They got to the brain. The other kid said something about "hot feelings going straight to the brain." Karl said the kid didn't know what he was talking about. The kid asked Karl what made him such an expert on the brain.

250

Karl said he had a brain-damaged brother. The other kid said: "Your brain's damaged too." Whereupon Karl punched him out.

November 7, 1975

Foumi's found a site for Day Care. Family Service in Santa Monica. It doesn't have the bricks and the lawns of the Episcopal church but it is more centrally located. And the director seems to want us.

November 8, 1975

I took Noah to our pediatrician for his annual physical. The doctor reports that he is in good shape. He asked me what Noah was learning in school these days. And I was stumped.

November 9, 1975

Karl enjoys having Grandma in the house, treats her as if she's a new friend. Noah's attitude is one of indifference tempered by wary respect: he obeys her in his indolent way. The burden of Grandma's presence falls most heavily upon Foumi. It's never easy to have one's parent in the house.

November 10, 1975

Our day-care center has been approved by the state as a servicing agency. That means there could be financial support forthcoming. Hallelujah!

November 13, 1975

The parent of one of Noah's former classmates took her son out of Camarillo. Six years old, he was in the same ward with teenagers. And he was literally climbing the walls to escape their attacks.

November 15, 1975

Noah was up at 3:00 A.M. and chewed his shirt to a thread during the long night. And this morning he's been pinching everyone. I guess he's trying to tell us something. But what? What? I never knew that the most agonizing word in the English language could be *what*.

November 17, 1975

Piano lessons. Soccer practice. Karl seems to be enjoying a normal boyhood. But sometimes I'm simply too intense with him. A Jewish mother must be especially hard to take when she comes in the guise of a balding father.

November 18, 1975

The family has become accustomed to Grandma. We bought her an electric blanket, doored off the den, and everyone respects her nocturnal privacy. But Karl worries about her: "She's seventy-one and maybe she'll die while she's here."

November 19, 1975

What do you do when your refrigerator breaks down at eight o'clock on a Saturday night? When, naturally, there's no repairman in sound of even his own answering service? First, you take the food out of the freezer and ask a neighbor to hold it for you. Second, you go to the liquor store and pick up several bags of ice to put in the cooling compartment. Then on Monday morning, after the repairman officially pronounces last rites, you buy a new refrigerator. Not on the basis of comparison shopping. Not on the basis of *Consumer Reports*. But on the basis of how soon it can be delivered.

So we have a new refrigerator. In coppertone.

November 20, 1975

Hollering and whooping, his eyes puffed, Noah this morning has been trying to tell us that something is wrong. He can't

252

tell us where the pain is and we can't tell him that the pain will pass. I don't know what hurts whom the most.

November 21, 1975
One of the mothers at Noah's school was watching her son loping through the climbing ladders. "Somewhere in the jungle," she said, "there must be a monkey with brains."

November 25, 1975
I awoke from a bad dream this morning:
In addition to Noah, Foumi and I had had another brain-damaged child, a girl who focused in and out, who had normal spells, then fantastically abnormal ones. We had put her in an institution on Staten Island. And I had forgotten about her. I had even forgotten her name, Emily. I asked Foumi how could we possibly have forgotten our own daughter? And how was it that we never had news of her. And Foumi said that she had instructed the teachers there never to get in touch with us, told them that we didn't want to know anything about Emily. Emily, it seemed, had not lived with us for very long; we had never really become attached to her. And I said to Foumi: "That's exactly what we should have done with Noah—gotten rid of him before we became attached to him."

.

November 26, 1975
Foumi has been complaining about the life of a writer. Last night she said to me: "It's terrible to be a writer. You must always live in the past." I didn't say anything but I could have answered: What other place is there? In reliving the past in the guise of the present, a writer is doing nothing less than constantly resurrecting himself.

November 27, 1975
Here are some statistics: One out of four children in this country is born with a birth defect; one of eight is serious. One

out of every ten children suffers from some form of brain damage; one out of every thirty-five has mental retardation. These numbers come from a documentary on "Birth in America" I watched on educational television last night. What really hit me though was the alarm it sounded about the dangers of local anesthesia and induced birth; both sins visited upon Noah. Perhaps there may have been a genetic proclivity or predisposition in Noah for brain damage, but certainly the birth process and the obstetrician nailed down the job.

Indeed, my selection of the obstetrician was a grim joke. I've been more careful in buying a car than I was in choosing her as our doctor. I fell victim to reverse prejudice. The good lady was married to a Chinese man so I thought she could identify with us. Maybe she could. But she just wasn't a very good doctor.

First, she put the normally ninety-five-pound Foumi on a diet during pregnancy so that she could have an easy delivery. Second, she X-rayed Foumi late in pregnancy when Foumi mistakenly thought she had swallowed a chickenbone. Third, she induced the labor so she could have an uninterrupted Fourth of July holiday. Fourth, she gave Foumi a local anesthetic, contravening our wishes and instructions, so that she could have an easier time "sewing up."

Come to think of it, we may be lucky Noah isn't any worse off than he is. But it's all mea culpa.

November 28, 1975

Noah likes to hear me whisper. He laughs every time I whisper. I should whisper more, control myself more, shout less, and rant less. But then maybe he won't find my whispering so funny.

November 29, 1975

Foumi and Grandma are sewing away in the den, preparing pants and quilted pajamas for Noah. Grandma seems all right now, but last night she gave us a scare. She suddenly complained of dizziness, and had to lie down for a spell.

One of Noah's old UCLA behavior-modification-trained therapists dropped by for a visit. She tried to convince Foumi that we ought to try teaching Noah speech again, the behavior modification way. Foumi said: "No way."

Speech is a small part of Noah's total problem, but I do think Noah is beginning to kind of talk on his own anyway. Not much—but anything is better than nothing. He imitates a "Good morning," a "Good night," and an "I want to eat" sound. And yesterday, during our walk, I distinctly heard him say to a dog: "Go away."

We had a picnic at the beach with some people from Japan. How gracious they were, how considerate. Karl had a good time and even Noah liked the excursion. He behaved beautifully. Either he's becoming easier to handle or he just likes Japanese people.

Noah was scratching and pinching me furiously last night. This morning I asked Adele Mortin, his schoolteacher, whether Noah had been pinching her lately. No, she said, he had stopped his pinching completely.

I guess it just leaks out at home. Noah has school behavior and home behavior—just like any other kid.

Someone told me of a child like Noah who turned out to be susceptible to certain allergens. Perhaps we could experiment with Noah's diet: cut out milk and eggs, eliminate wheats and flours, do selective rotation, and find out if he reacts to these allergens—the way some people react to alcohol. But why bother? I know deep in my heart that Noah is suffering from something a lot more serious and complicated than an allergy.

December 17, 1975

At dinner Karl mentioned one of his recurring dreams. It began with Noah's being cured. I said we all had that recurring dream. But, said Karl, his dream was a nightmare. Why was it a nightmare? "Because Foumi became brain-damaged."

December 18, 1975

Noah has become more picky with his food lately. Perhaps his dietary needs are changing. But his tastes still remain gourmet. Uninfluenced by peer tastes, the only fast food he'll still go near is pizza.

December 19, 1975

A Christmas party at Noah's school yesterday. All the children seated around a horseshoe table. And Noah's behavior was absolutely marvelous. Everyone was sure he would tug at Santa's whiskers. But Noah did no such thing. He knows when not to push—or pull—a good thing.

December 20, 1975

My neighbor, Dick, told me that he and his wife keep remarking to each other about how good-looking Noah is. I said: "Noah doesn't have anything else to do but be good-looking."

December 21, 1975

Last night Foumi cut Karl's hair, some of which was growing down over his eyes. He said that he wasn't going anywhere until it grew back. This morning he lay in bed with the blanket pulled up over his head. And he didn't get out of bed until a friend came bearing Christmas gifts.

December 22, 1975

I took Noah to Karl's soccer game. I don't understand the sport but I love the way the kids look in their uniforms—like children in a French movie. Noah seemed to enjoy the game for a while until I literally had to sit on him: he wanted to run out onto the field too.

December 24, 1975

Foumi received a letter this morning from the parent of a child attending a special school in Tokyo—the school that had impressed Foumi. The parent wrote that the school didn't pay the teachers enough; and that though it had some good teachers it also had too many young teachers who didn't know what they were doing. So the whistle has been blown on Tokyo. But only for the time being. I wasn't looking so much for a solution for Noah as a way for us to live in Tokyo, to have the freedom to move around we would have without a Noah.

December 26, 1975

Where hath Christmas gone? Karl made a big thing out of it and I went along with him. I bought him a magic set and got a plywood board so I could set up his old electric trains. Noah has been his enigmatic self. Sometimes enjoying his sojourn at home, sometimes mysteriously unhappy.

For the first time I have been considering keeping Noah with us until we get old, until the end of our natural lives. But even that might be a cruelty to him; he would someday have to adjust to an institution at an advanced age without any previous training. His life, no matter how I look at it, can have no happy ending. His future, at best, crouches at the feet of my whims.

December 27, 1975
During the holiday season I overheard a discussion between Karl and a friend of his. "If God's so great," Karl was saying, "how come he made a Noah?"

"Yeah," the friend acknowledged. "God sure blew it with Noah."

I have my own theological observation to make: *Soul* and *spirit*, the stuff of old-fashioned religion, are nothing but vague descriptions of precise right-brain functions. Modern psychology and psychiatry offer hip restatements of these religious tenets—or abstractions—in the guise of science. And thus the brain remains the captive of the new and old religionists, outside the clutches of real science.

Poor Noah. He poses insoluble problems, but root ones. And all the vested institutionalized sentimentalities of society conspire against him.

December 28, 1975
These days Noah and I scramble up and down the cliff trails on our afternoon walks, an important part of the day for each of us. I think he derives a sense of accomplishment as he develops his coordination, exercises his judgment. And I like the simple servitude I perform in the cloak of a leader.

December 31, 1975
Noah and I took the longest walk we've ever taken together. Down the cliff trails and through the mobile-home court to the beach, where we walked along the water's edge for about a mile, Noah pouncing beside his shadow in the sand as the sun set. Then we came back through the canyon. And there was nary a complaint out of him. He is getting to be a big boy in terms of his physical proclivities, his endurance, his agility.

January 2, 1976
Foumi wasn't feeling well, so I celebrated the new year by taking Noah out to a friend's in Malibu and walking along the

258

beach there, my friend and I talking, Noah trailing behind us. My friend said he noticed that I didn't talk so much about putting Noah in an institution anymore.

I said: It was still a day-to-day situation. If Foumi or I became ill, for example, he would have to go. But right now we do enjoy Noah, as a love object, as a living presence. And Noah is funny. His ritualistic behavior, his attempts to avoid study or work or any chore which demands even a minimum of exertion, can still make us laugh. Anyway, I said, at this point I couldn't visualize my life without Noah. Just as I once could not visualize my life with a Noah.

My friend said it certainly sounded as if I wasn't ready to part with Noah.

I said I wasn't. Any more than he was ready to part with his home, which the state beach commission was requisitioning to make way for a parking lot for the public beach. That will happen inevitably. Meanwhile he enjoys his house and we enjoy our kid.

I think everyone has a Noah, something dear and treasured that will be foreclosed too soon. Only ours is of our blood and tissue.

January 6, 1976

This is one of those periods in which we think Noah is trying to speak. So I try to talk more to him, to reply to his yelps and whines as if they were words.

January 8, 1976

Sometimes I think it's my feelings that are grotesque, not Noah's behavior. Here is a nine-and-a-half-year-old boy, physically fully developed, that I constantly want to sweep up in my arms and hug and kiss. I'm the freak.

But then I become philosophical and realize that every parent wants to do it with his kid, even with his twenty-year-old kid. Being a parent is just as confusing as being a child ever was.

January 11, 1976

Who says Noah can't communicate? At dinnertime he'll enter the kitchen and start peering over the stovetop to check on what's cooking. Then, after reconnoitering once or twice more, he'll take his seat at the dinner table, lean on his elbows, and actively wait in anticipation.

January 16, 1976

Noah's era of good feeling continues. I drive him to school each morning. Foumi works with him each afternoon. I take him for a twilight walk. He spends his evening happily loped over the love seat or twiddling with the drapes. But I have to be careful when I talk to him. The longer I keep up my one-sided conversation, the more he thinks I'm bawling him out for doing something wrong. A side-effect legacy of behavior mod, I'm afraid.

January 20, 1976

Grandma took the bus into Westwood by herself this morning. A brave act for a seventy-year-old woman who can speak no English. Oh that Noah could one day take a bus downtown by himself!

January 21, 1976

I received a call from a woman who has identical twins, one of whom is normal, the other diagnosed as "autistic" at UCLA. At that time the diagnosing doctor said: "There goes our theory." Because that child's malady obviously could neither be attributed directly to environment nor genetics. Which leaves a slowly manifesting birth damage to the brain, one that might be derived from a virus or an anesthesia, as the most logical cause.

We brought some kids, normal and special, to Family Service. We wanted to try out the room; they wanted to see if our presence would disrupt their other activities. Our kids made their noise and it didn't seem to disturb anyone. The room they will rent us is far from ideal. But it will do. We will finally have our day-care center.

January 29, 1976
If Noah preoccupies me less, he still governs my values completely. Because of Noah, most "serious problems" seem neither serious nor problems to me. My positions, different to begin with, are now totally deviant. Could it be that Noah has recreated me into an original?

February 1, 1976
A group of parents are forming another group. They called to ask if we would join. But it has the word *autistic* in it so we could not consider being a part of it. These parents remained resolutely uneducable.

February 4, 1976
I was so busy I did not take Noah for his walk yesterday. And he was up half the night wailing, wassailing, and singsonging. But I don't think he stays up solely because of a lack of fatigue. Even without our communal exercise his day is busy enough. I sometimes think he just stays up late to complain—to bemoan his lot—in the only way he knows how.

February 5, 1976
The mother of a brain-damaged girl called last night. Her daughter is in the hospital, her stomach has been cut open, and they extracted from her intestines several pieces of plastic

mattress cover. It seems she had been suffering cramps for several days. At the institution in which she's in residence they thought she had the flu, gave her antibiotics. When that didn't work they finally took her to the hospital where she underwent emergency exploratory surgery.

Now the poor girl is heavily drugged, her arms and legs are tied down, she is being fed intravenously, and they are afraid that she'll pull out her stitches. She is like Noah, unable to communicate anything. And the same thing could happen to him. He likes to put things in his mouth.

February 7, 1976

The gulf between Karl and Noah widens. Karl continually matures while our expectations for Noah diminish. But I do think Noah has a sense of humor.

This afternoon I returned home late. Foumi had evidently already started Noah on his walk, so I went looking for them. Turning a corner I saw Noah and Foumi coming toward me. I walked briskly by them as if I were a stranger. Noah seemed to notice me but kept walking straight ahead, looking around and back at me noncommittally. I turned around and followed after him, walking right by him again. This time he looked me straight in the eye as I passed and began to laugh, as if he were trying to tell me that the joke was on me.

February 8, 1976

Yesterday's mail brought a big manila envelope from Japan containing a brightly covered yellow book. Foumi's book. The book she's written comparing education in America and in Japan.

I never wanted to be married to a writer. I know the breed too well. But how happy I am that through writing, Foumi, like myself, has achieved some measure of identity. And how proud I am of her.

The brain-damaged girl had to be operated on again because of an infection from her unmoved feces, the antibiotics not working. The poor child's continually drugged, being fed intravenously; she's suffering intolerably. If she were a household pet—instead of an incomplete human being—she would have been put to death already.

Karl worries about his hair. He's trying to train it to fall to one side, is beginning to be vain about his appearance. Boys grow, but Noah still has his lovely androgynous appearance.

I was playing with Noah last night, hugging and rolling with him across my bed, when suddenly he bit me under the arm.

Foumi is busy interviewing people for the day-care center. It's hard to find the right staff. Most people are either too young or too inexperienced.

Foumi and Karl and Grandma and I have begun playing Simple Simon Says every night, trying to coax Noah into the game. We can get him interested for a few seconds, then he resists and runs off, escapes into another room. It's still so hard to get him involved in anything.

I think we've found the right people for the day-care center. Foumi and I asked ourselves the simple question: Would we feel confident having this person in charge of Noah? And in the case of these two people the answer was a resounding yes.

February 23, 1976

The UCLA Placement Office called and said that in the future they could not make any job referrals to our day-care center because of my wife's racial attitude. I was shocked. I know Foumi doesn't have a smidgen of race prejudice in her bones. Reva Jones, one of the two teachers we've hired, is black. I couldn't understand what they were talking about.

Until I tracked it all down. And then we had a good laugh.

It seems Foumi told a job seeker over the phone yesterday that we weren't interested in any more "applicants." The sensitive job seeker evidently thought Foumi had said "Africans" and had reported it to the dean.

February 25, 1976

Last night I heard another institution horror story. This time about a brain-damaged kid in Camarillo who had been found bleeding from a broken nose, no one near him, no one on the staff knowing what had happened.

March 1, 1976

Last night we took Noah out to eat pizza. How he loves pizza. As we left the restaurant he said distinctly, "Good. Good." And when Foumi asked me whether something was to the left or to the right, the Sphinx repeated, "Right. Right," exhausting his language supply for the year.

March 3, 1976

Noah was up early again this morning, tantrumming, scratching himself fiercely, crying furiously. I hate Noah when he begins to cry, to wake me, to abuse my night's sleep. But what if Noah weren't home doing that? Where would he be? In a foster home. In a state institution. And how much more abused would I feel? How much emptier would I feel? There would be a dullness in my life—and a constant fear.

March 5, 1976
Foumi is amazing, her perseverance pays off. This news story is from today's Los Angeles *Times*:

NEW PALISADES DAY CENTER TO OPEN MONDAY

The new Palisades Day Care Center for Developmentally Disabled Children will open Monday, March 8, at Family Service of Santa Monica, 1539 Euclid St.

The nonprofit center will offer extended day care and supervised training for children suffering from brain damage, autism, neurological impairments and Down's syndrome.

It will be open weekdays from 2:30 to 5:30 P.M., and Saturdays, holidays and vacation periods from 10 A.M. to 4 P.M.

It will serve up to 10 children from 5 to 12 years of age, according to the director, Mrs. Foumiko Greenfeld.

14

March 7, 1976

Tomorrow is a day of starts of good causes: Our day-care center opens. And my play, *I Have a Dream*, based on the writings and speeches of Martin Luther King, Jr., which I've been working on since last summer, goes into rehearsal.

March 9, 1976

We've immediately run into a problem with the day-care center. Family Service, our landlord, told us they wanted a screen put up outside the room we're renting so that their clients wouldn't see our children. This infuriated me. It was as if we were running into the Episcopalian church crap again. I had a long talk with the F.S. president, only to discover that if not in bed with Freudians we were renting from them.

March 10, 1976

I read a piece in a magazine by a father who claims to have "cured" his "autistic" kid. What rot! If this father had talked about a specific area of the brain that was not functioning and how it had begun to function again, then I would have to listen. Instead, he only talked in general, vague terms and after reading the piece twice I still don't understand exactly what the man did and what he thinks he's accomplished. It's amazing that the brain—the most complicated organ in man—is the one treated most simplistically.

March 14, 1976

Karl spent the day with me, inspecting his parental activities. I took him to the *I Have a Dream* rehearsal in the morning and he was unusually quiet, almost respectful, though he did tend to become bored the second and third times a scene was repeated.

In the afternoon we went to the day-care center. We have six children. And that's all we want for now. And, in addition to our two aides, we had two volunteers there. But what the children enjoyed most, I think, was when Karl began to play catch with them. They were flattered. The same way I used to be flattered when one of the big kids on the block would play with me. To brain-damaged children, no matter what their ages, any normal child is a big kid.

March 20, 1976

The day-care center is going well. We're proving that parents can run things, even better than professionals. But it also means instead of worrying about one brain-damaged child, Foumi and I now have to worry about six.

March 21, 1976

I'm not sure the day-care center is so good for Noah. He and I had stopped taking our evening constitutionals because of his long, structured days. So last night when I took him for a walk he was like a young colt being let out for the first time. He went back and forth on the bluff, cavorting and running—and Noah has the normal kid's need to run.

So many of his needs are those of a normal child. I keep forgetting that. I also keep forgetting that much of his bizarre behavior is nothing more than his only means of communication. For example, lately he has been lifting up our bedcover and removing the thin quilt beneath it and taking that back to his bed. Foumi figured out that perhaps he's been trying to tell us that his own thick quilt is too warm. Last night we gave him the thin quilt. And he slept better than he has in weeks.

March 24, 1976

The six children at our day-care center:

An eleven-year-old boy who calls it "the second school."

A beautiful blonde nine-year-old girl who runs wild and talks only in echolaliac—parrotlike—bursts.

An eleven-year-old girl whose speech seems normal but who can barely walk a straight line.

An eleven-year-old boy who can quickly learn to solve a puzzle but can even more quickly break a window or jam a toilet.

A cute little Down's syndrome boy of ten who seems very frail and gentle—until he pinches you.

And Noah. Whose general lack of abilities places him at the bottom of the group.

Our six kids.

I love the kids. The only qualms I have are about the facility. It ain't the Ritz. And some of the parents are a nuisance in the way they forget to pick up their children on time. But I guess they're entitled to their lapses. They have enough to worry about.

April 7, 1976

I went to Washington for the opening of *I Have a Dream*. All the technical cues—the complete sound track—that the director had kept telling me not to worry about should have been worried about a lot more. But that's show business. The audience loved it.

I was very moved on opening night too. Especially when Coretta King came onstage during the curtain calls and joined the cast in singing "We Shall Overcome." And at the party afterward, when I was introduced to Coretta, she turned away from the leaders and dignitaries clustered about her and embraced me with tears in her eyes.

As always, though, the best part of being away was coming back. How I loved the moment I walked in the door last night. The cat eyed me strangely, Noah shyly, Karl expectantly (he knew I would have gifts for him), and Foumi with quiet delight. I hugged and kissed everyone, the paterfamilias home again. Life in Washington without them had been mostly an empty hotel room and long, solitary walks.

April 9, 1976

At Noah's school this morning I asked Adele Mortin how to treat two of the kids in our day-care center. Both are being treated much too leniently by their parents. They throw things, they have tantrums, they are hyperactive. "Now," said Adele, "you see what teachers have to put up with. It's not easy."

She's right. Noah is easier than most. Some of the other kids, allowed to run wild at home, want to run wild at school and at Day Care too.

April 10, 1976

The wages of the day-care business: Our eleven-year-old girl fell and broke her elbow. I rushed her to the emergency room at the hospital. She was a brave girl through it all. "The doctor won't give me shots?" she kept asking tearfully. "No," I kept promising her. She'll have to keep the arm in a cast for six weeks.

April 20, 1976

The day-care center continues to take up Foumi's time. Always one problem after another. Now one of our teachers is leaving, going back to Georgia. The day-care center also takes up my time. Every two weeks I prepare a payroll. Just like a Republican. And all the forms I have to fill out will make me one.

April 21, 1976

Grandma knows how to deal with Noah. They communicate on a common ground—neither speaks English.

April 23, 1976

We've hired a new teacher and we're losing one of our day-care kids, our beautiful blonde nine-year-old girl. She's going into a residential school up north. And I can't fault her mother for sending her there. She's a widow and it's been an awfully tough haul for her. It's amazing that she's been able to keep her girl at home this long.

I'll be curious as to how that place works out. It may be a place for Noah.

April 25, 1976

Last night Foumi and I were talking about Noam Chomsky and how right he was: Speech is a birthright, something that comes biochemically as part and parcel of the birth process, like little Contac pills timed to go off only during the first few years of life.

And then this turn-the-clock-an-hour-ahead morning I heard Noah in the hallway. I called him to our bed and he begrudgingly lay down next to me for a while, fighting off my affection. Finally, he sat up and said in a low but distinct monotone whisper, "Iwannaeat."

270

April 26, 1976

For the first time yesterday Karl professed interest in something Jewish. He asked about having a Bar Mitzvah. His reason: some kids in school had told him about all the gifts you get. I said if he wanted a Bar Mitzvah he could have one. But he would have to study Hebrew and I could not guarantee the quantity of gifts. I think that settled the matter.

April 28, 1976

An old army buddy of mine has a place in Mariposa, near Yosemite. He's been suggesting that I might want to take Karl fishing there. And now is the time to do it, before Grandma leaves in two weeks for her trip to England. I mentioned the idea to Karl and he jumped at it. Foumi's face turned sour. It's one of those damned-if-I-do-damned-if-I-don't problems: It's good for Karl if I go father-son fishing with him. It's bad for Foumi and Noah to be without my presence over a long weekend.

May 5, 1976

I pulled Karl out of school and spent three days with him on a fishing trip. My friend's camp was a mobile home, an interior like a Holiday Inn, an exterior of eyesore aluminum, but sitting right above a small lake framed by tall pine trees and a clear blue sky. We had all the conveniences—electricity, hot and cold running water, gas heat, and flush toilets—plus pure rolling hill country air. We had great mornings in bed joking with each other before cooking breakfast. And then out on the lake we would catch a slew of perch which we cleaned and ate for lunch. The second time out on the lake, though, Karl didn't catch any fish for a while and tears began to stream down his cheeks. Then he got a few bites and all was well again. I wasn't too much help during the lean period. I know even less about fishing than Hemingway knew about stickball.

Karl had a good time. He enjoyed the experience of being away on a trip with his father. And without a Noah, I told my-

271

self driving back, I could be a better father to Karl, devoting more time and energy to him.

But then Noah greeted us with such a sullen look when we walked in the door last night that I realized a normal Noah might give us all an even tougher time. If sibling-jealousy looks could kill, I was a goner.

May 10, 1976

I think I can see the beginning of a mean cast coming over Noah's face, that glazed, psychopathic look that suggests the capability of anything. And I can see by my own reaction that it is the kind of look that will get him beaten up later. One is always tempted, almost feels challenged, to knock some sense and direction into that kind of impenetrable look.

May 13, 1976

Our new teacher, Katie Irving, and Reva Jones, our veteran teacher, are working very well together at the day-care center. I continually marvel at how Foumi has managed to put it all together.

May 14, 1976

Noah has taken to a security blanket again. Something we thought we were long done with. When he goes to sleep at night now he must have one of his old quilts rubbing against his face. And in the morning when he rises he takes his quilt to the living room and rests on the love seat until he is fully awake.

May 15, 1976

I dread bath nights. It means most of my evening is given up putting Gulliver to bed.

May 16, 1976

At lunch I was buttering some matzoh. Noah reached over and touched a piece, as if to stake it as his own. Successful communication.

May 17, 1976

A brain is a mechanism, not a gift of creation; a brain has components, is not an abstract unity. Just because much of our thinking is verbal, it does not follow that all of our brain functions are verbal. Indeed, the very part of the brain that deals the most with emotions has probably the least to do with words. Yet we tend to treat the brain as if it were a dime serial, a continuing literary experience whose operation can best be understood through an analysis of plot devices.

May 18, 1976

Karl brought home his sixth-grade group picture. It's a far cry from the kind of picture we used to take, all of us in suits, solemn faced in neat rows, in front of the school. Karl's picture is in front of the school too, but it looks more like a picnic, the kids in sports clothes, piled in pyramids, making various gestures, some even obscene. I guess another generation has truly passed.

May 19, 1976

This morning we had one of those great all-American, half-Jewish, half-Japanese scenes: Noah was slow in waking. And when Foumi tried to prod him out of bed, he pulled her hair. I freed a screaming Foumi and led a protesting Noah to the breakfast table. He took a bite of his egg and then left the table. I booted him in the ass as he passed by me.

I soon heard Foumi in the living room loudly complaining that Noah had spit out his egg. By this time I was trying to short-order-cook a hamburger for Karl who had suddenly decided that he couldn't look at an egg. Now both

Foumi and Karl began attacking me for having booted Noah. This made me angrier with Noah. I forced him back to the breakfast table. But then when he reached over and put his hand right into my peanut-butter toast, I overreacted and rapped him across the wrist.

Now Noah was angrily slapping at his own face and Foumi and Karl were berating me and it was getting late and everyone was blaming everyone else and Noah kept screaming away. Finally, we decided the hell with his breakfast and dressed him and brushed his teeth and got him into my car. I drove him to school, and by 9:15 the worst part of my day was over.

At school Adele Mortin told me that to overreact is natural. She also showed me some of the work Noah has been doing on peg boards—much the same work he has been doing with Foumi, organizing shapes and forms and colors. Which means there are parts of his brain that function, that can be taught. So it's the age-old question: How can we communicate the thoughts which are nonverbal? What is the language for which there is by definition only a nonlanguage? How can we talk to Noah without using words? How can he communicate to us the thoughts (the right-brain functions) that are neither clothed in nor influenced by language?

May 22, 1976

I was instructed by the state to bring Noah to a local pediatrician for a medical exam. It was strictly a bureaucratic procedure, a medical check on Noah's handicapped status. The pediatrician made us wait an hour and five minutes past the appointment time. And when the nurse finally ushered us into his office, he had no idea about Noah's background; he had not even looked at the preliminary questionnaire. Noah took one look at the man and knew he didn't know a damned thing; he began to tantrum in protest. I chastised the son-of-a-bitch for not doing his homework, for trying to rip off some easy taxpayer dollars. Noah, thinking my fury was directed at him, bit my hand. Lucky for the doctor. I was one step away from slugging him.

May 23, 1976

How I love Noah. A love beyond sex. A love beyond need. A love based on service. A love in fact. He can be so endearing—putting his face up to mine to be kissed. I guess every pet has its wiles. But he is my pet.

May 25, 1976

Getting the day-care center going has given Foumi enormous confidence and a great sense of accomplishment. But we're also paying the piper. Noah is actually learning less. He's beginning to forget the Chinese characters Foumi worked so hard to teach him.

May 26, 1976

For a while a woman at Family Service was giving us a hard time. She is their Director of Children's Services, and although our day-care center is an autonomous rent-paying organization she had somehow decided that we were in her charge. I thought we had corrected her on that point. Then an article appeared in a local paper mentioning that Family Service had a day-care center for disabled children and that this woman was operating it. I checked with the writer, who said that was the information she had received from this woman.

I'm not against anyone who works hard getting a little glory. But this woman, who has been a constant impediment, now seems to be trying to appropriate the fact of our existence to her credit. It's unreal. But then everything about our children is unreal.

May 27, 1976

I have come to regard the day-care center like one of those bad-news, good-news jokes—but in reverse. We now have several kids to worry about—not just Noah. That's bad. We also have several more kids to love. And that's good. I never really appreciated the other children as individuals until they became our responsibility.

275

Last night Noah suddenly became sleepy and exploded in tantrum, slapping himself repeatedly on his face and head. This especially upset me because I had just read in the newspaper about the problems they were having at the "autistic unit" at Camarillo. And since the Spastic Children's Foundation can offer us no lasting commitment to a constantly growing Noah, Camarillo would seem, now, to be Noah's eventual repository. The problems there are the usual ones: overcrowding and understaffing and parental complaints of injury and neglect. But I don't like to be reminded of them, I don't want to think about Noah's fate or future. My future, my fate, is death and I can accept it. But Noah, for all his innocence, faces a future in limbo, a fate in purgatory. And I don't know how to deal with that.

May 30, 1976
A holiday morning: Foumi has been planting, now she's working with Noah. Karl has gone to the cliff to fly his kite. And I have been typing, trying to send my small ideas soaring.

Very small ideas. Very little soaring.

But so goes a family—the holiday I am really celebrating.

June 1, 1976
Karl tells me he criticized a friend's kid brother for the way he answered the phone. And the kid replied: "I can answer the phone a lot better than your kid brother."

June 2, 1976
I often complain about Noah's early rising. But it's also hard for Noah to get up if he's slept deeply. Because he wakes in stages: First he hides his head under his quilt in bed. Then he leaves the bed, taking the quilt with him, and ostriches on the love seat. This morning Foumi sat down beside him on the love seat and tried to hug him. He was elusive but lovely—a big,

276

overgrown baby. I looked at Foumi. We were thinking the same thing. She began to weep.

June 4, 1976
Last night Noah awoke me around four o'clock and I lay in bed the rest of the night wondering about him. What difference is it to him whether it's night or day? Who knows exactly what happens in terms of his perceptions? Simple, spatial relationships —all sorts of basic perceptions that we take for granted—may not be granted to him.

The only thing I know about Noah is his existence mocks all other values. I look at Noah and realize there can be a life without any of the standard definitions, any of the *givens*. Noah exists. Simple as that.

June 9, 1976
This afternoon Karl's teacher told me Karl had made fun of Noah, put him down by referring to him as a "Bozo" in front of the other kids, in other words, criticized Noah defensively before anyone else could. When I confronted Karl he exploded in a cascade giveaway of guilty tears.

Karl and Noah. Noah and Karl. Who will prove the bigger problem yet?

June 14, 1976
I'm having Karl write the story of his life. In short takes. In simple sentences. I correct them and then he types them up. One of yesterday's sentences: "I first liked my mother more than my father but gradually it became about even."

I worry a lot though about training him without killing his creativity. At the same time I don't want him to wind up an illiterate either.

June 18, 1976
Last night we cut Noah's toenails. It is now a three-person job: the third person is Karl. I hold Noah down, Karl keeps his foot straight, and Foumi trims the nails.

We have to keep his fingernails short these days too. When he tantrums he digs his fingers deep into you.

June 20, 1976
The difference between Karl and Noah: When I wrestle with Karl affection flows physically. But if I wrap my arms around Noah he just stoically endures it.

June 21, 1976
Each night there is some paperwork involving Day Care. But we do have something going—something small, but something.

Noah goes to school each morning at 9:00. At 2:30 a cab takes him to our Day Care. He is home at 5:45. It's a schedule he—and we—can live with.

It disturbs me, though, that he barely talks at all anymore. Except for a perfunctory, all-purpose "Bye-bye."

June 23, 1976

Some parents will be the end of us. Foumi works so hard—long hours, without pay—running the day-care center. A mother calls and makes an appointment to see Foumi about her child who she says desperately needs an after-school program. And then the desperate mother doesn't show up.

June 27, 1976

This morning I told Noah to put out the light as he was leaving my room. He did so but then also closed the door. I shouted after him to leave the door open. He reopened the door, snapped the light back on, and then closed the door again. So a lot of his brainwork is actually situational guesswork.

June 30, 1976

The best thing about the L.A. school system is their summer programs. Most children matter-of-factly attend them whether they are behind or ahead in their schoolwork.

Karl is going to summer school at his new junior high because it's a good way for him to adjust to the change from elementary school. But last night I looked at his math work. Again they have him doing magic boxes. His math hasn't changed since he was in kindergarten. In trying to make math more interesting, I think modern educators have, instead, made it more difficult by making it less systematic. They make the same mistake that occurs in special education: trying to adapt the brain to the subject rather than adapt the subject to the brain. It's amazing how the brain, which is the learning mechanism, is constantly ignored.

July 1, 1976

Last night we were making preparations for Karl to celebrate the birthday of his friend Erich. We had to take him shopping for a gift, we had to confirm the arrangements with Erich's parents for a day at the Magic Mountain Amusement Park. Indeed, for days Karl has been full of nothing but Erich's birthday celebration. And then about 10:30 Foumi turned to me and said, "You know, we've completely forgotten. But tomorrow is Noah's birthday."

Talk not, get not. It's so easy to ignore Noah. Karl demands and gets more of my conscious attention. Sometimes I can return to the house and not even acknowledge the presence of Noah with a greeting.

By way of a birthday celebration this morning, Foumi and I were recalling when Noah would greet each kid in our neighborhood by name, when he would come to the table and talk in full sentences—"I want to sit down and eat grapes." Before he was two, before he walked.

Oh that Noah could talk again!

July 2, 1976

I made Karl one happy boy. I picked up Fourth of July fireworks. Karl said "Thank you" as he began to inspect the assortment. He had never before said "Thank you" with such feeling.

But last night I got annoyed with him. He simply does not know his math fundamentals. Not the least of the Freudian crimes is the havoc they have wreaked on our educational system. One learns only through drills; in that way rote actions are imprinted into the brain. The psychogenic fraternity knows nothing about the way the brain works, the mechanical inputs necessary, the rote work involved in learning. So our kids lack fundamentals. Fundamentals. *Attitudes* and *environments* and *receptiveness*—without fundamentals—still do not constitute learning.

July 6, 1976

We operated our day-care center straight through the bicentennial weekend. But Noah got in a day of swimming and Karl had his fireworks party at the beach and also marched in the local Fourth of July parade, playing a triangle in a children's band.

After the parade we all went to a picnic. And though Noah did his hoop-and-whee dance to the satyrs in the host's garden, he was no great behavior problem. He loved eating hot dogs and corn on the cob and watermelon and drinking prodigious quantities of canned soda. Except Tab. He didn't like Tab.

July 12, 1976

We visited some friends who have a pool. I took Noah in for a dip and then dressed him. He went back into the pool with all his clothes on.

July 15, 1976

Karl watched the balloting with great interest as Jimmy Carter smiled to nomination victory. Noah showed his dental work too, sucking on the fringes of our bedspread.

281

July 16, 1976

Trouble in day-care city. We're losing Katie Irving, our teacher who has worked out so well with Reva Jones. So it's back to the interview grindstone for Foumi. Our August program is our crucial one. We'll be going full-time, six days a week, for the whole month. There just isn't anything like it. Somehow everybody else closes down in August so that the teachers can get vacations, which leaves the kids out on a ledge.

July 19, 1976

I now can let Noah go into the water by himself, wearing a life jacket and tube, because Karl will hover about him, playfully yet protectively.

July 20, 1976

A parent we know who has long been a Cassandra, constantly telling us that it does not matter what the parent of a brain-damaged child does because the child will end up in an institution, has finally conceded: "The longer you keep the child home, the better. Because in an institution the control is out of your hands."

And control with these kids—as in art, as in life—is all.

July 21, 1976

It's amazing how every four years Foumi, Karl, and I sit before the TV set during the Olympics and become experts in gymnastics ("She should only have received nine points on that") and swimming ("His stroke is too regular"). I guess instant expertise accompanies instant fame in Warhol time. Also instant disappointment: I had never heard of Shirley Babashoff until last week and already she's let me down.

But we also had our own Olympic event in the house. Bowing. We kept trying to teach Noah how to bow. First, he would fight us off. But we worked through his resistance until he was willing to bow from his head. But getting him to bow from the waist was another story. Finally, he did—to rousing cheers.

282

July 22, 1976

Noah jabs into my face, his hand reaching out, a kind of warding-off radar. Then his fingers probe hard: karate fingers.

July 23, 1976

Karl remains a great joy to the other kids when he shows up at the day-care center. It takes a special kind of ordinary kid to mix with ordinary special kids. He must be interested, he must have compassion, he must have a sense of humor, he must not feel condescending, he must not be afraid.

July 28, 1976

We took Noah to the Board of Education for a committee evaluation on his placement for the next school year. Noah sat like a charm, a model child, throughout the discussion. We were even complimented on how well behaved he was. For a moment I was even afraid that Noah might blow it for us and would be assigned to a normal school. For the function of the committee was to decide whether or not there might be a place for the child within the public school system or whether the child should be placed in a private school, his tuition paid by the state, because the city lacked the proper class.

The committee agreed to recommend that Noah be funded at his present school next year. They also, in effect, gave us the choice of selecting his chief diagnostic label. We asked that Noah be classified as "severely retarded." Because, for better or worse, that most precisely describes his present condition, his current capacities.

July 29, 1976

I took Karl to the circus at the Forum. He loved it but I was disappointed. No jugglers. No sword swallowers. No sideshow. A skimpy production overall. It wasn't as good as the circuses I remember. But then, when Karl takes his kid to the circus, it probably won't be as good as the ones he remembers either.

283

The girl we hired as Katie's replacement at the day-care center didn't work out. She was someone in love with the idea of special education but afraid of the children. After a nervous day we came up with a replacement. One of the teachers at Noah's school last year has agreed to fill in. We don't know too much about her, but we're delighted to have found her.

August 1, 1976

We've had guests, friends from the East, New York intellectuals who have had a difficult time through the years, but whose kids have turned out all right. I stop and catch myself. How can I—of all people—talk like this, describe people in this manner, imply a judgment based on the way children turn out? Look at Noah.

Yet it's so easy to make the child the measure of the family, the family the measure of the life. And how we so want to measure our lives, to assign marks to them as if in that way we somehow make marks with our lives.

When we have guests, I watch Noah objectively regard us impersonally, and notice how much the boys have changed. Now Karl, beneath his long hair, is the sensitive one, the Luftmensch; and Noah seems more the earth man, the full-bodied laborer, the peasant farmer. Even though he doesn't work.

The visit of friends is a time for thinking—and refocusing. We all need witnesses to our performances, audiences to our lives.

August 2, 1976

Noah has a sense of justice. He never cries if I chastise him when he's done something wrong. He only cries if he thinks he's right and I have wronged him.

August 3, 1976

Every night after dinner Noah clears the table, drinking the dregs in every cup, licking at the remains on every dish, but nevertheless getting all the dishes to the sink where Karl sponges them and places them in the dishwasher. Then Noah wearily wipes the table. He has to be urged on, prodded from dish to dish, spot to spot, and sometimes it seems more effort than it's worth. But finally he does ooze satisfaction, the thrill of accomplishment.

August 4, 1976

Last night Karl and I walked and talked along the bluff. When I look at Karl now I can see the beginnings of his spring-up look: he'll be a slight, lean kid. I pray he'll be a terrific kid. I look at some of the siblings of brain-damaged children and they're usually overindulged wrecks, a little hyperactive themselves.

August 7, 1976

There is always a problem with the day-care center. Now an alcoholic is coming around, trying to volunteer. Problem people gravitate to problem situations.

August 9, 1976

Every once in a while I project the future: I see Foumi at seventy-five, Noah at forty, and myself mercifully dead.

August 10, 1976

When I took the boys swimming yesterday Noah did not want to go into the water at all: the difference between the water temperature and the air temperature was too great. Finally I pushed him down the pool steps and then gradually he did get used to the chill and enjoyed floating about. Meanwhile, Karl and I raced around the pool, me playing the role of fellow kid and enjoying it.

Noah began to cry loudly. I couldn't figure out why unless it was because he was simply jealous. Until I saw a hornet sitting on the other side of his face.

I would have forgotten the incident completely. Except he came home from Day Care the other day with a fat swollen finger, a bee sting victim.

August 11, 1976

I still enjoy my walks with Noah. Especially after sundown. Afraid of the dark, he is truly dependent, holding on to my hand like a lover. And when a dog barks he tries to shelter himself within my body. All but climbing up and into it.

August 13, 1976

Foumi worries too much about the day-care center. She worries about finding another site, hiring a new teacher, having enough kids for next year. She does not realize that so much of living in America is playing it by ear.

August 16, 1976

I no longer work with Noah at all. Working with him means looking forward to future results and I want my life with him to stand still.

August 17, 1976

A night with Noah: He plants himself on the love seat. Or drapes himself on a couch. And does absolutely nothing. Except throw pillows on the floor and scatter the magazines and books that lie on end tables. Innocent enough. And if he has a tantrum we know eventuaily it will pass. We are lucky compared to the parents of the more violent children.

But there are also several quiet disturbances that can take place of an evening. For example, we look up: Noah is not on the couch. Or the love seat. Or in the den.

There is a trail of pants and underwear, leading to a bed on which he is sitting. En route there is an open bathroom door. Within one or another—or both bathrooms, equitably distributed—is a bowel movement. If we are fortunate, no bedcovers are stained; if not, it is washing-machine time. In any event, Noah has to be wiped and redressed.

The worst thing, though, is the time that is spent consciously and unconsciously aware of Noah's nothingness. It is debilitating, enervating, contagious. I think there must be a Gresham's law in relation to energy: Bad energy drives out good energy, negative energy drives away constructive energy. By bedtime I often find I have dissipated the evening much as Noah has. I have done nothing.

August 18, 1976

We took the day-care center kids swimming at the St. John's Hospital pool in Santa Monica. I arranged it almost like a military expedition. Three kids and a teacher and a volunteer in each car. Two volunteers waiting at the pool, ready to help the kids get into the water, while the other volunteers were parking the cars. By the time the kids were in the water, we had one adult covering each kid.

It was fun watching them. Each kid had his own pool style. One perched on the first step into the pool, lying across it as if it were a shelf, and never proceeded farther into the water. Another got into the water and tried to drink half the pool. One boy found a spot and jumped up and down in place. Another boy leaped in and out of the pool, never swimming between jumps. A girl talked her usual streak as she socially splashed about. Noah giggled and bounced, as he hugged the lip of the pool.

I was glad to see Noah with peers enjoying himself. But I also realized again how essentially lazy all these kids are and how frightened they are of new activities. Or is that the same thing?

August 20, 1976

When I look at Karl, I marvel at growth. When I look at Noah, I ask, in puzzlement: What is life?

287

August 24, 1976

Day Care was supposed to make our lives simpler. But our temporary teacher is complaining of nose aches, claiming they're the result of Noah's butting his head against her on our swimming expedition. I've learned that one of our parents has been charging another parent six dollars daily to car-pool her child. And now there is a bus strike, denying Reva Jones, our teacher, her only means of transportation.

August 25, 1976

I woke up from a nightmare: a Hieronymus Bosch version of Noah in the future—broken arms, battered eyes, a choked throat.

August 27, 1976

I had lunch with an old friend, someone I had not seen in years. As we brought each other up to date, she observed, "Noah seems to fill your life." At dinner I reported that comment to Foumi. Foumi shook her head and smiled. "No one understands. Noah empties your life."

September 1, 1976

Foumi hired a new teacher for the day-care center, a young Chicano male. She thinks it will be good for the kids to have a man around.

September 4, 1976

Noah is still afraid of our cat, T.G. Always gives him a wide berth. This morning Noah was standing atop the end table surveying T.G. And T.G. was looking up at him like a dog who has chased a cat up a tree.

September 7, 1976

Our family had a mini-vacation at a motel on Mission Bay in San Diego. Noah did not sleep at all for two nights. Still Karl and I had fun, swimming and paddle boating and bike riding. Grandma, back from England, and Foumi enjoyed the San Diego Wild Animal Zoo. What Noah liked best was returning home.

September 8, 1976

I looked over the newspapers that had collected while we were gone. I came across a piece on how scandalous the conditions are in the "autistic" ward at Camarillo State Hospital, the patients often physically abused, continually drugged. I wonder if I should show it to Foumi.

September 9, 1976

With Noah I feel we are living out the end of a thinning skein. Now he's started putting his fingers in his mouth—a habit I just can't stand.

September 10, 1976

Today is one of those endlessly rainy fall days, a day that harks back to Westchester County. To Japan, to Brooklyn Heights, to Greenwich Village, to Germany, to Saturday afternoon high school football games in Brooklyn before sparsely filled stands —a day, in short, that reverberates throughout my life. And here I am sitting at a typewriter, listening to a brain-damaged child squeal. Is that what it all comes down to?

September 16, 1976

Foumi is tired and annoyed. Tired of not being appreciated for all her work at Day Care. Annoyed because some of the parents don't even care enough to come and see what's being done for their children. I told Adele Mortin, Noah's schoolteacher, about it. She said: "Parents of ordinary children are the same way. They just want to drop their children off and run."

September 17, 1976

Last night when Noah came out of his bath I noticed with a start that he had an erection. The future is almost upon us. He is, after all, ten years old.

September 18, 1976

The bus strike plays havoc with my schedule. Just as I have to drive Noah to school each morning, I have to drive Reva Jones home from Day Care every evening. Instead of being a driven writer, I have become a driving writer.

September 21, 1976

Last night my play, *I Have a Dream*, opened on Broadway. And I wasn't there. Not because of Noah. But because of the carpetbagging director and producers. I couldn't decide what would be worse—celebrating or commiserating with them.

Meanwhile, my lawyer has called from New York to tell me that the first reviews have been raves, that the play should do well during its ten-week run.

September 22, 1976

It's a good thing I did not go into New York. This morning Foumi complained of a severe toothache. So after driving Noah to school I had to take her to our dentist in Venice. He referred her to a dental surgeon in Brentwood. We drove there and had the tooth extracted. Then in the afternoon the taxi company neglected to pick up our Day Care children. So I had to ferry them to our site in Santa Monica. When I returned home I found Karl waiting for me to take him to the Palisades shopping section so he could buy a jockstrap for gym and sign up

290

for drum lessons. After that, it was back to Santa Monica to pick up Noah.

Being a Broadway playwright is not all it's cracked up to be.

September 23, 1976

Karl likes junior high, thrives on being one of the big kids now. And I hear the beat of a pubescent Noah. Again I noticed him having an erection.

Meanwhile, there are still the old problems. Last night Noah let loose with a mammoth bowel movement. I wiped him, the first wipes. Then I gave him some toilet paper with which to wipe himself. He did so expertly even though there was nothing left to wipe. Then he put the paper into his mouth.

September 25, 1976

Karl has been working on a collage for school. And Foumi has been helping him with it. When I saw her contribution, the work she had *helped* him do, once more I mourned all the unpainted pictures, the empty canvases, all the artwork she has not done these last—or lost—ten years.

September 26, 1976

I don't understand modern education. I found out Karl's collage was for English. But he couldn't even spell the word. I wonder if his art teacher will have him doing conjugations.

Also, last night Karl described Japan as "a spin-off of Asia." Which shows how kids learn the language in Varietyland—or at my dinner table.

October 4, 1976

Yom Kippur. A day for Jewish guilt. For all the things I no longer do for Noah. Such as run after doctors. Or seek out new miracle cures. I just try to take him for granted.

291

Which means: I take for granted that I have to live in a house with blankets chewed, pillows strewn about, chairs upturned. I take it for granted that I have to be constantly wary of his bowel movements, ready to wipe him as soon as he finishes, otherwise he will choose a bedspread, a towel, sheets—anything —for that purpose, or simply come to rest upon a chair or couch. I take for granted that I have to wash him and bathe him every other night. I take for granted that I have to sit with him as he eats and that I have to brush his teeth twice a day and that he has to be coached in the acts of dressing and undressing and cannot put on his own shoes or tie the laces. I take for granted that I must walk with him in the evenings, that I must drive him to school each day, that I must pick him up in the late afternoons. I take for granted that I constantly have a baby to care for.

I also take for granted that what I do is so little, that what Foumi does is so much more.

October 5, 1976

Maybe we should start a night-care center too. Noah was up at 2:30, whimpering and yelping. I took him to the bathroom and back again, and tucked in his covers, but still he would not go back to sleep. And neither could I.

October 7, 1976

Noah amazed me. Since he was up all night I expected him to nod off during the day. But no—he didn't get to bed until after ten tonight. The kid has an unusual metabolism. So what else is new?

October 10, 1976

We will miss Grandma when she leaves on Tuesday, returning to Japan. Her presence has enabled us to lead an almost normal social life; we could go out of an evening without too much hassle.

October 14, 1976

The newspapers are again full of stories about Camarillo State Hospital, Noah's eventual repository. The District Attorney is investigating the death of some eighty to ninety patients there. I phoned a parent whose child was in Camarillo, asking how the kids could die there. "Easy," she said, "an overdose of drugs. The patients are constantly drugged and what happens is this: An attendant gives a patient a shot. Another attendant comes by and gives the same patient another shot."

October 17, 1976

Karl slept over at a friend's house last night so Foumi and I could linger in bed this Sunday morning. When Noah awoke he came and rattled our bedroom door. We were *in flagrante delicto* at the moment. Finally he gave up and wandered into the living room. "If he came in," laughed Foumi, "maybe it would have cured him."

October 21, 1976

Noah continues to chew on his shirt collars, to remove his shoes at school, to do a quick strip act whenever he has the chance, and is generally becoming, in a word—or rather two words—more difficult.

October 23, 1976

I had not planned to vote at all but I finally registered only because Karl observes what I do and it would have set a poor precedent for him. Among the wages of paternity will be a decision in a voting booth.

November 1, 1976

I worked with Noah yesterday for the first time in months, having him match objects in terms of size and shape and colors. It was disappointing for me. So much time and effort invested in him, so little progress made.

293

November 2, 1976

Election Day. Karl went with me to the polling place, an ordinary residence just two blocks down the street from us. Here I had to punch a card that I guess would later be tabulated by IBM machines. (I voted softly, very softly, on tiptoes, because between Carter and Ford I could not make an enthusiastic choice.) Then Karl and I took a walk along the cliff talking about elections and issues. Karl told me that he's opposed to abortion and that he was taking that position in a debate in his health class. "If people don't want babies," he said dogmatically, "they shouldn't make love." I know I signed a form saying he could receive sex education. Still I wonder how much he's received.

November 4, 1976

Open house at Noah's school last night. I overheard some "new" parents talking about "breakthroughs." I just worry about Noah's "fallback" position—and mine.

November 5, 1976

The parent of a brain-damaged child in a residential school tells us she always hears glowing reports from the social worker. But when she goes there herself her daughter seems very skinny and her mouth always reeks with the garliclike smell of infection.

November 8, 1976

Noah has taken to moistening the tips of his fingers with his tongue—as if he were about to turn the page of a book—and then touching a wall, a surface, an object, or a person instead. It's a habit he picked up from one of his day-care classmates and it annoys me greatly. Yesterday he did two other things that upset and frightened me:

I was watching television in the den. I thought Noah was in

the living room. When suddenly he attacked me from behind, scratching at my face, clawing at my throat, and going off in a painful yowl himself after I beat him off.

Later, at dinner, for no discernible reason he turned to me and pulled my hair. I can only suspect that on both occasions he suddenly had a pain—a toothache, for example—and he was reacting to it, assigning me as the cause of it, and hence also the source of possible alleviation.

Both incidents frightened me. Not physically but psychically. I do not look forward to a future in which he could overpower me.

I do not look forward to the future anyway. In today's newspaper I read that there would be more hearings on the many suspicious deaths in Camarillo and Norwalk state hospitals. Evidently most of the deaths were caused by overdosages of drugs, dispensed like salted peanuts, to keep patients in somnolent states.

November 9, 1976

Karl saw *Day of the Dolphins* on television. He was impressed with the fact that the dolphins had been taught to speak in much the same way we had once tried to teach Noah speech. Of course, George C. Scott succeeded with the dolphins while we failed with Noah. "We blew it," said Karl. "We should have tossed Noah into a tank."

Meanwhile, Noah keeps touching everything with wet fingers. He knows it's wrong for him to do so too. Every time I chide him for it, he does not howl with righteous indignation. He just tries to make peace with me—and returns to his compulsion.

November 10, 1976

God, did Karl look handsome when I dropped him off at school this morning. But so did Noah. I have handsome kids. The ironic heirs of a bald man.

November 11, 1976

Day-care woes: We've learned some other facilities are still receiving transportation money from the state while we're scraping the bottom. By starting our day-care center, I have learned a lot about how badly and unfairly government functions—not only on the state level but also on the federal level. For example, everyone talks about federal aid for day care, but there is no federal aid when the need is the greatest—to provide day care for the developmentally disabled.

November 12, 1976

Karl said he wants to play the harpsichord. I told him: "No, I want my son to become a boxer." I shouldn't tease like that. My street smarts are sometimes pretty dumb. I apologized to Karl, but it was too late to heal the damage.

November 14, 1976

Karl's team is having a disastrous soccer season. They've lost all five of their games. But Karl is now one of the better players on the team, so he is actually getting more in self-esteem out of the sport.

November 16, 1976

Yesterday was Foumi's birthday, forty-six big ones. We celebrated it by quietly lunching out. And now Karl's birthday is shifting into the spotlight. Or rather he's shifting it into the spotlight. This morning he let me know it was only ten shopping days away. He also informed me that he wasn't sure he would play with his friend Warren, who was thirteen yesterday, until after his own historic birthday. "Because right now Warren is two years older than me and that's too much," he said. "I'll play with Warren again when I'm twelve."

November 17, 1976
I asked Karl: "What does it feel like being in a family with a brain-damaged brother?"
Karl shrugged. "I don't know what it feels like being in a family without a brain-damaged brother."

November 19, 1976
I'm near the end of the line with Noah. His new habits really offend me. I have to do something. And I won't even be able to send him to Camarillo as a last resort. They keep uncovering more manslaughters there, more evidence of monumental neglect.

November 20, 1976
Now Foumi's in a funk. Noah's touching his fingers to his tongue every few moments is driving her berserk too. So are the daily disclosures of the maltreatment at Camarillo and the other state hospitals. We had known all about it. But there is nothing worse than seeing in public print what you know through personal observation. Newspapers make the obvious official, objectify the correlative.
So we both feel terrible. There is no escape down the road. There is only a pursuit after us.

November 22, 1976
Last night Karl and I were watching television in my room, slumped on the floor with the bed as a backrest, while Foumi watched her Japanese program in the den. I asked Karl if he ever worried about Noah. "Sure, I worry about him," he said. "But I try not to worry too much, otherwise my whole life will be depressed."

November 23, 1976
I had lunch with a friend, trying to unburden myself of many of my Noah woes. But it didn't help. The newspapers are still

297

full of Camarillo and I still don't see any solutions in sight. The best solution in terms of my problem would be to kill Noah. To take him out rowing and drown him, a true *An American Tragedy*. First, I would begin to take him out on weekends. Establish the custom, the pattern. He is a danger in a boat. He could actually become unruly. It could happen.

If I were to snuff him out in the open with a shotgun I could get as much as fifteen years. I can't see ending my life in jail. I can't see ending my life, period. I know that before I would kill myself, I would kill Noah.

November 25, 1976
The day began with Karl coming to our bed. And then I called Noah. And he came, briefly dipping his head toward Foumi when I told him to kiss her. And I felt like crying. Either the holiday season or my age makes for a sentimental morning.

November 26, 1976
This is really the historic day of this bicentennial year: Karl's twelfth birthday. I gave him his gift—ten bicentennial silver dollars and ten paper ones—before breakfast.

November 27, 1976
Yesterday I managed to avoid Noah completely. It's a game I now play. Dodge Noah and win a day.

November 28, 1976
Most states these days use brain activity—or the lack of it—rather than heartbeat, or its absence, as the legal definition of death. If we carry that point to its logical extreme, why can't a creature such as Noah—who has no meaningful brain activity as translated into purposive behavior—be put to death? He is no more than a pet and he should be put to death just like any pet when no one is willing to take care of him any longer. The

only way I can keep my own head is to regard him as a pet. Because if I regard him as anything else I will destroy myself. He is my luxury, my whim, my hobby. He is not my son. He is my pet.

A horrible weekend.
I thought continually that soon I will have to kill Noah. The monster that has long been lurking in him increasingly shows its face. And just as the day may come when I can no longer bear to take care of him, I could not bear to see him mistreated—or maltreated—in a state hospital like Camarillo or Letchworth Village.

He will become a hopeless grotesque with less than endearing manners. He keeps putting his fingers to his lips and then spit-touching the nearest object or person. He pinches, he scratches, he pulls hair. This morning he suddenly pulled Foumi's hair after she had chastised him for his finger-spitting. I heard her crying and rushed to free her from his grasp. "I will soon be bald or gray," she moaned.

Killing him will be a kindness. His brain has stopped working; he has not been functioning anyway. I dread it but I see myself killing my son not as myth but as fact. My dreams now are dreams of prison. Isolation. A winding down of my life in solitude. It seems absurd, I know. But could I ever bear to see Noah suffer, killed softly and cruelly, day after day? No.

There is a man from Santa Barbara who killed his brain-damaged son a few years ago. He put a gun to the boy's head and squeezed the trigger, then called the police. He's in prison now. But he'll get out eventually.

November 30, 1976
E. E. Cummings wrote of an "intense fragility"; Noah has an intense vulnerability. He was sick yesterday. He always gets sick after a holiday.

299

December 2, 1976

I'm so sick of Noah, it's sickening. I have so little love for Noah these days, and he senses it. Ever since his teeth have become loose, he's begun scattering his spittle about, and disrobing, and his eating habits have become poor. I don't care what he's trying to tell us. I just look at his elongating body and I don't feel much love. In fact, I feel fear—and hate.

December 6, 1976

I awoke to a vomiting Noah. I cleaned him, all the rug stains, and tried to let Foumi have a late day. I also tried to make peace with Noah. I stopped slapping his hand whenever he put his fingers to his lips. But there was no peace.

December 9, 1976

A bad week. A crisis time. We have to do something about Noah. He is in a constant irascible mood and we are always beside ourselves. We are nervous, on edge, contentious. We upbraid each other; we are at each other. We have to get away from the problem—or send the problem away. Even get Noah away for a year. It is no solution but it would buy us time. Foumi, especially, seems to have had enough.

Noah is ten and a half now. He has a sullen look, drooping eyelids, like one forever caught in a bad photograph. I think he's more aware of his prison than ever before. He cannot tell us anything and that frustrates him. We cannot tell him anything and that frustrates us. He cannot even be told, for example, to blow his nose or clear his throat to avoid a small discomfort. He cannot be offered the surcease that even the worst of pains will pass. And lately he's been especially unhappy because his teeth are changing. Imagine feeling your teeth with your tongue and suddenly they are loose and shaky and then one day they are not there. And you have no way of knowing exactly what is happening to you as you seem to be literally falling apart. No wonder he's upset, poor thing.

300

One of those all-time classic days, the kind of Noah day that I had long forgotten, that I had hoped was long since over. I drove Karl to school this morning and upon my return I thought I would steal a moment or two in the car, reading the newspaper. But Foumi was at the door, calling me into the house. I thought it was a phone call from New York. But no. When she had gone to awaken Noah, she had found him in a pool of urine and excrement. Excrement all over the bed, all over the rug, all over Noah himself.

We spent the rest of the morning cleaning up and bathing Noah. Washing the mattress cover, the sheets, his pajamas, his quilts, his pillows. Trotting the mattress out to the deck to dry. Cleaning the bedroom walls and the children's bathtub and the house itself. It is two o'clock and I have finally come to my office, not to work but to get away.

Perhaps Noah lately really doesn't like me, my drill sergeant's way with him. Whether it is because of his "normal" development or my "abnormal" treatment of him, I really do feel a hatred from him these days. I see it in his eyes.

But I don't care if I am hated by a monster. I am beginning to hate him. He is no longer cute, he is hideous, he *is* a monster. My son, the monster, is Rosemary's Baby, the *Exorcist* child, King Kong. I live with the symbol of escapist mass entertainment in my own house. He is my grim reality.

One of my best friends, an old army buddy, called me. He has big C. Oh, how words can govern attitudes. I was in a state of shock. Until I talked about it to Foumi and gradually she reminded me that cancer was just another word for sick.

Noah has been much better the last few days. He doesn't finger-spit as much and hasn't violently attacked anyone. He is smiling and has a good appetite. So Foumi and I are going at each other less and enjoying him more. Foumi thinks perhaps Noah is just going through "the tens," the "difficult tens." I would like to think so too.

December 17, 1976

Whatever the cosmic reason—perhaps even the Yuletide spirit in the air—Noah continues to be much easier to take.

December 18, 1976

We had a lovely Christmas Parents Day Party at the day-care center Saturday and we're still basking in its afterglow. Our volunteers Patty Norian and Murray Sobel, and our music specialist, April Cole, and our occupational therapist, Betty Ann Altman, were there; our staff was there; and the parents were there—some of them seeing for the first time what their children could do. Such looks of joy and gratitude on their faces: Learning of a son's perfect musical pitch. Watching a daughter do the Virginia Reel. Seeing a son's macrame-weaving. And the children, of course, were delighted with their Christmas presents.

We have to keep the day-care center going. We have established something important. There is no way we can stop it now. I feel the thrill of proprietorship—albeit nonprofit; I feel such pride in what Foumi has accomplished. It is the most creative thing that artist has managed since Noah was born.

It's ironical: If Noah has proven debilitating to our dreams, he has also provided the material for a kind of realization of ourselves. It's not the realization either of us anticipated or wanted, but then one cannot predetermine the scenario one is destined—or doomed—to act out, either.

The girl from Osaka and the street kid from Brooklyn wind up doing some good. Which ain't bad.

December 19, 1976

Who is to say that what is best for Noah may not be best for us as a family? Why should our family be dedicated to my writing or Foumi's painting or Karl's maturing? Why can't our family be dedicated to the care of Noah? What finer principle? After all, everything we do—in spite of how we try to squirm out of it—is because of Noah anyway.

December 20, 1976

Noah mirrors my mood. If I use violence on him, he responds with violence. If I use sweetness, he is sweet. There is no way to overwhelm him except on his terms. He's my Foumi all over again.

He's also the child in our day-care center who I think has shown the least improvement. (Except in jealousy. When I gave my attention to some of the other children at the party, he didn't seem too happy about it.) And of the five kids who come regularly, I have to admit that Noah is the worst of the lot in terms of potential. But still he has much more potential than he actually realizes.

How much these kids need encouragement! How much all kids need encouragement! I wonder if I don't tend to get too down on Karl sometimes, if I don't give him enough chance to breathe in the heady air of success.

December 21, 1976

Noah was about to tantrum when I began dressing him this morning, pushing away the pants that I was trying to get him to poke his legs into. I took another pair of pants from the bureau. He poked his legs through docilely. He simply had not liked the other pants. He's entitled to likes and dislikes in clothing.

December 22, 1976

If we did not have the day-care center going full-time from 10:00 to 4:00 each day during this holiday period, today would have been the fifth straight day of having Noah at home without a thing to do.

December 24, 1976

Noah found the candies under the Christmas tree and began his celebration one day early. His prerogative.

December 27, 1976

On Christmas Eve, Karl was morose. He thought he might not be getting a gift from us at all; he had seen no new package take up dramatic residence under the tree during the afternoon. (I had slipped his gift unobtrusively beneath a large one.) Finally, I told him it was there and pointed it out to him. He picked up the small package, examined it disappointedly, and asked me what it was. I told him, "Perfume." He looked at me positively amazed. I told him that I always like to get perfume for a person I loved, that I had decided it was the most memorable gift I could get him because I was sure it was one he would never forget. He thought I was joking, or worse than that, teasing, but he also was not quite sure, either.

So on Christmas morning I was delighted to see how genuinely happy—or relieved—he was as he came into our bedroom proudly sporting his new watch.

December 31, 1976

I had a dream last night. Noah was in an institution. All the children were at the swimming pool. Noah took off all his clothes and went into the water. He came out of the water and promenaded about, still naked. A little boy came over to me and said that Noah shouldn't be walking around like that, it wasn't good for the other kids. I asked the director of the place, a woman named Ruth, who that little boy was. She said that he was the staff psychoanalyst's son. I said if an analyst could help Noah, I would be pleased. She laughed. And then somehow she was gone.

I had come to the place with Karl, a Karl who was his true current age of twelve. Noah, however, was in his teens. I left Karl in the recreation area and went to look for the director because I wanted to talk further with her: I wanted to learn exactly what they were doing for Noah in that place. I found the director, this woman named Ruth, making rounds in the Women's Ward. But somehow I never could get any satisfactory answer out of her even though she was most cordial to me. She just kept finding other people to talk to, other work that had to be done. There were constant interruptions of every sort. I became worried about where I had left Karl, I had forgotten exactly where the institution's recreation area was. Somehow I became convinced that I had lost him, lost him forever. And frantically I went off searching for him, not even knowing where to begin my search.

It was then that I woke up.

I went into Noah's room. He was naked, under his quilt, somehow having stripped.

January 1, 1977

I told Karl about my dream. He, in turn, told me about a recent recurring dream of his.

"You die. And then Noah suddenly becomes normal. So Foumi goes and kills the fathers of the other kids in our day-care center. But those kids stay brain-damaged. And Foumi gets caught and has to go to jail."

"And then what happens?" I asked.

"I don't know," said Karl. "I always wake up."

January 2, 1977

Yesterday I took Karl to the Rose Bowl game. We lost our way getting there. And getting back. I lost a pair of eyeglasses and an umbrella handle. And worst of all, Michigan, my alma mater, lost the game.

Noah was hard to wake this morning, but glad to be going back to school—reminding me again how much he needs a structured day, an ordered existence, as fixed a frame of reference as possible.

Yesterday, I bawled out Karl because of his spending habits, the way he constantly alchemizes his money into polymer—all those plastic models of ships and planes that proliferate in his room. I can't step into his room without inadvertently destroying an aircraft carrier.

And today Karl's been a perfect angel. I think a normal child—like an abnormal child—likes controls, discipline, limitations set within well-defined boundaries.

It's spring again. And this afternoon Foumi and I will drive up to Santa Barbara, leaving Noah and Karl behind in the charge of Katie Irving, the former teacher at our day-care center. I am really looking forward to our holiday. We will sit in the sun, walk along the beach, swim in the pool, and fill out day-care center tax forms.

As usual, Santa Barbara remains the California of our dreams: the air so clear, the sky so blue. We ate too much and napped a lot and went swimming, and visited the art museum and enjoyed the carefree childless life. No meals to prepare, no wondering where Noah was or what Karl was up to, we lolled in a happy limbo. It was the first time we were without the kids since Karl's Y camp and Noah's Spastics stay coincided a year and a half ago.

But just two days away from the kids and I don't think I could have stood a third day. I bemoan the kids, especially Noah, but

I cannot visualize a life without him. Just as I cannot visualize a life without Karl. Without Foumi. No matter what I say, no matter what I do, I love Noah more than I can do or say. I want him in my house. I want him in my home. That is his place.

January 17, 1977

Yesterday as we packed for home Foumi shrugged and smiled. "Back to reality."

Karl was delighted to see us. He was full of talk about how he spent his weekend. Saturday he had lunched at a restaurant with a friend. It was the first time either of them ever had waiter service without an adult presence. And it seemed the uncertainty of how much to tip when it was all over had ruined their enjoyment of the meal.

Noah was so happy to see us too. While Katie was reporting that he had had a good weekend and behaved well, he was leaping and jumping and smiling. I could even detect the traces of a "Good morning" sound in his greeting. And I noticed two more teeth, two back teeth, were gone.

And from a freshened—or refreshed—point of view I could accept, as he put his fingers in his mouth and withdrew them moistened in abrupt gestures, that he was telling me, as he has been telling me for months and months, that some of his teeth were missing—the big news in his life.

The urge to communicate is there, the need to communicate is there. And that urge and that need are nothing less than the breath of hope itself. Life itself.

I can never kill the dream that is my son.

16

January 25, 1977

Karl had to write a report for his health class. This is what he handed in.

INTRODUCTION

I have a brain damaged brother. His name is Noah. My brother is a ten year old boy who can't talk, read, write and can't do most things a boy his age can do, such as throw or catch a ball. He goes to a special school and a special day care center in the afternoon. He has black hair and a charming smile. Noah stands about 54½ inches tall.

He has a disease for which there is no cure and there is no known cause.

These next few pages will tell you what it's like to live with a brain damaged brother.

A DAY WITH NOAH

In the morning, Noah usually gets up early and chants a low humming noise. Then in about fifteen minutes, he will walk down the hall to the living room where he sits on a certain love seat which he has made his. He waits for somebody to come out and make breakfast. After breakfast my parents help him dress, brush his teeth, and take him to the bathroom.

If nobody teaches him he wanders from bedroom to bedroom, from living room to den. He knocks over pillows and blankets and chews on anything soft. Sometimes he takes off his shirt, sometimes his pants, sometimes his socks, sometimes everything. While doing this he is emitting the same noise as when he got up—or he is giggling or laughing or screaming. But sometimes he is saying things in his own gurgled way.

Since he can't talk my mother teaches him through sight. She has him sort and match colors and shapes. He can also associate certain Chinese characters with definite objects. For example he can associate the Chinese character for *car* with an automobile model.

For lunch he eats a very nutritional meal. He always gets protein first, then vegetables, then starch. We rarely give him any sweets because no dentists can handle him.

After lunch he does the same thing he did before breakfast which accomplishes nothing—unless he studies.

When dinner is served he usually waits until the family has started to eat before he comes to the table. Even then it is hard to keep him seated. During dinner he bounces up and down. He eats with his hands and eats quickly to get to the starch.

When dinner is over he wanders around for a while. To put him to bed you have to change him, brush his teeth and make him go to the bathroom. It seems he is always cutest right before he goes to bed.

THE PROBLEMS

The problems are naturally more than the advantages. Noah has temper tantrums quite frequently. In these tantrums, he runs through the house pushing things all over and messes up the house. All or most of these tantrums seems to start for no reason at all. I guess when you can't talk, tantrumming is one of the few ways to communicate. Sometimes while people are watching T.V. or reading, he will stick his hand in your face. He usually is giggling while doing this, so I guess he is just teasing. If he gets mad while eating he will stick his dirty hands on your shirt and get it all messy. To leave Noah alone is a great risk because if he swallows something he shouldn't or gets hurt he can't tell anybody. So that's why we never leave him alone.

ADVANTAGES AND HUMOROUS THINGS

To be honest I do tend to take advantage of the fact that my brother is brain damaged. Like sometimes I get more attention than I deserve and I also get more things because he naturally doesn't buy anything.

Humorous things are not very common. But when they happen you almost cry because you know he tried so hard. Just recently he put his legs through his shirt sleaves, as if it were a pair of pants when he was trying to dress himself.

And when he gets into bed at night he often stands up straight as a board and falls backwards and then slips under the covers.

THOUGHTS ABOUT NOAH

I really don't know what my feelings about Noah are. Because I don't like thinking about the future for him. Once in a while I get mad at him for what he is because we can't take trips and do the things a normal family does. But I shouldn't get mad at him. It's not his fault that he is the way he is. Right now he is very cute and charming.

BIBLIOGRAPHY

1. "A Child Called Noah" by Josh Greenfeld
2. An interview with my parents, Josh and Foumi Greenfeld
3. Every day of my life

ABOUT THE AUTHOR

Josh Greenfeld is a journalist, novelist, playwright, and screenwriter who lives in Pacific Palisades, California. In addition to *A Child Called Noah*, he has written the novels *O for a Master of Magic* and *Harry and Tonto*, the plays *Clandestine on the Morning Line* and *I Have a Dream*, and was nominated for an Academy Award for the screenplay of *Harry and Tonto*.